Cases in Strategic Marketing Management:

*Business Strategies
in Muslim Countries*

Cases in Strategic Marketing Management:

Business Strategies in Muslim Countries

Professor John A. Quelch
London Business School

Prentice
Hall

Upper Saddle River, New Jersey

Library of Congress Cataloging-in-Publication Data

Quelch, John A.
    Cases in strategic marketing management : business strategies in Muslim countries /
John A. Quelch
      p. cm.
Includes index.
ISBN 0-13-028357-6
    1. Marketing—Islamic countries—Case studies.   2. Marketing—Islamic
countries—Management—Case studies.   I. Title.
HF5415.12.I74 Q45 2000
658.8′02—dc21

                            00-020496

VP/Editorial Director: James C. Boyd
Editor-in-Chief: Natalie Anderson
Senior Editor: Leah Johnson
Managing Editor: Bruce Kaplan
Editorial Assistant: Rebecca Calvert
Assistant Editor: Anthony Palmiotto
Senior Marketing Manager: Shannon Moore
Director of Production: Michael Weinstein
Production Manager: Gail Steier de Acevedo
Production Coordinator: Kelly Warsak
Permissions Coordinator: Suzanne Grappi
Media Project Manager: Cindy Harford
Manufacturing Buyer: Natacha St. Hill Moore
Senior Manufacturing and Prepress Manager: Vincent Scelta
Cover Design: Bruce Kenselaar
Full Service Composition: BookMasters, Inc.

Printed in the United States of America.

10 9 8 7 6 5 4 3 2 1
ISBN 0-13-028357-6

CONTENTS

CHAPTER

1

INTRODUCTION

One-fifth of the world's population is currently Muslim. By 2025, 30% will be Muslim including 60% of the population under the age of 18. There are 45 independent Muslim states and of all the world's religions, Islam has perhaps the strongest hold on its followers. Yet, in this age of globalization, few Western multinationals have done more than scratch the surface of the marketing opportunity that Muslim societies represent. Although the emerging markets of Asia, Latin America, and Eastern Europe have attracted considerable foreign direct investment, relatively little interest has been shown in the Muslim societies of the Middle East and Central Asia. It is true, however, that Muslim countries in Asia—notably Indonesia and Malaysia—have attracted attention. Reflecting this lack of interest, foreign direct investment as a percentage of gross domestic product is lower in the Middle East and North Africa than in any other region. Only 1% of international capital flows go to the Middle East. The region accounts for only 5% of U.S. international trade (Ajani, 1997).

There are three possible explanations. The first is cultural distance. The cultural gaps between Western and Muslim societies are often perceived to be greater than those between Western and Asian societies. The peaceful countenance of Buddha seems to many Westerners more approachable than Mohammed. Growing numbers of Westerners traveling to and working in Asia, fueled further by the opening of China, have spawned greater cross-cultural understanding.

A second, though related, explanation is the threat of terrorism. It is as unfair to describe the United States as a violent society, based on the acts of a few well-publicized gunmen, as it is to dismiss all Muslims as terrorists based on the acts of Hamas and like-minded opponents of the state of Israel. Although there are over 6 million Muslims in the United States, Muslims are still widely viewed with suspicion. The lack of cultural understanding was evident in 1997 when Nike eventually recalled shoes with a logo that offended Muslims because it resembled the word Allah in Arabic. Travel, trade, and foreign investment bridging the West and most Muslim countries have not developed to the same degree as they have in other emerging markets—except again in those Muslim countries located outside the Middle East region and that are less strict in requiring public adherence to Muslim tenets.

A third explanation is that many Muslims, imbued with the pride of Mohammed, have not quite recovered from being under Western colonial rule. They are, perhaps understandably, determined to reassert their religious and cultural independence. Those in the oil-rich countries of the Gulf region are, thanks to the short-term profiteering of Western suppliers in the 1960s and 1970s, quite wary of Western businessmen bearing fruits. The vagaries of business negotiations and the investment of time to build trust are simply too much for many Western businessmen with a no-time-to-waste attitude and countless deals on offer in other emerging markets.

Muslim countries are far from homogeneous. Just as cultural values, consumer behaviors, and marketing practices differ among Christian societies, so the same is true of Muslim nations. In some cases, the entire population is Muslim and Islamic principles, embodied in the shariah or holy law, are the basis of all law and social discourse. In other countries, Islam may be one of several official religions and Muslims may barely be in the majority. The absence of a core country in the Muslim world perhaps makes Islam harder for outsiders to understand. Indonesia, the most populous Muslim country, is on the geographical periphery of the Islamic world (Huntington, 1996).

Even in the heart of Muslim civilization—the Middle East—there is considerable political and cultural fragmentation. There are dramatic differences in stages of economic development between oil-rich Muslim countries such as the United Arab Emirates, with a per capita income among the world's top ten, and neighboring Yemen, among the world's poorest. There are many unresolved rivalries and border disputes, for example between Egypt and Sudan over water rights. Political leaders from Iran and Syria compete in the Arab world for recognition as the true leader of Islam. Meanwhile, intra-regional trade languishes. Trade among Arab nations accounts for less than 1% of combined imports and for only 8% of combined exports (compared to 20% in the Mercosur region of Latin America). The region's total non-oil exports amount to less than Finland's (Khalaf, 1997).

Yet, after the Asian financial crisis of 1998, the collapse of the Russian economy, and still another setback to Brazil in its effort to become the economic powerhouse of Latin America, battle-weary Western multinationals are, at the start of the twenty-first century, taking a more cautious view of emerging markets. In some cases, this is resulting in a reallocation of investment from the developing to the developed world. In other cases, multinationals are more open to new opportunities, looking to investments in the Middle East and Africa to diversify their portfolios. Finally, there are smaller Western companies, especially those headquartered in Europe rather than North America, for whom Muslim countries are geographically closer, not seen as so threatening, and represent a market opportunity overlooked by their larger competitors.

Economic progress in certain Muslim countries has been encouraging. During the 4 years after 1995, Egypt demonstrated how proper economic management can stimulate growth of over 5% per year. Egypt has provided exporters with access to imports at world prices and to export financing. It has opened up trade restrictions and financial markets, streamlined licensing requirements, reduced customs fees, and lowered borrowing costs. Labor markets have been liberalized (but unemployment remains high). Finally, privatization, essential to attracting foreign investment, has been embraced and some protective public sector subsidies reduced or phased out (Khalaf, 1998). The top global investment banks have been opening Cairo offices as a result (Hubard, 1997).

The political climate in the Middle East also appeared more promising as the new millenium approached. The 1995 Amman Summit spawned the Middle East and North Africa development bank with a $5 billion capitalization (Gardner, 1995). Despite repeated political setbacks, business people in Israel, Jordan, and Palestine have established over 35 joint ventures and realize, for example in the tourism industry, that a multi-country approach will attract more investment (Porter et al., 1997). In 1999, Iran, regarded as an habitual funder of Middle East terrorism, began reaching out to its less aggressive Middle East neighbors, inviting a high-level Saudi Arabian delegation to visit in 1999. Power passed peacefully in Jordan from the formidable King Hussein to King Abdullah, who quickly proceeded to discontinue sanctuary for the Hamas terrorist group within his borders. And, after a brief flirtation with a right-wing government, Israelis elected Prime Minister Barak to continue the assassinated Prime Minister Rabin's work for peace. The high quality business community in Israel is an important force for progress in the region, not merely in its own right, but as an example to motivate other Middle Eastern countries as to what a vibrant business sector can achieve (Marcus, 1996).

It is true that in many Muslim countries, the politically powerful have been content to leave the nuts and bolts of business to others. For example, Indian managers are employed widely in the countries of the Gulf, and in Malaysia and Indonesia, Chinese expatriates have played a formidable role in business life. Gradually, however, the caliber of Muslim management talent is developing as wealthy families, concerned about succession planning, send their sons and daughters to be educated in London and New York. At the same time, they may return with pleasant memories of liberal Western lifestyles and thereby add to the intergenerational tension that can be detected barely below the surface in many Muslim countries.

RELIGION AND SOCIETY

Strict followers of the Koran say it bans all interest, not just usury, because interest forces borrowers to shoulder all the risk while rewarding the owners of the capital. According to some, Islam teaches that money should not be created out of money but by taking risks on productive investments. This results in a high percentage of assets being held as cash. It constrains economic development, savings, and home ownership (because interest cannot obviously be charged on mortgage loans). However, through a variety of techniques, Islamic finance has designed analogues to central bank bills, treasury bills, and corporate notes that are shariah compliant. Investments can be made in inventory and work-in-process financing and in plant and equipment leases. There are lists of stocks that are compliant and mutual funds in which Muslims can invest knowing that all the stocks in the portfolios comply with Islamic principles (which ban gambling, the drinking of alcohol, eating of pork, and prostitution). There are over 100 banks with deposits between $50 and $80 billion specializing in Islamic banking. Because most investors do not want to put their money into high-risk projects, Islamic banks provide fixed rate products that provide a predetermined return as a result of investing in short-term commodity trades and trade-finance deals. Malaysia, in an effort to become a center for Islamic finance and the gateway for Middle Eastern investments in Asia, has encouraged Islamic unit trusts, brokerage houses, and insurance companies (Khalaf, 1995).

Westerners often recoil from what they perceive as the subordinate status of women in strict Muslim societies. Women cannot go into public places unless veiled and in company. In Saudi Arabia, women cannot drive. The purpose is to protect them from the unwanted attentions of men. Such restrictions plus the fact that few women work in strict Islamic societies mean that they are unlikely to ever be truly competitive in the world economy. On the plus side, family values and the upbringing of children receive great attention. Violent crime, drug use, and prostitution are less evident in Cairo, the largest Muslim city in Africa, than they are in Johannesburg, the largest Westernized city. Incidentally, Muslim women have always had the right to own property independent of their husbands, while British women only obtained the same right in 1870—and Pakistan, Bangladesh, and Turkey have all had female prime ministers (Mazrui, 1997). Even in Saudi Arabia, 3,000 women are now working in the private sector and the Internet is giving new opportunities to Saudi women to set up businesses from their homes (*The Economist*, October 2, 1999).

These customs affect marketing practices and what products sell. Perhaps surprisingly, cosmetics sales, adjusting for per capita income, are as strong, if not stronger, in strict Muslim societies. Women wearing the veil pay particular attention to eye liner and mascara. Within their homes, Muslim women socialize frequently with each other and Western brands of cosmetics are well-known, used, and discussed at such get-togethers. Home exercise machines are popular because women cannot easily visit the local gym or health club.

Restrictions on what women can wear in public do not mean that fashionable clothing and lingerie are not of interest to wealthy Muslim women. In Egypt, where the law has permitted women to go unveiled in public since 1923, many women wear headscarves instead of veils, a growing percentage wear make-up, and the Salaam Centre for Veiled Women makes colorful veils and hijab for the woman who wants to identify publicly with Islam but not to the extent of wearing the black chador.

NEGOTIATING AND SELLING

Western businessmen operating in Muslim societies have learned the value of long-term relationships cultivated over many years. During the oil boom of the 1970s, many Western companies were able to extract perhaps unreasonable profits from oil-rich countries whose rulers were signing deals without necessarily the best financial advice. As a result, today there is a greater wariness of the unknown vendor, and a stronger pool of local and expatriate managers who advise the sheikhs and emirs of the Middle East before they enter into deals. Many of the important local families have also sent their sons to colleges and business schools in the United States and Europe. In addition, the region is now spawning a new elite of sophisticated Middle Eastern investors and entrepreneurs, led by Prince Alwaleed bin Talal. The prince, the world's richest non-American businessman, took a substantial stake in Citibank when its stock price was less than half today's valuation. American Express has successfully targeted this new class of businessman in Egypt using Western-style account management techniques, mobile phones to enable its account managers to respond quickly to clients, and short-term lending to build initial trust.

For the most part, however, business negotiations in the Muslim world are still complicated by the notion that a promise made to a nonbeliever in Islam has no validity. Salespeople familiar with Muslim cultures indicate that it is often necessary to keep asking in person to have a business promise fulfilled. Personal trust is more important than any written contract. Trust is hard to establish. It may take as many as nine sales calls to build trust with a Saudi prince's financial advisers and with the prince himself before a contract is agreed. The conversation in a good sales call will often focus on social issues and the prospective customer's hobbies. Hard selling and disparagement of competitors should be avoided. Once trust is established and the sale made, the buyer will likely want to do a lot more business with the supplier. The decision process is lengthy but, once made, the switching costs are high. For the multinational company, an ideal salesperson is an expatriate who speaks Arabic and who has infinite patience. The salesperson will find that appointments are not always kept and that the people whom he or she is supposed to meet are unexpectedly out of town or at the airport in order to be seen as a part of the crowd meeting a foreign dignitary. The salesperson's patience may be taxed to the limit before a decision on a contract is taken, but once taken, an impatient flurry of activity may follow with the salesperson pressured to deliver immediately much more than was agreed. Perhaps this overgeneralizes but many Western businesspeople, accustomed to being able to parachute into a city, cut a deal, and leave on the next plane, do not appreciate that time has almost a different meaning in Muslim societies (Williams, 1998).

A good salesperson will know further that, in Muslim societies, hospitality offered must be accepted. When visiting a home, a gift from the visitor to the male head of the household, offered with the right hand, is appropriate. As in many societies, the living room where guests are received contains material possessions designed to indicate the wealth of the family. To consume the food and drink offered is to honor the host (Laffin, 1985).

ADAPTING THE MARKETING PROGRAM

The same marketing principles apply in Muslim countries that apply in Western societies. However, cultural differences require adaptations to the marketing approaches used by Western companies. The level of adaptation required depends on the product or service being sold and the degree to which Muslim religious edicts are followed in everyday society. In addition, Western multinationals may find it less economical to adapt their marketing programs to smaller Muslim countries.

Product Policy

Most Western marketers find that demand for their products in Muslim markets is limited only by available disposable income. As in many emerging markets, there is an inherent belief that the Western-made brand is superior in quality to any local equivalent. The size of most Muslim markets is too small to facilitate economic local production of equivalent products. In addition, the status of owning and using Western brands is also evident. Some segments of society, however, reject the use of Western brands as incompatible with their Islamic principles and demand for some product categories—such as expensive Western-style toys—is simply not well-developed. In Iran and Egypt, government and religious officials have tried to develop demand for appropriately attired female dolls to counter the inroads being made by Mattel's Barbie line (Jehl, 1999). On the whole, however, assuming package labeling is adapted to local language and content requirements, most Western brands are well received.

However, product categories where price premiums are charged for intellectual property find Muslim markets especially challenging. Egyptian law gives only weak 10-year patent protection on the process by which a drug is produced—often easily circumvented—rather than on the final product. Knockoffs of pharmaceuticals developed by Western multinationals typically sell for one-fifth the brand-name prices in Egypt where two-thirds of all drugs are made by local companies. Western multinationals have been trying to bargain investment capital in return for tighter intellectual property laws. When they have made investments, the results have not always been as expected. The founder of the first private pharmaceutical company in Egypt sold out to Glaxo, then subsequently opened a rival plant nearby (Pearl, 1996).

Of course, marketers of food products must be careful to avoid using any pork-based additives in their manufacturing processes, and all alcohol is banned. During the Muslim holy month of Ramadan, fasting is mandatory until sunset. Accordingly, Western restaurant chains must adjust their menus, opening hours, and store delivery schedules.

Many adaptations required of Western marketers are what would be required in any emerging market. For example, Kellogg's has to market not only corn flakes but the concept of a Western-style breakfast. Nestle and Knorr have to reassure Muslim mothers that their soups are healthy and not a cop-out from homemaker responsibilities.

Pricing Policy

The pleasure of bargaining still characterizes transactions in Muslim societies. If an excessive opening price is quoted, it is preferable to avoid being upset or dismissive but, rather, to demur and wait to be asked what price you would be prepared to pay. When selling to Muslim countries, Western salespeople sometimes complain about a high degree of price sensitivity and an apparent unwillingness to appreciate superior quality and value-added services. This is often a reflection of a lack of trust on the part of the buyer. Many Western salespeople are inclined to give up too soon rather than patiently educating the prospect through a series of meetings to understand why a higher price is fair. To test the fairness of the prices quotes by pharmaceutical companies, Middle East governments now often look at the prices of the same or comparable drugs in the countries from which vendors are securing their supplies.

Added-value sales promotions—as opposed to direct price cuts—are not as effective as in the West. A cosmetics company offering a gift with purchase promotion, for example, may find that the gift is simply regarded as irrelevant. Where price sensitivity exists, it is best to focus on the core product rather than attempt to distract. Perhaps in time, consumer behavior in Muslim countries will change and consumer-promotion offers will become increasingly effective. Such a trend is unlikely to be aided by flawed promotions such as Lancome's invitation to Middle East consumers to enter a contest requiring completion of the last line of a Shakespeare sonnet in English.

Given the prohibition on interest in Muslim countries, it might seem unlikely that consumer credit or layaway schemes could be offered. However, if an Islamic bank extends the credit, the payments can be considered to include not interest but the cost of the capital.

Finally, because trade flows between Muslim markets are not well established, it is possible for owners of global brands to maintain price differentials from one market to another on the same product, in relation to the economic prosperity or stage of category development in each market.

Marketing Communications

Advertising in print and electronic media is available in all Muslim countries. Cultural nuances make it difficult to effectively use a single advertising campaign or execution in all markets, just as would be the case in Western Europe. In Saudi Arabia, restrictions on the attire of women shown in advertising are especially restrictive. Although satellite channels permit pan-regional advertising to be placed, Western multinationals must be alert to possible adverse reaction from the Saudi authorities to any spill-over satellite advertising that deviates too far from their local norms (Koranteng, 1997).

As in many emerging markets, the initial focus of consumer-products advertising must be on building brand-name recognition and an understanding of the benefits and how to use the product. Although perfumes, of course, require no explanation, skin care regimes and household cleaning products do. Kodak has found it challenging to find the right message to promote photography in countries that are largely desert and do not see photography as entertaining. Kodak has focussed on the family involvement and perceived status that goes along with being a good amateur photographer.

As in many emerging markets, direct mail is not extensively used, partly as a result of the unreliable postal system. In strict Muslim societies like Saudi Arabia, however, women can only receive mail via a post office box number. As a result, direct mail targeting women is often screened by husbands and fathers, but cosmetics companies have found it effective for announcing new products and delivering samples. Because few women are working outside the home and direct mail is relatively underdeveloped, response rates in countries like Saudi Arabia can be surprisingly high.

Companies relying in the West on party-plan selling have found establishing their businesses in strict Muslim societies difficult but not impossible. Although women are restricted in public, this makes for a strong and vibrant family life behind the scenes. Add to family-networking opportunities, time availability, and the propensity to shop if one can afford to do so, and the conditions are ripe for Avon and other party-plan companies to succeed.

Distribution Policy

Restrictions on foreign ownership, the perceived risk of investment, cultural complexities, and modest market potential have resulted in many multinationals electing to serve Muslim markets through local agents and distributors, often associated with prominent families and appointed on an exclusive basis. Such arrangements sometimes result in mutually beneficial long-term relationships. Kodak, for example, has worked with the same distributor in Saudi Arabia for over 40 years. In other cases, however, the distributor, exclusively representing several Western brands, may not be giving enough sales push for the likes of world headquarters. If a multinational company decides to change distributors, the result may be an acrimonious and drawn-out litigation that can cost a brand dearly in its efforts to build long-term market share.

In some cases, multinationals do not perceive each small Middle East market to have sufficient potential to warrant appointing a separate distributor, so a master distributor might be appointed to oversee, say, all the Gulf region countries.

Partly because of restrictions on interest from bank deposits, franchising has proved to be an increasingly popular investment. Because the financial risk is largely borne by the franchisee, multinationals such as McDonald's see the appointment of local nationals as franchisees as a risk-free way to globalize their brands. Fewer government approvals are needed because local investors are involved. The Saudi government and others have developed model franchise agreements to govern such arrangements (Martin, 1999).

ORGANIZATION AND MANAGEMENT

Because Muslim countries span continents, there is hardly a Western multinational that addresses them as a group in its strategic thinking. In fact, it is remarkable—given the size of the worldwide Muslim population—how little attention Western multinationals are paying to this opportunity and how few Muslims are employed as marketing managers or strategic thinkers at the world or regional headquarters of these corporations. In the case of industrial marketers, for example, defense contractors and account managers based at world or regional headquarters will typically travel to Middle East countries, frequently building long-term relationships through well-placed local agents that are often close to the ruling families. Military spending in Jordan has recently been as high as 11% of gross domestic product, and in Egypt 6% compared to 3.6% in the average developing country.

Many multinational consumer goods companies, such as Procter & Gamble, draw only 1% or 2% of their sales from the Middle East and, therefore, organize export shipments to local country distributors from plants outside the region and from offices often located in Geneva. On the other hand, Nestlé, with a long history of investing in emerging markets, has five specialist factories in five Middle East countries: Ice cream is made in Dubai, soups and cereals in Saudi Arabia, ketchup in Syria, chocolate in Turkey, and yogurt and bouillon in Egypt.

With the opening of the former Soviet republics, some companies are using Istanbul, Turkey, as a base from which to penetrate Central Asia (Spain, 1997). Of course, Malaysia and Indonesia are typically treated as part of the Asia Pacific region or ASEAN subregion. An enigma is Pakistan which is sometimes handled by a multinational's senior executive for Europe, the Middle East, and Africa and sometimes by the senior executive for Asia.

Because of the rivalries among Muslim nations, it is often difficult to serve multiple country markets effectively from one local center. The convenience of flight schedules also bears upon the location decision. Perhaps aided by its insignificant size as well as its location, Dubai has emerged as an important entrepot and regional headquarters location for not merely the Gulf region but the entire Middle East. For example, Kodak oversees its Middle East distributors from Dubai with the Dubai operation reporting to a vice president for Europe, the Middle East, and Africa who is based in London. Bahrain, also small in size and by no means as oil rich as it once was, is also seeking to establish itself as a regional center, specializing in financial services.

Likewise, the nationalities of managers who can operate effectively throughout the region is also limited. Lebanese are widely acknowledged for their business acumen and Egyptian managers, often highly educated, are increasingly accepted throughout the Middle East. There is considerable interest in localization in Muslim societies and, as a result, multinationals using high quality Muslim managers or better still, local nationals, as managers are likely to be well received. In the late 1990s, the Saudi Arabian country manager of Pfizer's pharmaceuticals company was a Lebanese. The overall manager for the Middle East, based in Dubai, was a Moroccan who had taken over from an Egyptian. The days of the traditional expatriate, the manager who couldn't quite make it at London headquarters, are rapidly fading.

CONCLUSION

Muslim societies represent the final frontier for Western multinationals. Economic reforms and the spread of Western business practices are making these markets more accessible.

As the enormous—and rapidly growing—marketing opportunity represented by Muslim countries becomes better appreciated, Western multinationals will make more investments in the region, acquiring local companies or building greenfield plants, rather than merely exporting through local distributors who may not necessarily have the incentive or the skills to invest in building local demand. A growing commitment to Muslim countries will be followed by multinationals recruiting and developing local management talent to run their subsidiaries in Muslim countries.

References

Ajani, Fouad. "The Region Left Behind," *US News and World Report,* July 28, 1997, p. 40.

Gardner, David. "Peace Delivers The Summit, but Not the Goods," *Financial Times,* October 27, 1995, p. 10.

"How Women Beat the Rules," *The Economist,* October 2, 1999, p. 78.

Hubard, Mark. "Finance Houses Seek Foothold in Egypt," *Financial Times,* July 29, 1997, p. 8.

Huntington, Samuel P. *The Clash of Civilizations and the Remaking of World Order,* (New York: Simon & Schuster, 1996).

Jehl, Douglas. "Muslim World Promotes Its Own 'Decent' Barbie," *International Herald Tribune,* June 4, 1999, p. 2.

Khalaf, Roula. "Islamic Banking: Consensus Still Sought On Important Issues," *Financial Times,* November 18, 1995, p. I.

Khalaf, Roula. "The Pressures for Change Mount," *Financial Times,* Survey on Middle East and N. Africa Privatization, March 25, 1998, p. 1.

Khalaf, Roula. "World's Slowest Growing Developing Region," *Financial Times,* September 19, 1997, p. xxviii.

Koranteng, Juliana. "Saudi Ban on Dishes Doesn't Stop Viewing," *Ad Age International,* April 1997, p.i16.

Laffin, John. *Know the Middle East,* (London: Alan Sutton Publishing, 1985).

Marcus, Amy Dockser. "Business Ties Expand Among Palestinians, Jordanians and Israelis," *Wall Street Journal,* May 8, 1996, pp. 1, 8.

Martin, Josh. "Franchising in the Middle East," *Management Review,* June 1999, pp. 38–41.

Mazrui, Ali A. "Islamic and Western Values," *Foreign Affairs,* 76:5 (September-October 1997), pp. 118–132.

Pearl, Daniel. "Big Drug Makers Push Egypt, Other Nations to End Their 'Piracy,'" *Wall Street Journal,* December 13, 1996, pp. 1, 8.

Porter, Michael et al. "Making Real Progress in the Middle East," *Harvard Business School Bulletin,* December 1997, pp. 24–25.

Spain, William. "Turkey Carving a New Silk Road," *Ad Age International,* March 1997, p. 18.

Williams, Jeremy. *Don't They Know It's Friday* (Dubai: Motivate Publishing, 1998).

CHAPTER

2

PENETRATING AN EMERGING MARKET

Daewoo's Globalization: Uz-Daewoo Auto Project

On a weekend morning in August 1997, Woo Choong Kim, chairman and CEO of Daewoo Group, was chairing a small-group discussion about Daewoo's business projects in Uzbekistan. Reviewing progress over the last 5 years, Chairman Kim was preparing for an upcoming visit to Uzbekistan. Daewoo's investments in the automobile, electronics, textile, and banking sectors were bearing fruit. Preparations for the rollout of its telecommunication business were going well. Uz-Daewoo Auto Co., which opened the way for cooperation with Uzbekistan, was stepping up its production as planned, but facing several marketing and operation challenges. While the Uzbekistan government was pushing for more export sales, current moves announced by Ford, Opel, and Kia threatened to increase competitive pressure on Uz-Daewoo Auto in both the domestic and export markets. A shortage of hard currency and the limited convertibility of the local currency (Sum) constrained further investment.[1] With two new investment projects outside the automobile industry proposed by the Uzbekistan government, Chairman Kim and his senior managers had to answer the challenges facing the automobile business and, at the same time, review Daewoo's overall strategy in Uzbekistan.

COMPANY BACKGROUND

Founded in 1967 as a small textile-trading company, the Daewoo Group was one of the world's largest industrial enterprises. As of June 1997, the group consisted of 31 domestic companies and 454 overseas subsidiaries and branch offices with more than 250,000 employees worldwide. The Daewoo Group was engaged in trading; in domestic and overseas construction; in shipbuilding; and in the manufacture of motor vehicles,

---

[1]As of July 1997, US$1 was equivalent to 64.2 Sum at the official rate, and to 141.3 Sum at the market rate.

Doctoral Candidate Chanhi Park prepared this case under the supervision of Professor John A. Quelch as the basis for class discussion rather than to illustrate either effective or ineffective handling of an administrative situation. Confidential data have been disguised.

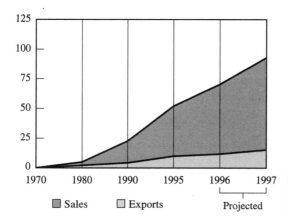

125 — 100 — 75 — 50 — 25 — 0

1970   1980   1990   1995   1996   1997

■ Sales   ☐ Exports   Projected

EXHIBIT 2.1 Daewoo's Total Sales and Exports in US$Billions: 1970–1997

heavy machinery, telecommunications equipment, consumer electronics, home appliances, textiles, and other products. Daewoo also had investments in financial and telecommunication services, and operated hotels worldwide. The Daewoo Group recorded total sales of US$68 billion in 1996 and ranked twenty-fourth on the *Fortune Global 500.* Exhibit 2.1 summarizes the sales and export growth of Daewoo, and Exhibit 2.2 breaks down Daewoo's overseas business network by region and by line of business.

EXHIBIT 2.2 Overseas Network by Region (as of June 1997)

	Subsidiaries	*Branches*	*R&D Centers*	*Construction Sites*	*Total*	*Cumulative Investment*[1]
Asia	135	68	3	29	235	$1,390 million
Africa/Middle East	24	27		40	91	$ 315 million
CIS	25	13	2		40	$ 270 million
Eastern Europe	37	6		1	44	$ 571 million
Western Europe	36	9	5		50	$ 364 million
Americas	54	20	3	1	78	$ 394 million
Total	311	143	13	71	538	$3,304 million

Overseas Network by Lines of Business

	Subsidiaries	*Branches*	*R&D Centers*	*Construction Sites*	*Total*	*Cumulative Investment*[1]
Trade	138	86			224	$ 910 million
Construction	41	21		71	133	$ 676 million
Electronics/ Telecommunications	74	24	9		107	$ 680 million
Automotive Industry	20	1	2		23	$ 767 million
Heavy Industry	11	5	2		18	$ 100 million
Finance	13	4			17	$ 125 million
Others	14	2			16	$ 46 million
Total	311	143	13	71	538	$3,304 million

[1]Investment amount = equity investment + loans to the subsidiaries

As of June 1997, Daewoo had investments in 380 projects in over 85 nations. Daewoo expected to increase its global network to 1,000 locations by the year 2000. Unlike many multinationals, since 1991 more than half of Daewoo's overseas investments had been concentrated in emerging markets, which management thought had the greatest potential for the coming century. By meeting the development needs of these emerging markets, Daewoo hoped to fully realize its commitment to "mutual prosperity."

Fully operational overseas investment programs included electronics and home appliances manufacturing in the United Kingdom, France, Spain, Poland, Mexico, Uzbekistan, and Kazakhstan. Daewoo also had investments in major vehicle and component production plants in Poland, Romania, the Czech Republic, Uzbekistan, India, China, the Ukraine, Vietnam, the Philippines, Iran, and Indonesia.

Daewoo aimed to be among the world's top 10 companies in automobiles, electronics and home appliances, heavy equipment manufacturing, shipbuilding, and telecommunication services by the year 2000. Chairman Kim had founded the company at the age of 31 and still exercised intimate leadership over key strategic issues in all 31 subsidiary companies. His entrepreneurial spirit, hard work, and business insights made him an important role model among younger Koreans. He authored the book, *It's a Big World and There's Lots to be Done,* published in August 1989. The Korean edition sold one million copies in record time. The English translation was published in 1992 under the title, *Every Street Is Paved with Gold.* Chairman Kim spent more than 260 days abroad every year, always worked more than 130 hours a week, and never took a vacation throughout his career.

COMPANY HISTORY

Daewoo Corporation was founded in 1967 as a producer and exporter of textile products. The company became the parent of what was known in 1997 as the Daewoo Group, which comprised 31 companies. Exports grew from US$580,000 in 1967 to US$40 million in 1972. In that year, the company became the second-largest Korean exporter and was awarded the "Order of Industrial Merit, Gold Tower" by the Korean government.[2] Daewoo Corporation went public in 1973 and diversified into construction, financial services, and apparel manufacturing, in each case by acquiring financially distressed companies. Predicting the imposition of textile-import quotas by the U.S. government, Chairman Kim strongly pushed for maximum textile exports. As a result, when the quotas were allocated among suppliers based on their shares of exports into the United States, Daewoo Corp. benefited by reselling a portion of its quota, as well as by making profits on its own export sales. According to a senior Daewoo executive:

> With the quota premium alone, we could have bought 10 top-of-the-line 20-story office buildings in downtown Seoul every year. With that much money on hand, we decided instead to pursue our entrepreneurial ambition and contribute to our country by doing real business.

Taking advantage of that success, Daewoo diversified further into heavy machinery industries in the late 1970s. It was the Korean government that pushed for this diversification. Due to the worldwide recession and the energy crises, the Korean gov-

---

[2]Korea's total exports were less than $2 billion in 1972.

ernment's industrial restructuring drive toward heavy machinery and petrochemicals faced great challenges. A senior Daewoo executive explained:

> Once we became famous thanks to a couple of successful turnarounds, the government and the financial community consistently pushed us to do more acquisitions. Some people criticize us for the acquisition drive, but we were compelled to acquire many of the current Daewoo companies. We turned Korea Heavy Industries into a profit in our first year running its operations in 1976, and dedicated the Okpo shipyard (currently the main facility of Daewoo shipbuilding) in 1981. We also acquired the 50% stake in GM Korea in 1978.

By 1979, Daewoo was Korea's biggest exporter and one of the five largest conglomerates in Korea. By 1981, the number of Daewoo overseas offices had grown to 65. In 1982, consumer electronics and telecommunications were added to Daewoo's business portfolio. Daewoo Telecom's 16-bit personal computer Model D became a popular choice in the U.S. market under the Leading Edge brand. Expansion into emerging markets that included several former communist nations laid the foundation for Daewoo's continued growth. Daewoo played a leading role in developing Korea's economic (and diplomatic) relations with Libya, Sudan, Iran, China, and Russia throughout the 1970s and 1980s. Korea's first commercial office in Eastern Europe was established by Daewoo in East Berlin in 1988, followed by other Daewoo offices in Prague in 1989 and Moscow in 1990. A refrigerator plant was dedicated in China in 1988. Daewoo formed the first Korean-Chinese joint venture in 1989 to produce color-picture tubes. Throughout the 1990s, Daewoo continued its leading role in building economic relations with Poland, Romania, and North Korea.

Chairman Kim and Daewoo people attributed the growth to their hard work and willingness to take on new challenges. Overcoming a variety of environmental threats and administrative challenges during the high-growth period, Daewoo built a refined and flexible management system supported by the entrepreneurial initiative of front-line managers rather than by management and planning processes. Industry insiders also explained Daewoo's growth in terms of its financial expertise, its use of governmental subsidies for turnarounds, and its exploitation of opportunities in both the domestic and international financial markets.

Above all, an international orientation had been the engine of Daewoo's growth. Having started as a trading company, Daewoo had developed competencies in international trade and finance from the outset. When Daewoo became one of the biggest Korean conglomerates in the early 1980s, its managers discovered that the 40-million domestic market was too small to fuel Daewoo's continued growth. So, international expansion was inevitable. Moreover, some of Daewoo's export goods were more technically sophisticated than the domestic market could absorb at that time. A senior Daewoo executive in the textile business stated:

> When we considered introducing some of the apparel products developed for export into the domestic market in the early 1980s, we realized that many of the incumbent firms would be driven out of the market. We decided to pursue the larger overseas market rather than trying to steal share from our weaker competitors in Korea. As we built our credential in international markets, our business partners offered bigger deals in a wider variety of businesses.

Exhibit 2.3 lists the principal Daewoo Group companies in Korea, and Exhibit 2.4 lists the principal overseas Daewoo subsidiaries.

EXHIBIT 2.3 Major Daewoo Group Companies (Domestic)[1]

	1996 Sales	Company	Business Fields and Products
Trading	$19.4 billion (Automobile-related: $12.5 billion)	Daewoo Corporation (General Trading Division)	Trading, Financing, Resource Development, Investment, Project Organization, Logistics
Construction and Hotels	$7.2 billion	Daewoo Corporation (Construction Division)	Architectural Works, Civil Works, Plants, R&D, Development Programs, Design Engineering
		Keangnam Enterprises Ltd.	Architectural Works, Civil Works, Plants, Engineering, Consulting
		Kyungnam Metal Co., Ltd.	Aluminum Extrusion, Curtain Walls, Frame, Profiles, Fabrication of Aluminum Sash
		Daewoo Development Co., Ltd.	Hotels, Museum
Heavy Industry and Ship-building	$5.1 billion	Daewoo Heavy Industries Ltd. (General Machinery Division)	Diesel Engines, Construction Equipment, Machine Tools, Factory Automation, Defense Products, Materials, Precision Machines, Aerospace Products, Machinery, Equipment
		Daewoo Heavy Industries Ltd. (Shipbuilding Division)	Shipbuilding, Offshore Platforms, Specialty Vessels, Repair and Conversion, Offshore Workshops, Drilling Rigs, Steel Structures, Industrial Plants
		Korea Industrial Systems Co., Ltd.	Computer Numerically Controlled Equipment
Automotive Industry[2]	$4.5 billion	Daewoo Motor Co., Ltd.	Vehicle Manufacturing (Passenger Cars, Buses, Trucks)
		Daewoo Heavy Industries Ltd. (Public Motors Division)	Minivehicle Production
		Daewoo Automotive Components Ltd.	Alternators, Cranking Motors, Ignition Coils, Distributors, Brake Systems, Catalytic Converters. Steering Systems, FWD Axles, Compressors. Car Air Conditioner, Components, Radiators
		Daewoo Precision Industries Ltd.	Automotive Components. Materials Nuclear Fuel Components, Machinery, Pneumatic Tools, Defense Industry Products
		Koram Plastics Co., Ltd.	Rim Bumpers, Battery Cases
		Korea Automotive Fuel Systems	Automotive Fuel Systems
		Daewoo Motor Sales Co., Ltd.	Vehicle Sales

Category	Sales	Company	Products / Services
Electronics and Telecom-munications	$4.2 billion	Daewoo Electronics Co., Ltd.	TVs, VCRs, Microwave Ovens, Audio Systems, Home Appliances
		Daewoo Electronic Components Co., Ltd.	E-Tuners, Hybrid-Ics, DYs, Capacitors (Film, Aluminum. Electrolytic, Tantalum), FBTs, Thermistors, Relays, Keyboards, SAW Filters
		Orion Electric Co., Ltd.	Monochrome CRTs, Electron Guns, Color CRTs, Electron Gun Parts, Computer Monitors, Flat Panel Display Devices (LDC, PDP, and ELD)
		Orion Electric Components Co., Ltd.	Color CRT Manufacturing, Sales
		Daewoo Electric Motor Industries Ltd.	Motor Manufacturing
		Daewoo Telecom Ltd.	Computers, Peripherals, System Integration, Telecommunications Systems
		Daewoo Information Systems Co., Ltd.	System Integration, System Products, System Services
Finance and Services	$1.2 billion	Daewoo Securities Co., Ltd.	Brokerage, Underwriting, Overseas Investment, Settlement and Standing Proxy, Dealing, Mergers and Acquisitions
		Daewoo Economic Research Institute	Advanced Analysis of Economic Factors
		Daewoo Capital Management Co., Ltd.	Korea Fund Advisor, Investment Advisor, Portfolio Manager
		Korea Financial Service Co., Ltd.	Factoring
		The Diners Club of Korea	Credit Cards
		Dongwoo Management Co., Ltd.	Building Maintenance
		Daewoo Venture Capital Co., Ltd.	Technical and Financial Support to Small and Medium-Size Enterprises

[1]This figure is the annual consolidated sales by domestic companies.
[2]Daewoo's automobile-related sales by overseas subsidiaries were estimated to be $8.6 billion as of 1996.

EXHIBIT 2.4 Major Daewoo Group Subsidiaries (Overseas)

	Western Europe	*Business Fields and Products*
United Kingdom	Daewoo Worthing Technical Center	Car Design and Engineering
	Daewoo Electronics U.K.	Home Appliances Manufacturing
France	Euro Daewoo	Heavy Machinery
	Daewoo Cars	Car Sales
	Daewoo Electronics Manufacturing	Home Appliances Manufacturing
	Daewoo Orion	CRT Manufacturing
	Daewoo Automobile France	Car Sales
Germany	Daewoo Automobile Germany	Car Sales
	Daewoo Motor Engineering	Car Engineering
	Euro Daewoo	Heavy-Equipment Sales
	Eastern Europe	
Poland	Daewoo-FSO Motor	Passenger Car Manufacturing
	Daewoo Motor Polska	Commercial Vehicles Manufacturing
	Centrum Daewoo	Car Sales
	Daewoo Electronics Poland	Home Appliances Manufacturing
Romania	Daewoo Automobile Romania	Passenger Cars Manufacturing
	Daewoo Mangalia Heavy Industries	Shipbuilding and Repair
	Daewoo Romania Bank	Banking
Czech Republic	Daewoo AVIA	Commercial Vehicles Manufacturing
Hungary	Daewoo MBM	Bearing Production
	Daewoo Bank	Loans, Trusts
	Daewoo Securities	Securities Brokerage
	Daewoo Leasing	Leasing
	CIS	
Uzbekistan	Uz-Daewoo Auto	Passenger Cars Manufacturing
	Uz-Daewoo Electronics	Home Appliances Manufacturing
	Uz-Daewoo Bank	Banking
	Uz-Daewoo Textile	Cotton Fabrics
	Uz-Daewoo Telecom	Telecommunications Services
Kazakhstan	Daewoo Almaty Electronics	Home Appliances Manufacturing
	Kazaktelecom	Telecommunications Services
Ukraine	Auto ZAZ	Passenger Cars Manufacturing
	Dniepr-Daewoo	Telecommunication Equipment Manufacturing
	Asia	
China	Daewoo China	Holding Company
	FAW-Daewoo Automotive Engines	Engine, Transmissions
	Shandong-Daewoo Automotive Components	Automotive Components
	Daewoo Cement Plant	Cement Production
	Guilin Daewoo Bus	Buses

EXHIBIT 2.4 *(continued)*

Asia	Business Fields and Products
Daewoo Heavy Industries Yantai	Excavator Manufacturing
Beijing Lufthansa Center	Hotel, Office, Apartments
Yanbian Daewoo Hotel	Hotel
Guilin Sheraton Hotel	Hotel
Shanghai Business Center	Business Center Construction
Heilangijang Electronic Technology	Telecommunications Services

Vietnam		
	Daeha Business Center	Hotel, Offices, Apartments
	Daewoo Hanel Electronics	Home Appliances Manufacturing
	Orion Hanel Picture Tube	CRT Manufacturing
	Vietnam Daewoo Motor	Passenger Cars Manufacturing
	Firstvina Bank	Banking
	Saidong Industrial Zone Development	Plant Site Development

India		
	Daewoo Motors India	Passenger Cars Manufacturing
	Daewoo Securities India	Securities Brokerage
	Daewoo Power India	Power Plant Construction

Africa and Middle East		
Iran	Kerman Motor	Passenger Cars Manufacturing
Morocco	Rabat Hilton Hotel	Hotel
Sudan	International Tire Manufacturing	Tire
	Port Sudan Spinning Mill	Cotton Yarn
Algeria	Algiers Hilton Hotel	Hotel
Nigeria	Daewoo Nigeria	Construction
Angola	Oil Exploration Project	Oil Exploration

Latin America		
Mexico	Daewoo Electronics, Mexico	Color TV Manufacturing
	DECOMEX	Home Appliances Sales
	DEHAMEX	Home Appliances Manufacturing
	Daewoo Electro-Components Mexico	Components Manufacturing
	Daewoo Orion Mexicana	CPT Manufacturing
Chile	DECSA	Home Appliances Sales
Peru	Oil Exploration Project	Oil Exploration
Colombia	DECO	Home Appliances Sales

North America		
United States	Daewoo Motor America	Car Sales
	Daewoo International America	Trading
	Daewoo Electronics America	Home Appliances Sales
	Daewoo Securities	Securities Brokerage
	Daewoo Machinery	Heavy Equipment Sales

Overseas automobile investments were central to Daewoo's globalization and growth strategy in the 1990s. Faced with stiff competition in a slow-growth domestic market, Chairman Kim took charge of the automobile business and led the series of overseas automobile investments detailed later. In addition to the automobile projects, overseas investments were also initiated in electronics and telecommunications services. Daewoo was running mobile communication services in China and Uzbekistan. Local banks and financial institutions were established in 18 nations. Daewoo's bid for Thomson Multimedia was still on hold.[3] As of June 1997, Daewoo had invested $3.3 billion in more than 380 overseas projects. Chairman Kim anticipated $15 billion worth of overseas projects by 2005. According to the plan, Daewoo would employ 250,000 foreign workers at 1,000 overseas subsidiaries and branches that would help generate a group total of $177 billion in revenues by 2000.

Daewoo's Automobile Business: 1972–1992

Daewoo Motor Company (DMC) was the automobile subsidiary of Daewoo Group. In 1972, General Motors had set up an automobile plant (GM Korea) as a joint venture with a Korean local partner. Daewoo acquired the local partner's 50% share of GM Korea in 1978 and assumed management responsibility. The company was renamed Daewoo Motor Company in 1983. DMC was the market-share leader in the domestic compact car market (considered the "luxury" end of the market at that time in Korea) and was second in the domestic subcompact car market until the mid-1980s. As a partner in GM's "world car" project, Daewoo invested $1.1 billion to set up a new production line for the Pontiac Lemans (a 1500cc subcompact) targeted at both the United States and Korean markets, and started production in 1986. Exports to the United States began in April 1987. Domestic sales of the Lemans were encouraging at first, but exports were fewer than expected. According to a DMC executive, Daewoo gradually saw the need to pursue a more independent strategy:

> GM considered DMC as just one more factory in its worldwide network serving the Korean domestic market (60,000 vehicles/year) and providing low-cost vehicles for the U.S. market (40,000 vehicles/year). However, DMC wanted to pursue a larger market opportunity. The relationship soured and Daewoo set up a minicar plant with cooperation from Suzuki in 1988. In 1991, the new plant located in Changwon started to produce the Tico (with an 800cc engine) and the Damas (a light commercial vehicle) based on the design platform of the Suzuki Alto.

By mid-1991, the divergence of interests between Daewoo and GM had become acute, and industry insiders began to forecast the possible breakup of the joint venture. Meanwhile, in the late 1980s, domestic competition became tougher. Hyundai, Daewoo's

---

[3]In February 1996, the Chirac government announced a privatization plan for Thomson S.A., the French conglomerate comprising Thomson CSF (defense and electronics), Thomson SGS (semiconductor), and Thomson Multimedia (TMM: consumer electronics and telecommunications equipment). TMM had acquired 100% of GE's Audio & Video Division including GE's 100% share of RCA in 1987. In 1996, Daewoo announced its plan to bid and was selected as the final bidder for TMM. The deal was put on hold due to the pressure of domestic politics in France. If Daewoo succeeded in the bid, it would become the biggest consumer electronics company in the world.

biggest domestic rival, introduced new compact (2000cc Sonata) and subcompact (1500cc Excel) models with enhanced features, thanks to continued research and development (R&D) investment and technical assistance from Mitsubishi. Hyundai launched the Excel and the Sonata in the U.S. market in 1986 and 1988 respectively. Kia, which has been a small number-three manufacturer with a limited product line until the mid-1980s, was permitted by the Korean government to enter the passenger vehicle segment in 1984. Kia introduced subcompact and compact cars in 1986 and 1990 respectively. Ford and Mazda had equity stakes and technology licensing agreements with Kia. Kia's 1300cc subcompact model (Pride) was exported to the U.S. market as the Ford Festiva. Under the trade liberalization program, import tariffs and sales taxes on vehicles imported into Korea were scheduled to be lowered gradually. In the face of stiff competition, market growth was expected to slow down due to growing traffic congestion on the roads, increasing parking charges, and reduced tax incentives for buyers. Exhibit 2.5 shows trends in automobile ownership in Korea.

Faced with mounting competitive pressures, DMC had several problems. A labor strike in 1986 that lasted three months diluted the launch of the Lemans. Anther strike in 1990 was also timed to coincide with a model change, and further hurt DMC's market position. The Changwon minicar plant did not suffer from labor disputes, but market demand for its minicars did not meet expectations due to the increasing consumer preference for bigger cars. One analyst in Seoul stated:

> During the turnaround of Daewoo Shipbuilding Company in the late 1980s, DMC did not get enough top management attention, which drives the resource allocation process at Daewoo. DMC management underestimated how quickly its domestic rivals were closing the technology gap. DMC focused on short-term profits and only invested enough to give periodic facelifts to the existing products. DMC tended to rely on technical assistance from GM rather than make the effort to develop new technologies internally; this threatened DMC's position as the technology leader among Korean automobile manufacturers. Faced with mounting competitive pressure from domestic competitors with redesigned and improved product lines and the prospect of a breakup with GM, DMC's market position looked increasingly fragile by 1992. Morale and production quality were also deteriorating.

This analysis was not shared by DMC managers. According to a DMC executive in Seoul:

> I agree that the market response for the 1992 model was lower than expected. However, we were not ignorant of the need for technology investment. As the joint venture with GM increasingly seemed likely to limit the growth of our automobile business, we knew we had to prepare to be technologically self-sufficient. The problem was the magnitude of investment commitment required to achieve this.

The Globalization Drive Since 1992

In 1992, Chairman Kim decided to take charge of DMC's strategy. Relying on his previous turnaround experience at Daewoo Shipbuilding Company, he first mandated closer cooperation between DMC and other Daewoo Group companies and developed new foreign markets for existing models. An aggressive grassroots sales campaign was launched to place Daewoo cars with all Daewoo employees and their relatives and

EXHIBIT 2.5 Trends in Automobile Ownership in Korea

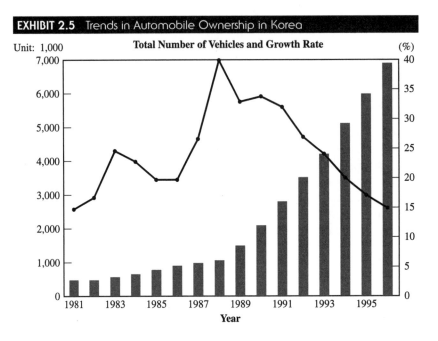

Total Number of Vehicles and Growth Rate

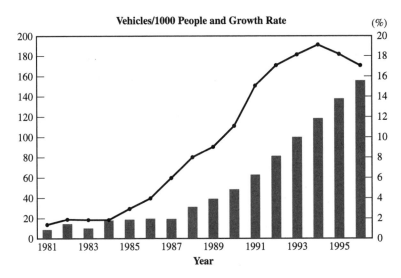

Vehicles/1000 People and Growth Rate

friends. Financing assistance to DMC was provided by the entire network of Daewoo companies. Second, Chairman Kim initiated major new-product development efforts. Three new passenger vehicle projects were started in fall 1993, each led by young general managers, and the organization was reshaped to meet the challenge. Following the breakup of the joint venture with GM in the winter of 1992, Chairman Kim merged the minicar plant operation into DMC. While searching for a technology-cooperation partner, DMC bought automobile R&D firms in Worthing, United Kingdom, (new model design and development) and Munich, Germany (engine development), which would be the basis for a global R&D network in collaboration with the existing R&D centers both in and outside of Korea.[4] Third, Chairman Kim set out to restore employee morale. He met all 12,000 DMC employees in 100 group meetings, which helped him secure support for implementing the changes needed to restore DMC's competitive edge.

Globalization was crucial to this effort. Chairman Kim believed that Daewoo had a unique strength in international operations (in comparison with other domestic competitors and foreign companies) and built his strategy on this. He exploited foreign markets with existing products and set up sales beachheads that would ensure sufficient demand to generate the scale economies needed for the next generation of models. After initiating exports to Western Europe in early 1995, DMC achieved 1% market share in the United Kingdom within 10 months. This confirmed Chairman Kim's belief in Daewoo's ability to penetrate new markets. Beyond the sales generated, Daewoo acquired invaluable learning about the automobile export market. Responses from emerging markets were even more favorable. Beginning with a knockdown plant in India (where Daewoo acquired existing facilities owned by Toyota and a local company) and the Uz-Daewoo Auto project in Uzbekistan, Daewoo acquired RODAE (the biggest automobile plant in Romania) in 1994 and FSO (the biggest automobile plant in Poland formerly owned by the government) in 1995. The Uzbekistan project encouraged other emerging market governments to work with Daewoo. Between 1992 and 1997, Daewoo also invested in production facilities in Vietnam, Indonesia, Philippines, the Czech Republic, Iran, and China. Daewoo's corporate size (sales of $65 billion in 1996), its financing capacity, and its global-business network facilitated these transactions. Exhibit 2.6 and Exhibit 2.7 detail Daewoo's automobile operations in Korea and overseas.

Daewoo sold 636,000 vehicles worldwide in 1995 and 857,000 in 1996. Around half of the sales outside Korea were sold in emerging markets, the other half in developed markets. DMC was the eighteenth-largest auto producer in 1996 with $12 billion sales and 27,000 employees, but aimed to be in the top ten by 2000. In that year, DMC expected to produce 2.5 million vehicles, valued at $40 billion. DMC's domestic production capacity goal of 1 million vehicles was accomplished with the dedication of Daewoo Motor's Kunsan plant in 1997.

Some industry experts raised concerns about this drive for scale. Given the overcapacity in the global automobile industry, they argued that fewer than 10 automobile companies could survive into the next century. However, Chairman Kim was confident that Daewoo's global strategy to achieve the necessary scale economies would work. He stated:[5]

> For the last 20 years, there have always been concerns about overcapacity in the global automobile industry. Daewoo is creating new demand in the emerging markets of Eastern Europe, the former CIS countries, and Asia.[6] With the rapid industrial development and the growth of consumer-buying power, Daewoo can benefit from being the first mover in these markets. Of course, Daewoo will also pursue opportunities in developed-country markets. There, we will define unique market niches and adopt differentiated

---

[4]Daewoo was also planning to open an R&D center in the United States as of July 1997.

[5]*The Monthly Chosun,* February 1995.

[6]The CIS (Commonwealth of Independent States) included the independent republics that formerly comprised the Soviet Union.

EXHIBIT 2.6 Companies Affiliated with Daewoo's Automobile Production

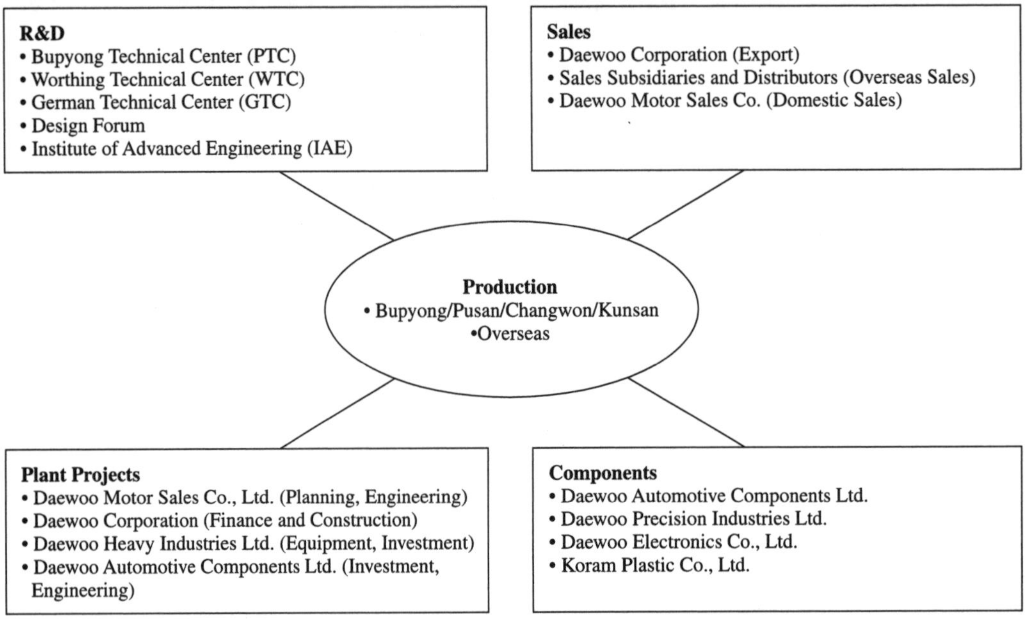

R&D
- Bupyong Technical Center (PTC)
- Worthing Technical Center (WTC)
- German Technical Center (GTC)
- Design Forum
- Institute of Advanced Engineering (IAE)

Sales
- Daewoo Corporation (Export)
- Sales Subsidiaries and Distributors (Overseas Sales)
- Daewoo Motor Sales Co. (Domestic Sales)

Production
- Bupyong/Pusan/Changwon/Kunsan
- Overseas

Plant Projects
- Daewoo Motor Sales Co., Ltd. (Planning, Engineering)
- Daewoo Corporation (Finance and Construction)
- Daewoo Heavy Industries Ltd. (Equipment, Investment)
- Daewoo Automotive Components Ltd. (Investment, Engineering)

Components
- Daewoo Automotive Components Ltd.
- Daewoo Precision Industries Ltd.
- Daewoo Electronics Co., Ltd.
- Koram Plastic Co., Ltd.

EXHIBIT 2.7 Daewoo's Domestic and Overseas Automobile Operations

A. Domestic Plants

Location	Products	Capacity/Year 1997
Bupyong	Passenger Cars	500,000
	KD (Knock-Down Kits)	200,000
Pusan	Buses	6,000
Changwon	Minicars/Light Commercial Vehicles	240,000
Kunsan	Passenger Cars	300,000
	Trucks	20,000

B. Overseas Plants

Country	Plant	Products	Capacity (by 1998)
Poland	DW-FSO	Passenger Cars (local model)	120,000
		Commercial Vehicles	40,000
	DMP	Passenger Cars	20,000
		Commercial Vehicles	45,000
Romania	RODAE	Passenger Cars	200,000
Czech Republic	Avia	Commercial Vehicles	25,000

Location	Product		1994	1995	1996
Uzbekistan	UZ-Daewoo	Passenger Cars			150,000
		Mini-Commercial			50,000
India	DDML	Passenger Cars			160,000
		Commercial Vehicles			10,000
China	Guilin	Bus			5,000
Iran	KMC	Passenger Cars			25,000
Philippines	TAMC	Passenger Cars			10,000
	FDIC	Large Bus			500
Vietnam	Vidamco	Passenger Cars			25,000
		Large Bus			2,000
Indonesia	PT.SD	Passenger Cars			3,000

C. Domestic and Export Sales: 1994–1996

Location	Product	1994	1995	1996
Domestic[1]	Passenger Cars	284,734	233,555	278,617
	Commercial Vehicles	24,863	20,886	21,460
	Subtotal	309,597	254,441	300,077
Export[2]	Passenger Cars	107,283	262,185	348,545
	Commercial Vehicles	3,640	3,044	5,168
	KD[3]	—	15,672	118,199
	Subtotal	110,923	280,901	471,912
Total		420,520	535,342	771,989

[1]Domestic sales in Korea
[2]Exports of finished vehicles from Korea
[3]Exports of knock-down kits from Korea

marketing strategies. Our U.S. market launch in 1998 will show the way. To seize the opportunity in emerging markets, Daewoo is acquiring existing plants in those countries. We cannot rely on direct exports of finished vehicles because they will inevitably come up against trade barriers. Acquisitions save time and money for both sides. The capital-intensive nature of the automobile industry is such that it takes around $1,000 fixed cost per unit of annual production to build a new plant; with careful renovation of existing plants, a large part of this cost can be saved. Daewoo's expanded market base will be the basis for achieving the necessary scale economies.

To remain competitive in the international market, we have to commit to an annual product development investment of $1 billion across five platforms. We need 300,000 to 400,000 unit production for each platform (including the variants such as convertibles and wagons), totaling two-million units of annual production. At this level of production, per unit R&D cost can be kept under $500. This is why leading automobile makers are maintaining production output of over two million vehicles per year. To maintain consumer interest, Daewoo is planning to introduce two or three new models every year. We launched the Lanos (a 1500cc subcompact) and the Nubira (an 1800cc or 2000cc subcompact) in 1996, and the Leganza (a 2200cc or 3000cc compact) in 1997. Export of these new models will begin in late 1997. Overseas plants will soon switch their production lines to these new models.

As of July 1997, more industry insiders were accepting the logic of Daewoo's move toward globalization. As one put it:

> Korea's domestic automobile market is too small for three producers (Daewoo, Hyundai, Kia). With the expected market entry of Samsung in 1998 (based on a technology licensing agreement with Nissan) which will add capacity to produce 200,000 vehicles a year, competition in the domestic market will intensify further. At the same time, tariff and nontariff barriers on foreign cars coming into the domestic market will be lowered. Korean producers are losing their cost advantage due to rising wage and land costs. Exports to emerging markets will be restricted by protective trade policies to nurture their industrialization goals. Overseas production is therefore essential. Without it, even the export of components will become economically infeasible in the near future. Current overseas moves by Hyundai and Kia prove this point.

As of July 1997, Daewoo's three new models were enjoying strong sales in Korea. Both the Lanos and the Leganza broke the first month sales record for a new model, and DMC was regaining market share leadership. The Leganza would be launched in the United States in 1998.

HISTORY OF THE UZ-DAEWOO AUTO PROJECT

Daewoo and the Uzbekistan Economy

Uzbekistan was liberated from the former Soviet Union in August 1991. Under President Kharimov's strong leadership, Uzbekistan was actively pursuing industrialization. Located in the middle of the historic Silk Road trading route in Eurasia, Uzbekistan had a rich heritage of Islamic culture and was geographically positioned to serve as a distribution center of Central Asia. Exhibit 2.8 and Exhibit 2.9 report key economic indicators of Uzbekistan, while Exhibit 2.10 shows a map of Uzbekistan. The population of 22 million was well educated; the adult literacy rate was 95%, 80% of the adult population had secondary education, and 16% had higher education. Uzbekistan was the world's fourth-largest producer of cotton (1.5 million tons/year) and had important deposits of gold (70 tons/year: 25% of former CIS annual production), natural gas (40 billion cubic meters/year: 5% of former CIS annual production), copper, molybdenum, zinc, and tungsten. Uzbekistan was agriculturally self-sufficient (mainly through rice). Soviet assembly plants in machinery, aircraft production, and steel refining had created a skilled labor force. The political environment was stable. Though still experiencing high inflation and a shortage of hard currency, Uzbekistan had the best record

EXHIBIT 2.8 Key Economic Indicators for Uzbekistan

		1994		1995				1996			
		3 Qtr	4 Qtr	1 Qtr	2 Qtr	3 Qtr	4 Qtr	1 Qtr	2 Qtr	3 Qtr	4 Qtr
Industrial Production	Monthly ave.										
General Index	1990 = 100	93.4	130.7	72.7	82.2	99.4	n/a	n/a	n/a	n/a	n/a
Cement	1,000 tons	428	328	261	276	322	280	211	305	307	248[1]
Mining											
Lignite	1,000 tons	336	298	221	234	269	278	232	239	253	190[1]
Natural Gas	mil cu meters	3,313	4,207	4,406	3,968	3,544	4,066	4,526	3,879	3,564	4,069[1]
Crude Petroleum	1,000 tons	326	402	437	430	439	464	402	432	398	461[1]
Employment											
Industry	1,000	1,100	1,084	1,120	1,110	1,100	1,070	1,050	1,035	1,020	n/a
Unemployment, Registered		19.3	21.2	27.6	32.8	28.4	26.4	28.9	32.9	33.4	n/a
Wages											
Monthly Earnings	Sum	480	600	973	1,475	1,551	2,118	2,244	3,350	3,920	n/a
Construction											
Dwellings Completed	1,000	6.9	6.4	2.4	5.6	6.4	5.1	2.0	5.9	8.7	n/a
Foreign trade	Qtrly totals										
Exports	$ mil	449.2	1,276.3	449.0	779.7	577.8	1,243.5	453.4	518.1[2]	n/a	n/a
Of Which: CIS		224.1	998.9	478.7	442.5	255.6	252.7	109.5	109.6[2]	n/a	n/a
Imports		648.2	790.7	517.9	592.8	488.8	1,148.4	603.4	559.8[2]	n/a	n/a
Of Which: CIS		375.2	378.3	220.0	273.5	316.8	307.3	187.0	205.2[2]	n/a	n/a

[1]October only
[2]Total for April–May
Source: OECD

EXHIBIT 2.9 Former Soviet Republics: GDP and GDP per Head (at Purchasing Power Parity)								
	1989	*1990*	*1991*	*1992*	*1993*	*1994*	*1995*	*1996*
Armenia—GDP								
$ bn	17.6	17.0	16.1	7.9	6.9	7.3	8.0	8.6
per head ($)	5,062	4,804	4,469	2,143	1,853	2,051	2,124	2,275
Azerbaijan—GDP								
$ bn	21.8	20.0	20.7	13.8	10.9	8.7	7.4	7.6
per head ($)	3,076	2,804	2,872	1,866	1,474	1,163	986	1,005
Belarus—GDP								
$ bn	49.9	50.4	51.4	47.7	43.8	37.7	34.8	36.5
per head ($)	4,879	4,910	5,006	4,631	4,228	3,645	3,365	3,525
Estonia—GDP								
$ bn	7.7	7.4	6.8	6.2	5.8	5.8	6.1	6.4
per head ($)	4,896	4,670	4,334	3,988	3,803	3,836	4,067	4,349
Georgia								
$ bn	24.1	21.4	17.8	10.9	7.7	5.6	5.5	6.2
per head ($)	4,420	3,919	3,275	2,005	1,405	1,032	1,005	1,139
Kazakstan								
$ bn	71.9	74.6	72.4	64.7	56.0	43.0	40.1	41.4
per head ($)	4,327	4,477	4,304	3,827	3,316	2,523	2,416	2,507
Kyrgyz Republic								
$ bn	11.0	11.9	11.2	9.7	8.3	6.3	6.0	6.5
per head ($)	2,550	2,706	2,524	2,164	1,842	1,364	1,311	1,372
Latvia								
$ bn	14.5	14.6	13.6	9.1	8.0	8.2	8.3	8.6
per head ($)	5,437	5,471	5,118	3,462	3,070	3,209	3,288	3,463
Lithuania								
$ bn	33.0	33.9	30.0	19.2	13.7	14.2	14.9	15.8
per head ($)	8,945	9,121	8,031	5,141	3,681	3,813	4,025	4,255
Moldova								
$ bn	15.9	16.2	13.9	10.2	10.3	7.2	7.2	6.8
per head ($)	3,666	3,722	3,195	2,336	2,362	1,666	1,661	1,563
Russia								
$ bn	856.7	875.4	865.0	759.9	711.9	636.4	626.2	601.4
per head ($)	5,815	5,918	5,835	5,124	4,805	4,301	4,227	4,066
Tajikistan								
$ bn	9.9	10.2	9.7	7.0	5.2	4.5	4.0	3.4
per head ($)	1,915	1,920	1,770	1,248	916	781	693	577

	1989	*1990*	*1991*	*1992*	*1993*	*1994*	*1995*	*1996*
Turkmenistan								
$ bn	10.0	10.7	10.5	10.2	9.5	7.7	6.8	6.7
per head ($)	2,798	2,903	2,815	2,675	2,413	1,930	1,627	1,522
Ukraine								
$ bn	216.5	217.6	206.6	191.3	168.4	132.4	119.2	109.5
per head ($)	4,181	4,197	3,978	3,668	3,227	2,551	2,308	2,138
Uzbekistan								
$ bn	44.6	47.5	49.1	46.0	45.0	43.1	42.6	41.9
per head ($)	2,219	2,312	2,351	2,122	2,058	1,928	1,892	1,847

Source: IMF; World Bank, *Statistical Handbook of States of the Former USSR;* UN Economic Commission for Europe, *Bulletin for Europe,* Vol. 44, 1992: EIU calculations.

of macroeconomic stability among the former CIS countries in Central Asia. According to V. Golishev, the presidential economic advisor:

> During the first stage of economic reform (from independence to mid-1994), Uzbekistan created a new commercially based legal framework and started market reforms. During the second stage (from mid-1994 to 1996), macroeconomic stabilization was the main objective. While Russia experienced a 50% decline in GDP from 1990 to 1996, Uzbekistan's GDP fell only 18% and the country achieved 1.6% GDP growth in 1996. The national budget deficit has been less that 3.5% each of last two years. Inflation in 1996 was 5.6% per month (half of the 1995 level), and is expected to drop further in 1997. The labor market is stable with 4% unemployment despite 1.5% to 2% population growth each year. Now, the government is pursuing a stabilization policy together with privatization and price reform. We are also promoting the formation of small- and medium-size business through a variety of ownership structures. To attract foreign investment, additional tax and customs duty concessions are planned.

Some Western analysts were more cautious, pointing to the large current account deficit, growing external debt burden, continuing restrictions on currency convertibility, regulatory controls on banking transactions, and the legacy of the communist bureaucracy, all of which discouraged importers and investors, particularly small- and medium-size businesses.

A senior Daewoo executive involved in the Uzbekistan automobile project commented:

> In emerging markets, we always find that there is an opportunity on the other side of any threat. If everything were fine, these countries wouldn't need us. We jump into difficult markets and take advantage of the opportunities they present while managing the risk. By working hard, we build credentials with our partners (whether they are government officials or entrepreneurs) and find the best solutions for mutual prosperity. By being the first mover, we are in a better position to obtain cooperation. As a country becomes richer, it doesn't have to concede as much to later entrants.

EXHIBIT 2.10 Map of Uzbekistan

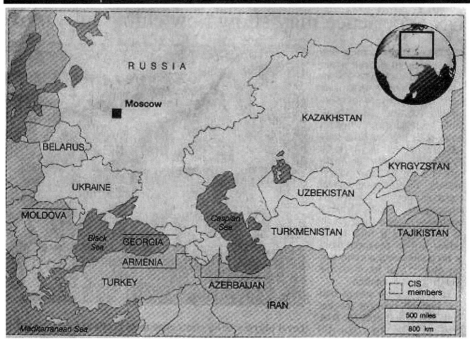

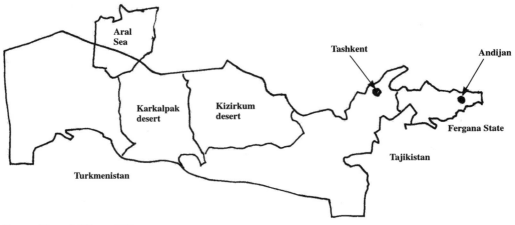

Source: Financial Times, 1997.

After gaining independence from the Soviet Union, Uzbekistan needed managerial talent, financial capital, and technology to realize its growth potential. Because Uzbekistan had to specialize in the production of cotton and other raw materials when it was part of the Soviet Union, it had relied on Russia for most of capital goods and consumer durables. President Kharimov's ambition was to turn Uzbekistan into a strong economic power in Central Asia through industrial development and export promotion. This required foreign investment. However, multinationals from the developed countries were concerned about political risk, macroeconomic instability, and various regulatory barriers. Siemens, Lufthansa, and Cargill had business interests in Uzbekistan, but none of them had been willing to commit to substantial investment. Japanese firms that had been active investors in developing countries in the 1960s and 1970s were also reluctant. It was Daewoo that first answered the call.

Daewoo's unique commitment to Uzbekistan was described by Golishev, the presidential economic advisor:

> Daewoo was the first foreign company to commit to a large-scale manufacturing plant in Uzbekistan. My country needs long-term, reliable partners, not casual partners in pursuit of a quick profit. The speedy entrepreneurial decision making of Daewoo management and the leadership of President Kharimov helped to overcome the bureaucratic obstacles. For example, it took only 24 months to build the Uz-Daewoo plant while it usually took at least three years to build an automobile plant in Korea. The Uz-Daewoo plant became the leading symbol of Uzbekistan industrial development. The day the plant opened was declared a national holiday (Uzbekistan-Korea Friendship Day]. Today, Daewoo's presence is not limited to automobile production. Daewoo is increasing its role in other key industries such as cotton, electronics, and telecommunications.

The Uz-Daewoo Auto Project

President Kharimov visited Korea in June 1992 and expressed interest in Daewoo's Changwon auto plant. Daewoo signed a 50/50 joint venture agreement with Uzautoprom[7] in August 1992 to build an automobile plant in Uzbekistan that would manufacture 200,000 vehicles annually including 100,000 Nexias, 50,000 Ticos, and 50,000 Damas. Exhibit 2.11 shows pictures and specifications of these models.[8] Construction of the Uz-Daewoo automobile plant began in 1994, and once completed in July 1996, it became the first modern automobile factory in Central Asia. Uz-Daewoo Auto would reach full-scale production by the end of 1997. Two-shift production commenced in February 1997, and three-team two-shift production was scheduled to begin in October 1997.

Located 350 kilometers from Tashkent and next to the rail link in Andijan, the plant offered good logistics. Previously, the plant had been used as a tractor assembly factory with 550 employees. The refurbished plant followed the same design as the Changwon plant in Korea. See Exhibit 2.12 for a plant diagram.

---

[7]Uzautoprom was the Automobile Manufacturing Association of Uzbekistan and was fully controlled by the Uzbekistan government. Hence, the project was effectively a joint venture between the Uzbekistan government and Daewoo.

[8]These brand names were the same as those used in Korea. Performance characteristics and specifications of the vehicles were almost identical, with minimal local adaptation.

EXHIBIT 2.11 Pictures and Specifications of Vehicles Produced by Uz-Daewoo Auto

NEXIA

GLE
- 1.5 SOHC engine
- Flush 13-inch wheel covers
- Power steering (option)
- Air conditioning (option)
- AM/FM stereo radio & cassette
- Power windows • Power antenna

GL
- 1.5 SOHC engine
- Front bucket seats, sliding & reclining
- Floor mat, carpet • Door pocket
- Door lock, manual • Speaker(FRT/RR)
- Variable speed wipe • Digital clock
- Remote trunk lid release, electric

TiCO

DLX
- Back glass - heated
- Driver's side map pocket
- AM/FM Stereo, Digital clock
- Speaker(LH/RH) • Manual antenna
- Air conditioning (option)
- Manual transmission (5-speed)

GLE
- Front bucket seats, sliding & reclining
- Full flat seat • Ventilator
- Manual transmission (4-speed)
- Door lock, manual
- Wiper speed • Cigar lighter

Both DLX and STD with 800cc 3 cylinder gasoline engine.

DAMAS

**MINI BUS
DLX**
- Wheel ctr cap • Headrest
- Air conditioning (option)
- Windshield washer - combined with wiper
- Back glass - heated • AM/FM stereo. ETR
- Driver's side map pocket • Manual antenna
- Speaker LH/RH (on door side)
- Capacity: 7 person

**MINI BUS
DLX**
- Door key - driver & codriver
- Front driver's seat, sliding
- Headrest (front - separate - slim)
- Air conditioning (option)
- Seatbelt warning - driver
- Capacity: 450kg

VAN
- Mud flap FRT & RR
- Head lamp - round (halogen)
- Door lock, manual, FRT
- Glove box • Locking fuel lid

All models with: Both DLX and STD with 800cc 3 cylinder
gasoline engine.

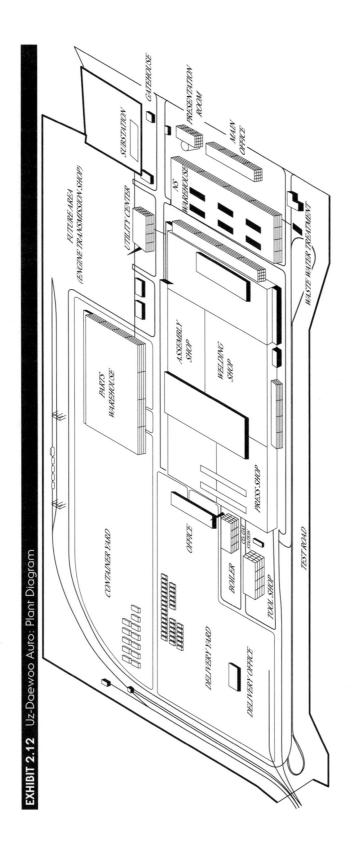

EXHIBIT 2.12 Uz-Daewoo Auto: Plant Diagram

GATEHOUSE

SUBSTATION

PRESENTATION ROOM

MAIN OFFICE

FUTURE AREA (ENGINE-TRANSMISSION SHOP)

UTILITY CENTER

NS WAREHOUSE

WASTE WATER TREATMENT

PARTS WAREHOUSE

ASSEMBLY SHOP

WELDING SHOP

CONTAINER YARD

OFFICE

PRESS SHOP

BOILER

TOOL SHOP

TEST ROAD

DELIVERY YARD

DELIVERY OFFICE

31

Production of the Damas, Tico, and Nexia models started on March 15, June 3, and June 17, 1996, respectively. Uzbekistan engineers and technicians (all of whom were trained at the Changwon and Bupyung plants in Korea) were in charge of production. Among the 3,200 workers at the factory, only 25 expatriate personnel were sent from Korea. Most of the local employees were in the 20 to 30 year age range with a technical school background. Some had previously worked in the old tractor factory. Jobs at the new plant were highly prized, even though the average worker earned the equivalent of $200 a month. Exhibit 2.13 documents the production and sales record while Exhibit 2.14 provides data on the long-term operating plan of Uz-Daewoo Auto Co.

The total project investment was $658 million of which shareholders' equity was $200 million and debt was $458 million. The Uzbekistan government provided 50% of the equity capital through Uzautoprom, and Daewoo Corp. provided the other 50%. Of the $458 million debt, $396 million was sourced through foreign loans ($222 million by the supplier's credit of Daewoo Corp. and $174 million by the National Bank of Uzbekistan) and the equivalent of $62 million was sourced through a local loan prepared by Asaka Bank. The Uzbekistan government provided a payment guarantee for Daewoo's $222 million supplier's credit. Following the "Uzbekistan cabinet decree on Uz-Daewoo Auto," the Uzbekistan government not only infused investment money but also provided administrative support for the project. A deputy prime minister was appointed to oversee and expedite the construction of the factory. The Uzbekistan government granted a five-year exemption for income tax, value-added tax, and customs on imported components, and promised to protect Uz-Daewoo's privileged position in the domestic market for 2 years.[9]

As of July 1997, Daewoo was meeting the expectations of the Uzbekistan government. The plant was credited with creating more than 10,000 new jobs, including jobs in construction, in auto dealerships, and in 10 local component companies established since 1996. A bank was set up to provide financial support for international trade and automobile sales. Technology transfer was achieved through the technology-licensing agreements and the personnel-exchange program for employees of Uz-Daewoo Auto and local component manufacturers. All of 3,200 employees of Uz-Daewoo completed a three-month training program in Korea; they were followed by dealer technicians and component manufacturer technicians. According to a senior executive in charge of the Daewoo Human Resource Development Institute in Korea:

> Both parties learn from each other. Our Uzbekistan friends learn technology and hard work in Korea, and both parties benefit from the international exposure. I heard that one day President Kharimov asked a Uzbekistan technician to say a few words in Korean when he visited the plant.

Uz-Daewoo's production capacity was scheduled to reach 300,000 units by the year 2000. In 1996, 26,000 vehicles were produced. The production goal for 1997 was 125,000 vehicles. Of these, 60,000 were expected to be exported to the Central Asian Republics and Russia (30,000 for each), and 50,000 were expected to be sold in Uzbekistan. The remaining 15,000 would be held in factory and dealer inventories. Of the 40,000 units actually produced by July 31, 30,000 were sold domestically and 10,000 were exported.

---

[9]The value-added tax was 18% in Uzbekistan. The Uzbekistan government imposed a 5.26% customs duty on auto imports from Russia and other former CIS countries and 60% customs duty on auto imports from non-CIS countries.

EXHIBIT 2.13 Uz-Daewoo Auto: Sales and Production Through July 1997

		Total	1996	1997	1997 (Monthly Data)						
					1	2	3	4	5	6	7
Production[1]	Tico	18,607	4,764	13,843	1,686	2,041	1,641	2,552	2,157	2,231	1,535
	Damas	14,420	8,664	5,756	1,012	415	493	992	1,077	1,026	741
	Nexia	35,111	12,229	22,882	2,984	3,496	2,418	4,313	3,545	3,616	2,510
	Total	68,138	25,657	42,481	5,682	5,952	4,552	7,857	6,779	6,873	4,786
Sales[2]	Tico	17,426	4,525	12,901	1,247	1,888	1,822	2,302	1,745	2,213	1,684
	Damas	14,105	8,266	5,839	1,031	576	472	836	1,148	870	906
	Nexia	33,601	11,345	22,256	2,152	3,192	2,980	4,054	3,281	3,030	3,567
	Total	65,132	24,136	40,996	4,430	5,656	5,274	7,192	6,174	6,113	6,157
Inventory[3]	Tico		239	n/a	678	831	650	900	1,312	1,330	1,181
	Damas		398	n/a	379	218	329	395	324	480	315
	Nexia		884	n/a	1,716	2,020	1,458	1,717	1,981	2,567	1,510
	Total		1,521	n/a	2,773	3,069	2,437	3,012	3,617	4,377	3,006
Domestic	Tico	16,833	4,220	12,613	1,240	1,851	1,654	2,257	1,739	2,208	1,664
	Damas	13,923	8,214	5,709	1,024	570	454	808	1,094	865	894
	Nexia	30,453	10,777	19,676	2,076	3,029	2,105	3,751	2,624	2,681	3,410
	Total	61,209	23,211	37,998	4,340	5,450	4,213	6,816	5,457	5,754	5,968
Export	Tico	593	305	288	7	37	168	45	6	5	20
	Damas	182	52	130	7	65	18	28	54	5	12
	Nexia	3,148	568	2,580	76	163	875	303	657	349	157
	Total	3,923	926	2,998	90	265	1,061	376	717	359	189

[1]Production since March 1996 for Damas, and June 1996 for Tico/Nexia.
[2]Sales: Domestic sales + Export sales (shipped from the Andijan factory). Sales since August 1996 for all three models.
[3]Inventory: Inventories at the factory at the end of the year or month (inventories at dealers are not included).

EXHIBIT 2.14 Uz-Daewoo Auto Long-term Operating Plan: 1996–2000

A. Long-term Production Plan (Units: 1,000 vehicles)

		1996	1997	1998	1999	2000	Other
Tico	STD	1	11	11	13	15	A/C: 35%[1]
	DLX	4	27	27	32	35	
	Total	5	38	38	45	50	
Damas	STD	1	1	4	5	5	A/C: 6%
	DLX	5	9	23	27	30	
	Van	2	4	11	13	15	
	Total	9	15	38	45	50	
Nexia	GL	5	29	30	36	40	A/C: 66%
	GLX	7	43	44	54	60	
	Total	12	72	74	90	100	
Total		26	125	150	180	200	Export 50%

[1]A/C = air conditioning

B. Local Content Plan (% of Value)

Year	1996	1997	1998	1999	2000
Tico/Damas	20%	30%	40%	60%	70%
Nexia	10%	20%	30%	40%	60%

C. Local Content Plan (parts added by year)

	1996	1997	1998	1999	2000
Locally supplied parts	seat, bumper, instrument panel (T/D), paint, trim part, wiring harness, brake/fuel pipe, blow molding, tuner, small plastic parts, small press parts	glass, muffler, fuel tank, carpet, insulator (T/D), large press parts, large plastic parts, battery, regulator, fastener	tire, brake disc, mirror, weatherstrip, speaker, instrument panel (Nexia)	engine parts, transmission parts, combustion switch, knuckle, brake hose, seat belt, speedometer, head lamp, parking brake lever	heater, caliper, brake system, shock absorber

The plant ran two shifts 250 working days a year, which could produce 40 vehicles per hour (20 Nexia, 10 Tico, and 10 Damas). Suppliers were selected ahead of production. By July 1997, six Korea-Uzbekistan joint ventures had been set up to work with Uz-Daewoo Auto, and small stamping parts were produced by wholly owned Uzbekistan companies. Uz-Daewoo was working closely to source components from other Daewoo plants such as RODAE of Romania and Daewoo-FSO of Poland. Imported parts and components were shipped from Korea to the Andijan plant by ship and train. Deliveries took 40 days. Local component sourcing was gradually increasing. In 1997, local content was expected to be 40% by value, including interior seats, bumpers, switchboards, and other components. By the year 2000, the value of locally made components was to reach 70%.[10]

In addition to the Uz-Daewoo Auto plant, Daewoo had many other investments in Uzbekistan. Cumulative investments totaled $1 billion by July 1997. Daewoo was the first Korean company to establish a trade office in Tashkent. Uz-Daewoo Electronics, a joint venture between Daewoo and the Uzbekistan government, was established in 1994, and by 1997, manufactured 400,00 television sets and VCRs, which were sold in Uzbekistan and Russia. In telecommunications, Daewoo provided 210,000 TDX lines to the Fergana region of Uzbekistan and was preparing for telephone and global satellite-delivered mobile telecommunication services. Daewoo also established the Uz-Daewoo Bank and was participating in the construction of railroads between China and Central Asia, as well as various natural resource development projects. Exhibit 2.15 summarizes the history of Daewoo's operations in Uzbekistan, and Exhibit 2.16 lists Daewoo's business activities in Uzbekistan. According to Daewoo executives, there was a certain complementarity between Daewoo and Uzbekistan. President Kharimov was impressed by Korea's history of government-led high-growth economic development in the 1960s through 1970s, and hoped that Uzbekistan might be able to replicate this experience. Daewoo's extensive experience in emerging markets was also valued by Uzbekistan officials. Daewoo's many lines of business and its sheer size also helped. According to a Western businessman in Tashkent:

> Size helps in Uzbekistan. Small companies are often frustrated by the regulations and bureaucracy. Given the limited currency convertibility and the

EXHIBIT 2.15	History of Daewoo's Operation in Uzbekistan
June 1992	Uzbekistan President I. Kharimov visited Korea
July 1992	Chairman Kim visited Uzbekistan
August 1992	Automobile joint venture contract signed between Daewoo and Uzbekistan government
September 1992	Daewoo Corp. opened trading office in Tashkent
May 1993	Electronics joint venture plant established
June 1994	Korean President Y. S. Kim visited Uzbekistan
February 1995	Uzbekistan President I. Kharimov visited Korea
May 1995	Trading joint venture (KOSMO) established
June 1995	Uzbekistan prime minister visited Korea
October 1995	$100 million cotton import contract signed
March 1996	Telecommunication joint venture plant established
May 1996	Mobile telecommunications (GSM) joint venture established
July 1996	Opening ceremony of Uz-Daewoo automobile joint venture plant (declared a national holiday)
May 1997	Daewoo Bank opened
June 1997	Daewoo textile plant opened
June 1997	Uzbekistan telecommunication minister visited Korea
December 1997	Automobile parts plant scheduled to open

[10]Local content referred to the proportion of locally made components and parts to the total value of the finished good.

EXHIBIT 2.16 List of Daewoo Businesses in Uzbekistan as of July 1997

Total investment amount: $1 billion
Total number of expatriate managers: 75
Total number of local employees: 6,000

Name:	Daewoo Corp. Tashkent Office
Business:	Trading office of Daewoo Corp. (trading and investment arm of Daewoo Group)
Figures:	$900 million sales in 1996
Employment:	1 expatriate, 14 local
Plan:	Increased cotton trade ($150 million in 1996 to $500 million in 2000), investment in cotton plantation (30K hectares/25K ton in 2000), $500 million investment in ginning plant (50K ton capacity)

Name:	KOSMO
Business:	International trade JV (trading electronics and automobile parts)
Figures:	$3.1 million sales in 1996
Employment:	1 expatriate, 14 local
Plan:	$22 million sales in 2000

Name:	Daewoo Textile Co.
Business:	Cotton yarn plant (13K ton/year: first case of 100% ownership by foreign investor) 70% of output is export, existing textile plant was renovated
Figures:	$60 million investment, $40 million export
Employment:	10 expatriate, 800 local
Plan:	Expansion into spinning, dyeing and apparel manufacturing, vertical integration of cotton-related operations

Name:	Uz-Daewoo Auto Co.
Business:	Automobile JV, 3 passenger car lines (Nexia 100K units, Tico 50K units, Damas 50K units), CKD assembly of bus and truck (bus 1K units, truck 110 units), 8 JVs for parts and 3 local firms under technology license
Figures:	$658 million investment, 200K production capacity
Employment:	25 expatriate, 4,000 local
Plan:	Increasing local content from 40% (1997) to 80% (2000), establishing national sales and service network

Name:	Uz-Daewoo Electronics Co. (36% stake for Uzbekistan government)
Business:	TV, VCR, car audio
Figures:	$20 million investment, $100 million sales in 1997 (expected): 30% for export
Employment:	7 expatriate, 660 local
Plan:	Extending local sales network (currently 14 outlets in Tashkent, 24 outside Tashkent), increasing local content

Name:	Daewoo Telecom Tashkent office
Business:	Trading TDX system and telecommunication equipment
Figures:	TDX 210K lines (nationwide)

Name:	Asloka-Daewoo Co. (49% owned by the Uzbekistan government)
Business:	Manufacturing, installation and maintenance of TDX system (since August 1996)
Figures:	$20 million investment, TDX 200K lines/year
Employment:	5 expatriate, 200 local
Plan:	Exporting 30% of output to CIS countries, main provider of National Telecommunications Network Plan (2 million lines over 15 years)

Name:	Uzbekistan Mobile Telecom System (division of Daewoo Corp.)
Business:	GSM cellular phone network ($50 million investment), local telephone network in Fergana region (JV contract signed in July 1996: $192 million investment), long distance provider (1 out of 3 providers: 2 others are Russian firms)
Name:	Uz-Daewoo Bank
Business:	Universal banking (mainly serving government-invested firms and Daewoo-related firms) (Daewoo Securities 55%, Uzbekistan partner 10%, EBRD 25%, Koram Bank 10%)
Figures:	$20 million investment by Daewoo
Plan:	Expanding service boundaries, expanding asset base up to $60 million by 2000

Currently Planned

Business:	Business center (400-room hotel, 22-floor office building, department store) foreign residential units
Situation:	JV agreement signed in July 1997, construction scheduled to start on December 1997

Source: Academic cooperation between Uzbekistan National Academy and Daewoo Research Institutes (Economics, Advanced Engineering)

various development needs, Daewoo's multiple lines of business help a lot. For example, it seems that Daewoo can buy cotton with local currency earnings and export it, which is impossible for me to do. While other firms are still hesitant to invest, Daewoo has a myriad of business opportunities to offer to Uzbekistan, because the company operates in so many fields.

Decision Making and Negotiation

Critical issues regarding the Uz-Daewoo Auto project and other Daewoo businesses in Uzbekistan were negotiated directly between President Kharimov and Chairman Kim. The two leaders had developed a great mutual respect since the start of the project. President Kharimov was believed to consider Chairman Kim and Daewoo his most important economic-development partner. It was Chairman Kim's strong entrepreneurial leadership that helped Daewoo open the new market and made things happen. According to a senior Daewoo executive involved in the Uzbekistan operation:

Chairman Kim always initiates our business deals and takes charge not only of strategic decisions but also of operational details. Experienced aides in the corporate office and operating divisions provide analysis reports to aid him in his decision making. However, it is usually Chairman Kim who senses the opportunities and judges the business prospects of each. He really thinks that every street is paved with gold. After a project has progressed to a certain stage, he focuses on key strategic issues and delegates operational issues to the corporate staff and local subsidiary managers. As the project matures further, the local subsidiary takes more of the initiative. Whenever necessary, Chairman Kim intervenes and deals with a problem, but the process is quite simple. With only a couple of phone calls or faxes, he cuts to the heart of the problem and identifies a solution. He also benefits from the wisdom of experienced executive assistants and front-line managers, but the process mainly involves very brief informal discussions. I've never seen him sit through a lengthy internal presentation. This business style is reflected in the simple internal reporting process of Daewoo. The direct experience of front-line managers is appreciated more than an ornate analysis written from behind a desk. Strategy is important. But it should be no more than a direction for the whole company. Bureaucratic haggling and sticking to routine procedures are the biggest enemies of progress in Daewoo. Having started as a trading company, Daewoo still values flexibility and deal making rather than building and running routinized operating systems.

Another senior Daewoo executive assisting Chairman Kim in managing overseas operations stated:

In emerging markets, the window of opportunity is not always open. Timing is often critical. Detailed environmental surveys or market research are important, but not always obtainable and often used for internal battles to make excuses or to avoid responsibility. In addition, market research studies often focus on the existing state-of-affairs, underestimating or ignoring future potential. We negotiate the environment. Chairman Kim visits the investment site, negotiates the deal personally, and makes an up-or-down decision. In this process, Chairman Kim carefully evaluates the business prospects and develop[s] solutions. Once faced with a decision, he spends enormous energy verifying investment information from various sources. In Uz-Daewoo Auto project, he visited Uzbekistan more than 10 times in a six-month period before he made the final decision to sign the agreement. This is one of the reasons why we have been able to penetrate so many emerging markets.

Some outsiders including business scholars, consultants, and business reporters criticized this entrepreneurial style. According to them, Daewoo relied too much on the entrepreneurial leadership of Chairman Kim, leaving little room for systematic management. There was also a concern that Daewoo was expanding much too fast and widely without sufficient core competencies and financial base. An investment banker in Seoul provided an interesting affirmative view:

When I first looked into Daewoo's investment decision processes, I was frustrated. Formal feasibility studies were often considered "ornamental" by the front-line managers and even by some of the financial managers. One Daewoo executive once told me that formal investment analysis is never sufficient to assess a project's feasibility without the benefit of business intuition. Now, I have a better understanding of Daewoo's way of doing business. First, Daewoo applies excellent project financing skills to its overseas investments. For example, in the Uz-Daewoo Auto case, Daewoo provides 50% of the equity capital over 3 years, and the debt is arranged with a payment guarantee from the Uzbekistan government. So, Daewoo can inject the initial portion of equity capital and reinvest the earnings from the project later on. Daewoo's financing terms and risk management approaches are quite creative. I've also found that the core of Daewoo's investment information is strictly confidential due to the nature of deals in emerging markets. This is one of the reasons why Daewoo's investment decision may seem improvised to outsiders.

According to a Daewoo executive who had helped Chairman Kim coordinate Daewoo's global operations for many years:

> We use quantitative analyses in our feasibility studies, but we do not rely solely on them in making our investment decisions. Daewoo's experience in emerging markets is very useful. Published data on emerging markets are not reliable and, due to political and economic volatility, are quickly outdated. Critical information bearing on the deal may come from the key players, but in many cases, they do not have the complete picture either. So, we learn as we go. For example, Daewoo and the Uzbekistan government invented a new approach to currency convertibility and import duties. Local experts can tell you something, but it is not a simple matter of retaining a consultant. Often, there is no base case for comparison. Strict confidentiality is essential, so only a limited number of people can be involved in the deal. As the deal is negotiated, mutual trust builds and we gain access to better information with the help of our ever-improving credentials. In this process, we can negotiate the details of the business environment in which we are going to operate. So, planning which market to enter while standing in front of a map of the world is impossible. Sometimes, we worry that there might have been better alternatives. However, it is impossible to know everything about every country in the world.

MARKETING

Market Size

A senior Daewoo manager involved in the deal commented on the size of the potential market and its relationship to the initial plant size and product mix:

> In the late 1980s when Uzbekistan was still a part of the Soviet Union, there were one million cars on the road in Uzbekistan. The typical Russian car used to sell in Uzbekistan for 6,000 rubles when the average worker earned 250 rubles per month.[11] Around 80,000 new cars were sold each year. A European Union study in 1996 suggested that Uzbekistan could absorb 4,000 imported cars per year based on the GNP per capita level. Considering the average age of cars on the road and a 10% annual replacement rate, annual demand for new cars in Uzbekistan should be 100,000 units. With 80% of the 14 million adults in Uzbekistan holding a driver's license, the long-term market potential is much larger. Considering an annual market demand for two million cars in the whole CIS region, we thought that 100,000 car exports to the neighboring countries was feasible. President Kharimov had initially suggested a 100,000-vehicle plant to produce the Tico and Damas models during his visit to the Changwon minicar plant. Daewoo subsequently offered to build a 200,000-vehicle-capacity plant. Originally, we planned to produce

---

[11]The typical Uz-Daewoo Auto employee earned 10,000 Sum a month in mid-1997.

40,000 Rabo (a small truck based on the Tico body); 60,000 Damas vans; and 80,000 Tico cars, but we subsequently changed our product mix to 50,000 Damas; 50,000 Tico; and 100,000 Nexia when we considered the market preference for larger, C-class cars.

As of 1995, there were 834,000 passenger cars and 266,000 trucks in Uzbekistan. The average age of vehicles on the road was 9 years. Ninety-five percent of the vehicles had been made in Russia. Table 2.1 shows the mix of cars on the road according to vehicle size class.

Sales, Distribution and Service

Exhibit 2.13 shows the sales and production history of Uz-Daewoo Auto. Of the 42,000 vehicles produced by the end of July 1997, 26,000 vehicles were sold for cash, 4,000 vehicles were sold via bank transfer, and 1,300 vehicles were exported. An additional 2,980 vehicles were in manufacturer's inventory, and 5,800 vehicles were in dealer inventory. Ninety percent of the exports were made to Russia, while the other 10% went to Kazakhstan, Kyrgystan, and Belarus.

At the company-owned flagship retail dealership in Andijan, the sales manager reported that 45 vehicles had been sold in May 1997, up from 20 in April. In a typical day, 50–60 customer prospects visited the dealership. No trade-ins were negotiated. All new cars carried a one-year warranty. The four sales people were paid salaries with no sales commission. Two spare parts sales people also worked at the dealership. Daewoo was not closely involved in domestic marketing. Uz-Daewoo Auto was in charge of production, nationwide promotion, and sales to dealers, and Uzautosanoat was in charge of distribution.[12] Due to high inflation (5% to 6% per month in 1997), Uz-Daewoo changed its price schedule every month subject to government approval. Table 2.2 reports the retail price tags at the flagship dealer. Table 2.3 shows the comparative cost structure for Tico and Nexia cars produced in Uzbekistan.

According to a Daewoo manager involved in the Uzbekistan operation:

> The retail price tags don't tell you the whole story. The high inflation and continuous devaluation of the Sum against the U.S. dollar creates an arbitrage

TABLE 2.1 Mix of Cars on the Road[1]		
	Mix of Cars on the Road: 1996	*1997 Forecast Mix of New Car Sales*
Class A	7,000 (0.9%)	1.5–2%, Tico has 100% share
Class B	88,000 (11.8%)	15%, Oka, Tavria
Class C	611,000 (81.7%)	80%, VW Golf, Fiat (Turkey), Nexia
Class D	12,000 (1.7%)	2–3%, Mercedes, BMW, Opel
Class E	29,000 (3.9%)	1–2%, Mercedes, BMW

[1]Across the whole CIS region, demand for Class C cars was 81% of the total while Class A cars represented only 2%.

Source: Interview with Mr. Yusupov, general director of Uz-Daewoo Auto Co.

---

[12]Uzautosanoat was an automobile sales and distribution company wholly owned by the Uzbekistan government. A ministerial level official was appointed the CEO of the company.

TABLE 2.2 Retail Sticker Prices on July 29, 1997[1]

	Local Currency: Cash	Local Currency: Bank Transfer	US$/Export
Nexia GL: Basic Model	$13,000	$15,600	$9,026
Nexia GL: Fully Loaded Model	$17,400	$20,880	$10,626
Tico: Basic Model	$6,790	$8,830	$4,800
Tico: Fully Loaded Model	$7,960	$10,350	$5,540
Damas: Basic Model	$9,110	$11,840	$5,900

[1]Exhibit 2.17 shows the exchange rate trends in more detail.

opportunity. If you can buy in U.S. dollars (at the official rate), you should earn an arbitrage profit due to the discrepancy between the official rate and the black market rate.

In Uzbekistan, Uz-Daewoo Auto had appointed 40 direct dealers, who in turn had appointed 150 subdealers. Eighteen of the direct dealers were wholly owned by Uz-autosanoat. Most of the dealers were former automotive service stations. Dealers earned

EXHIBIT 2.17 Exchange Rate Trend: Sum/US$

	Official Rate	Market Rate	Official Rate/Market Rate
1996			
January[1]	36.2	44.2	122%
February	36.4	45.5	125%
March	36.4	47.9	132%
April	336.9	49.3	134%
May	37.7	51.3	136%
June	37.8	51.5	136%
July	37.9	53.2	140%
August	38.6	56.1	145%
September	39.7	63.4	160%
October	42.3	75.5	178%
November	49.5	103.1	208%
December	52.9	109.5	207%
1997			
January	55.6	118.0	212%
February	56.7	126.6	224%
March	58.0	138.5	239%
April	59.3	150.0	253%
May	60.1	144.2	240%
June	61.8	142.8	231%
July	64.2	141.3	220%

[1]In January 1996, one U.S. dollar was equivalent to 36.2 Sum at the official rate (and 44.2 Sum at the market rate)

TABLE 2.3 Comparative Cost Structure for Tico and Nexia Produced in Uzbekistan: July 1997 (%)		
	Tico	*Nexia*
Factory Price	100.0	100.0
Cost of Goods Sold	71.1	72.1
Administrative Cost	9.6	8.6
Transportation & Other[1]	6.0	6.0
Profit Margin	13.3	13.3
Interest on Loans from Daewoo	7.1	7.1
Construction Fee to Daewoo	8.2	8.2
3% Royalty to Daewoo	3.0	3.0

[1]Transportation costs for imported parts were $3,200 per container for 2,000 containers per month (at full production).

a 5% retail sales margin on the Nexia and a 10% margin on the Tico and Damas. New dealers received discounts on purchases of their initial inventory. Outside Uzbekistan, Uz-Daewoo had appointed 22 dealers in Russia and other CIS countries. Of these, 5 were wholly owned, and 6 were partly owned by Uzautosanoat. By mid-1997, 1 billion Sum and $4 million had been spent to establish the distribution and service network. Uz-Daewoo and Uzautosanoat were planning to expand them. Further expansion of the service network would emphasize private service centers. Around 200 service centers were to be set up in Uzbekistan, and 50 of them were to be supplied with parts and components through Uzautosanoat. Dealer sales managers and service technicians received training provided by Daewoo in Korea as part of the personnel exchange program.

Uz-Daewoo Auto advertised daily on Uzbekistan's national television network. One advertisement showed the Nexia's maneuvering and performance capabilities in a circus arena, dodging the animals. Uz-Daewoo Auto's television advertising was part of an overall corporate image-building campaign by Daewoo, which would cost $1 million in 1997—almost one-quarter of all paid television advertising in Uzbekistan.

Competition

The Uzbekistan government was pushing Uz-Daewoo Auto to increase exports to generate hard currency. However, Daewoo claimed that sluggish domestic sales growth had limited the achievement of scale economies, and kept unit costs high. Smugglers from neighboring countries also restricted export sales. As long as the black market exchange rate of Sum/U.S. dollars was almost twice the official rate, export sales through official channels were problematic. In the absence of tight border controls, it was impossible to prevent smugglers from neighboring countries from bringing in U.S. dollars, converting them into Sum at the black market rate, and them smuggling Uz-Daewoo cars back to their countries.

Daewoo had hoped that Uz-Daewoo would be a useful production base for the growing Russia market. In Russia, imported cars from Uzbekistan had to pay a 5.26% tariff while those from Korea and other non-CIS countries paid 60%. Value-added tax in Russia was 20% (18% in Uzbekistan); the sales tax differential was absorbed by Uz-Daewoo Auto on officially exported cars. It cost $480 to transport a Nexia ($420 for a Tico) from Uzbekistan to Moscow.

Autovaz, the largest Russian automobile manufacturer that had formerly produced Rada, was producing and selling the VAZ2109 (1500cc) and the VAZ2110 (a new 1500cc model). Its production capacity was 900,000 vehicles a year, of which 600,000 were assigned for sale in the Russian domestic market. Table 2.4 shows price comparisons between Russian cars and Uz-Daewoo cars.

According to Yusupov, general director of Uz-Daewoo Auto, competition in the export market was tough and getting tougher:

> The Nexia is better equipped to compete in the export market. Traditionally, Russian and Uzbekistan consumers prefer C class cars (with engine sizes between 1500cc to 1800cc) due partly to rough road conditions. Uz-Daewoo should consider shifting the production mix in favor of the Nexia. Ford is planning a 50,000-vehicle-capacity plant to make Ford Escorts in Belarus; the retail price will be around $10,000 to $12,000. Opel (the German subsidiary of General Motors) has a strategic alliance with Autovaz to introduce Astras in 1998 which will be made in a 50,000-vehicle-capacity plant. Moscvich is also working on an alliance to produce Renault cars. Kia is planning a 50,000-vehicle-capacity CKD plant in Kaliningrad, Russia. There will be a flood of C-Class cars. Moreover, these competitors are spreading the word that the Nexia is no longer in production in Korea. Uz-Daewoo will be in trouble if Daewoo doesn't enable us to introduce a new model.

Daewoo managers also acknowledged the increasing competitive challenge, but viewed the situation differently:

> At present, Russian-made cars do not match Uz-Daewoo cars in terms of quality or performance. It will take some time before the competitive pressure materializes. Autovaz will only be doing joint CKD production of Opel's Astra and Calibra at the end of 1998. It will be another year before they start producing Open engines for those cars. There are many strategic alliances on paper, but as yet, no cars are rolling off production lines. Actions speak louder than words, and these deals always take longer than expected to bear

TABLE 2.4 Comparable Retail Car Prices in Russia

Russian Cars			*Uz-Daewoo Cars*		
Producer	Model	Price[1]	Producer	Model	Price
Autovaz	OKA	US$3,000	Uz-Daewoo	Tico	US$6,000
Tavria	Tavria	US$3,000			
Autovaz	VAZ2109	US$9,496	Uz-Daewoo	Nexia	US$12,000[2]
	VAZ2110	US$11,870			

[1]U.S. dollar prices were as of July 27, 1997, at the offical exchange rate.
[2]On the black market, the Nexia could retail for $8,000 if payment was made in U.S. dollars. The VAZ2109 sold for $8,500 on the black market.

fruit. Of course, Daewoo is preparing for the challenges. We will start producing state-of-the-art models (which are still under development) from 2000. The new model line will cover C, D, and E class cars. The Uz-Daewoo plant is designed to be able to shift to production of these new models.

Hard Currency Problem

Due to the shortage of hard currency in Uzbekistan, the convertibility of the Sum was strictly limited. Because the Uz-Daewoo project was designed to generate hard currency through exports, the Uzbekistan government gave Daewoo a higher priority in hard currency allocation for plant construction and component imports.[13] However, currency convertibility and repatriation of the earnings were ongoing challenges, and constrained further investment. Daewoo arranged foreign loans (under supplier's credit) from Western banks and institutions for its Uzbekistan projects, but recognized that it would take time for those projects to generate hard currency earnings. From the outset, Daewoo had been trying to alleviate this problem through becoming involved in the cotton business. From simple cotton exports, Daewoo was planning to expand its business into cotton plantations and spinning. Detailed operational decisions dealing with raw material allocation and pricing were still pending, but the business prospects were bright.[14] According to a Daewoo manager involved in the cotton business, a new textile industry complex in Uzbekistan that included the whole value-added processes from spinning to apparel manufacturing could generate $15 billion annual exports within 10 years.

Management Challenges

When construction work started on the plant, a task force was appointed by Chairman Kim to implement the Uz-Daewoo project. Kwan-Ki Lee (also the chairman of Uz-Daewoo Auto) was in charge of the team. Overall Daewoo operations in Uzbekistan were coordinated by Daewoo Corporation and reported to Chairman Kim. However, managing an operation in a remote foreign environment was still a daunting task. Early on, the telecommunications infrastructure was not reliable: In 1993, it could take 30 minutes to send a five-page fax from Seoul to Tashkent. Chairman Kim visited Uzbekistan whenever necessary. Lee and his staff were spending half their time in Uzbekistan and usually traveled on weekends to save time. Due to the variety of Daewoo's businesses in Uzbekistan, the company was planning to appoint a senior executive stationed there to coordinate all Uzbekistan operations. Because of both the cultural and physical distance between Tashkent and Seoul, life in Uzbekistan was still a challenge for Korean managers. All 20 Uz-Daewoo Auto expatriates in Uzbekistan had their families in Korea. There was no reliable international school in Uzbekistan. At first, they could only obtain Korean food through monthly shipments from Daewoo's Seoul Office. Managing cross-cultural conflict was also a challenge. It took great patience and understanding to persuade Uzbekistan workers to adopt attitudes of hard work and competitiveness.

---

[13]Due to limited hard currency reserves and a growing current account deficit, the Uzbekistan government allocated hard currency for each business.

[14]Due to the importance of cotton to the Uzbekistan economy, the Uzbekistan government was in charge of the quantity allocation and the pricing of cotton trade.

CONCLUSION

Preparing for his upcoming visit to Uzbekistan, Chairman Kim reviewed the progress of Daewoo's cooperative ventures there and reflected on the role that cooperative ventures with other companies and with national governments had played in the growth of Daewoo. Uz-Daewoo Auto was facing several challenges. Faced with the pressure from the Uzbekistan government for increased export sales, Uz-Daewoo had to meet various competitive challenges in both the domestic and the export markets. Smugglers from neighboring countries were a major obstacle to export sales. Several multinational companies planning entry in Uzbekistan were criticizing the benefits Daewoo had earned as a first mover. Although hard currency shortages and limited convertibility constrained further investment, the Uzbekistan government was offering Daewoo two new investment projects outside the automobile sector. Chairman Kim had to resolve these issues as he sought to advance Daewoo's overall strategic relationship with Uzbekistan.

CHAPTER

3

PLANNING A JOINT VENTURE

Milkpak Limited—International Joint Venture

On January 25, 1987, Syed Babar Ali, chairman, and Syed Yawar Ali,[1] managing director of Milkpak Limited, prepared for a meeting with a high-level team from Nestlé, a multinational food company based in Switzerland. Milkpak Limited, incorporated in 1979, was a pioneer in developing a Pakistani industry for ultra-high temperature (UHT) milk, a sterilized milk that did not require refrigeration when specially packaged. The increasing popularity of UHT milk caused company sales to increase from 96 million rupees (Rs) in 1982—Milkpak's first full year of production—to 340 million rupees in 1986. The company was increasingly interested in producing value-added products and was exploring a joint venture with a foreign company.[2]

COMPANY BACKGROUND

Milkpak was part of a family group of businesses—the Ali Group—that spanned a number of interests. Considered one of Pakistan's leading industrial families, the Ali Group was involved in razor blade and textile manufacture in addition to having holdings in the insurance industry. The group had major investments in the vegetable oil and soap industries and also managed Ford's auto assembly plant prior to 1973, when the government nationalized all of these businesses.

Milkpak was founded to create a market for packaging materials produced by Packages Limited, a leading company in the Ali Group. Packages Limited was established in Lahore, Pakistan, in 1956, in collaboration with AB Akerlund & Rausing of Sweden, to convert paper and board into packaging. Packages later integrated backward into pulp

---

[1]Yawar Ali was Babar Ali's nephew.
[2]Exchange rate in 1986: Rs 16.65 = $1.00.

Research Associate Afroze A. Mohammed prepared this case under the supervision of Professor John A. Quelch as the basis for class discussion rather than to illustrate either effective or ineffective handling of an administrative situation. This case contains some information from earlier cases on Milkpak prepared by the Lahore University of Management Science.

and paper manufacturing. The company supplied packaging materials to a variety of industries and also provided technical assistance to packaging plants in Africa and the Middle East. Packages manufactured its own line of facial tissues and other consumer products. In 1986, Packages' total sales were approximately Rs 633 million.

Milkpak was established following a 1976 review of the use of Packages' equipment. The Tetra Laminator, a machine designed for making packaging material for long-life milk, was used very infrequently. Packages purchased the Tetra Laminator machine in 1967 from Tetra Pak of Sweden, a company affiliated with Akerlund & Rausing. The Tetra Pak aseptic system[3] was developed to package UHT milk. The UHT process heated milk at temperatures of 130 to 150 degrees centigrade for 2 to 3 seconds. Milk thus sterilized had a shelf life of up to 3 months without refrigeration when packaged in Tetra Pak containers. The Tetra Pak system had special advantages for developing countries that lacked extensive refrigeration and distribution systems. Some of the packages were in the shape of tetrahedrons (a four-faced pyramid); rectangular packages that required heavier and more expensive paper were also available.

Packages found that there was one milk plant in Pakistan—at the time inoperative—designed to produce sterilized milk. The company leased the plant which had a capacity of 17,500 liters of milk per day, as a pilot project to test the market for UHT milk. Packages hoped that a successful pilot project would encourage entrepreneurs to produce UHT milk, thereby increasing the demand for Tetra Pak packaging. To implement the project, a number of challenges were surmounted, including developing a low-cost, locally produced paper for packaging and securing reliable sources of milk supply. The pilot project was deemed a success in 1978 when, with limited promotional efforts, sales reached plant capacity.

Milkpak was incorporated in January 1979 after Packages decided to invest in a 150,000-liters-per-day UHT milk plant, at a cost of Rs 90 million. Financing for the new company was obtained from Tetra Pak; Danish Turnkey Dairies, the equipment supplier; and several development agencies, including the International Finance Corporation and the German Development Institute. (Exhibit 3.1 summarizes Milkpak's ownership structure.)

Milkpak started commercial production of UHT milk in its new plant in November 1981. (Exhibit 3.2 provides Milkpak's yearly sales and profit and loss statements from 1981 to 1986.) By 1987, Milkpak's product line had expanded from UHT milk to include fruit juices and other dairy products, though UHT milk still accounted for an estimated 85% of company sales. In 1984, Milkpak started marketing the Frost line of fruit juices, introduced a few years earlier by Packages. Frost juices were premixed, in contrast to existing juices on the market that were available in concentrate form. Milkpak bought the Frost brand name and equipment from Packages, and in 1986 fruit juices accounted for 9% of Milkpak's sales. Additional products included butter, introduced in 1985. In 1986, the company launched a sterilized cream product, Balai, and also a cooking oil, Desi Ghee. These products were sold under the brand name Milkpak.

PAKISTAN

Pakistan was founded in 1947, when British India was partitioned into two nation states. Pakistan, established as a Muslim country, initially had two geographically separate

---

[3]An aseptic system is free from pathogenic organisms.

EXHIBIT 3.1   Ownership Shares of Milkpak

Investor	Ownership share (%)
Ali family	15.7
Packages Limited	7.1
IGI[1]	5.7
International Finance Corporation	5.7
Tetra Pak[2]	8.6
DEG[3]	5.7
DTD[4]	2.9
IFU[5]	2.9
Public shareholders	45.7

[1]International General Insurance Company, 99% owned by the Ali family.
[2]The Swedish manufacturer of the equipment used to make materials for the nonrefrigerated milk containers.
[3]The German Development Institute, a foreign aid and development institution.
[4]Danish Turnkey Dairies, Limited, Milkpak's equipment supplier and the provider of Milkpak's specialized extension services to Pakistani dairy farmers.
[5]Industrial Fund for Developing Countries, Denmark.

Source: Company records.

sections on either side of India. In 1971, the eastern wing of Pakistan separated to form Bangladesh. The western section, which remained Pakistan, had Urdu as its national language, with English widely spoken. By 1986, Pakistan had a population of over 90 million. Pakistan's GNP per capita was $380, although the country had large income disparities. (Exhibit 3.3 provides basic social and economic data about Pakistan[4].)

In the 1980s, Pakistan had political and economic policies that promoted the role of private enterprise in the country's economy. This climate was in contrast to that prevailing from 1972 to 1977 when the government was concerned about the high concentration of industrial ownership and nationalized a number of businesses. In the mid-1980s, the rate of growth of manufacturing output was 9.1% per year, while agricultural output grew at 4.6% per year; from 1972 to 1977, these sectors had grown each year at only 5.2% and 2%, respectively (Burki, 1986). Policy initiatives made in the 1980s offered safeguards against nationalization and sought to ensure the safety of investments.

Although the overall climate for private investment was favorable, businesses had to obtain a variety of government licenses and approvals before undertaking or expanding projects. These approvals differed according to a project's source of funds and specific characteristics. The government's permission for a project would address issues such as the amount of investment allowed, procedures governing repatriation of capital and profits, the amount of raw materials that could be imported, and the location of the industrial establishment. In practice, obtaining these approvals could result in project delays, although the Pakistani government was making efforts to facilitate the process.

---

[4]Background information in this section is from *Pakistan and the World Bank: Partners in Progress* (Washington, D.C.: The World Bank, 1986).

EXHIBIT 3.2 Milkpak Profit-and-Loss Statements: 1981–1986

	1986	1985	1984	1983	1982	1981 (2 months)
Net sales	340,343,535	251,835,221	214,662,630	137,310,716	96,129,181	9,409,358
Cost of goods sold	296,417,357	223,485,654	185,175,145	114,742,655	85,894,230	9,986,726
Trading profit	43,926,178	28,349,567	29,487,485	22,568,061	10,234,951	(577,368)
Selling, administrative, and general expenses	30,294,796	17,980,055	14,959,910	10,723,215	8,731,245	1,413,890
Operating profit/(loss)[1]	13,631,382	10,369,512	14,527,575	11,844,846	1,503,706	(1,991,258)
Other income	1,043,295	970,458	773,190	342,738	342,021	1,194,391
	14,674,677	11,339,970	15,300,765	12,187,584	1,845,727	(796,867)
Financial charges	7,495,788	5,258,607	5,828,054	5,713,972	6,868,285	900,448
Worker's participation fund	361,500	355,970	546,389	414,430	—	
	7,857,288	5,614,577	6,374,443	6,128,402	6,868,285	900,488
Profit before taxation	6,817,389	5,725,393	8,926,322	6,059,182	(5,022,558)	(1,697,315)
Provision for taxation	3,045,000	1,063,000	4,535,000	—	—	
	3,772,389	4,122,393	4,391,322	6,059,182	(5,022,558)	(1,697,315)

[1]The decline in operating profit as a percentage of net sales in 1985 and 1986 was primarily due to switching to an aluminum foil packaging paper that improved the shelf life of Milkpak brand milk, starting a new fruit juice plant, and increases in sales promotion expenses.

Source: Company records.

EXHIBIT 3.3 Pakistan: Basic Country Data

Area: 803,940 sq. km.

Agricultural land (1983): 254,900 sq. km.

GNP per capita (1984): $380

Energy consumption per capita (1983): 179 kg of oil equivalent

Population (1984): 93.3 million

Urban population (percentage of total): 30.1

Projected population in 2000: 143 million

Population density (1984): 116.0 per sq. km.

Population density of agricultural land (1984): 366.0 per sq. km.

Population growth rate (1970–84): 3.1%

Urban population growth rate (1970–84): 4.6%

Crude birthrate (1984): 41 per thousand

Crude death rate (1984): 11 per thousand

Life expectancy at birth (1984): 50.6 years

Infant mortality (1984): 116.2 per thousand

Access to safe water (1981): 34.6% of population
    Urban: 72.0%
    Rural: 20.0%

Population per physician (1981): 3,190

Average size of household (1979): 6.7

Secondary school enrollment (1983): 15%

Adult literacy (1979): 24%

Labor force (1984): 26.4 million

Labor participation rate (1983): 28.3%

Percentage of income received by:
    Highest 5% of households (1970): 17.8
    Highest 20% of households (1970): 41.8
    Lowest 20% of households (1970): 8
    Lowest 40% of households (1970): 20.2

Estimated absolute poverty income level[1] (1979)
    Urban: $176.0 per capita
    Rural: $122.0 per capita

Estimated relative poverty income level[2] (1979)
    Urban: $88.0 per capita
    Rural: $58.0 per capita

Estimated population below absolute poverty income level[3]
    Urban: 32.0%
    Rural: 29.0%

---

[1]Absolute poverty income level is the level below which a minimal nutritionally adequate diet plus essential nonfood requirements is not affordable.
[2]Rural relative poverty income level is one-third of average per capita personal income of the country. Urban level is derived from the rural level with adjustment for higher cost of living in urban areas.
[3]Percentage of population (urban and rural) who are the "absolute poor."

Source: Adapted from *Pakistan and the World Bank, Partners in Progress* (1986).

THE PAKISTANI DAIRY INDUSTRY

Fresh milk was traditionally supplied to urban consumers directly from farms on a daily basis.[5] Consumers obtained milk (1) directly from farmers or dairy colonies (these sources were sometimes referred to as peri-urban producers) that kept buffaloes in or near the towns, and (2) from milkmen who purchased milk from farmers. Milkmen would travel the countryside by bicycle, collect milk in 40-liter cans, and then sell it to contractors, who put ice in the milk and then transported it into the city. The milk was then sold to consumers at their homes and through retail milk shops, which did not have refrigeration facilities. The entire process, from milking the buffalos to selling the milk in the city, took place each morning. Although the system delivered fresh milk to consumers each day, it had drawbacks. In particular, adulteration of milk with impure water occurred at various stages in the distribution chain. In addition, the absence of a refrigerated distribution infrastructure led to milk spoilage and waste.

The problems of transporting and distributing milk resulted in shortages in major urban centers—Milkpak's target market. Shortages were exacerbated by the market seasonality in production and consumption of milk. Milk consumption peaked in summer. In contrast, milk production was highest during the winter months of December to March, called the "flush" season, and lowest during the "lean" season from May to August. Lower production during the summer was caused by hot weather and decreased availability of fodder. As a result of both of these factors, the Pakistani government adopted liberal policies toward the import of milk products. (Exhibit 3.4 provides data on Pakistani milk production and dairy imports.)

		Dairy imports		
EXHIBIT 3.4 Milk Production and Dairy Imports, 1975–1976 to 1985–1986				
Year	*Estimated milk production (000 tons)*	*Value (million Rs)*	*Milk equivalent (000 tons)*	*Imports/ production (%)*
1975–76	8,348	313.0	329.2	3.94
1976–77	8,524	251.0	165.8	1.94
1977–78	8,704	391.1	448.5	5.15
1978–79	8,888	321.6	237.0	2.67
1979–80	9,075	481.9	420.4	4.63
1980–81	9,267	552.3	352.8	3.81
1981–82	9,462	522.6	275.8	2.91
1982–83	9,662	736.8	357.4	3.70
1983–84	10,242	802.1	397.4	3.88
1984–85	10,856	712.0	315.6	2.91
1985–86	11,508	779.2	282.4	2.45

Source: Pakistan Economic Survey Data; imports data from Federal Bureau of Statistics. Adapted from Table 4.2 in *Pakistan's Dairy Industry: Issues and Policy Alternatives.*

---

[5]Background information in this case about the Pakistani dairy industry, including the UHT industry, is from *Pakistan's Dairy Industry: Issues and Policy Alternatives,* Islamabad: The Directorate of Agricultural Policy and Chemonics International Consulting Division, 1989.

Milk powder was a particularly important dairy import. Milk powder, mixed with water to make fluid milk, had an established place in the Pakistani market, especially in Karachi, where fresh milk supplies were insufficient to meet demand as a result of increases in population. In 1986, about 30% of the demand for fluid milk supplies in Karachi was met by milk powder. Demand for milk powder was met primarily by imports, which averaged 20,000 to 30,000 tons annually. Powder was imported both as a branded product, in tins, and also in bulk (25 kilogram bags). Bulk supplies were repackaged by retailers in 1½ kg[6] plastic bags. Branded milk powders were typically bought by higher-income consumers while the repackaged bulk supplies were purchased by lower- and middle-income consumers.

Efforts had also been made to establish an indigenous local milk processing industry. Packages' decision to invest in Milkpak was made in spite of a history of failed investments in the milk processing industry. During the 1960s and 1970s, Pakistani entrepreneurs established 23 plants in the dairy processing field, including several plants for milk pasteurization. The failure of at least 15 of this "first generation" of dairy processing plants was attributed to poor management, difficulties in obtaining fresh milk supplies, and the lack of an extensive refrigerated distribution infrastructure.

Milk Collection

To ensure a reliable and high-quality supply of milk, especially during the lean season, Milkpak focused attention on developing a system for milk collection and agricultural extension. Milk collection centers were established in areas considered rich in milk production. The company taught farmers scientific techniques of livestock care and breeding, provided veterinary services, and made available high-yielding fodder seed and cattle feed. Milk was supplied to the company by traditional milk contractors who bought milk from farmers. In addition, Milkpak helped establish village cooperatives and, through them, received milk directly from farmers.

During the flush season, Milkpak often had to refuse milk supplies. Milkpak's management visited dairies in India, including Nestlé's plant, to gain an understanding of how other dairies in a similar environment addressed problems of seasonality.

UHT Milk Processing

Processed milk was required by law to contain 3.5% butterfat and 8.9% solids not fat (SNF). Fresh milk usually had a higher fat content and a lower level of solids than required. As a result, before being heated to 130 to 150 degrees centigrade, the milk was decreamed to reduce the fat content. To raise the SNF level, skimmed milk powder and water were added. When there was a shortage of fresh milk, milk powder could be added to increase milk production volumes, although, at prevailing prices for imported milk powder, it was rarely economical to do so. The technology for manufacturing UHT milk was considered expensive, with processing costs accounting for about 25% of total product costs. (Exhibit 3.5 reports estimates of UHT processing costs, obtained from different manufacturers in the industry.) Packaging materials,

---

[6]There are 1,000 kilograms in a metric ton.

EXHIBIT 3.5 UHT Milk Production Costs	
Cost item	*Rs/liter*
Raw milk[1]	2.66
Value of cream separated[2]	(0.45)
Net cost of raw milk	2.21
Conversion to 1 liter volume at 3.5% butter fat	2.28
Skimmed milk powder[3]	0.72
Processing cost[4]	1.72
Packaging cost	1.77
Transportation cost	0.08
Market returns/replacement[5]	0.20
Subtotal	6.77
Processor's margin	0.04
Distributor's margin	0.19
Retailer's margin	0.50
Subtotal	0.73
Retail price[6]	7.50

[1]Price of milk at 5% butterfat and 7% solid not fats.
[2]Cream (50% fat) valued at Rs 15 per kilogram.
[3]Adding 19 grams of skimmed milk powder at Rs 38/kg.
[4]Includes depreciation and financial charges.
[5]Market returns are assumed to be 3%.
[6]Retail UHT milk price in Lahore zone. The price in other areas was Rs 8/liter.

Source: International Consulting Division, Chemonics. Adapted from Table 2.4 in *Pakistan's Dairy Industry: Issues and Policy Alternatives,* 1989.

which were heavily taxed, accounted for another 26% of Milkpak's production cost (*Pakistan's Dairy Industry,* 1989).

UHT Milk Marketing

Positioning

A major challenge facing the company was to introduce urban consumers to the idea of long-life milk. Consumers were concerned that sterilized milk contained preservatives or was somehow not genuine because, unlike fresh milk, the Milkpak brand contained no cream. In one early promotional campaign, households were given two samples of Milkpak, one for immediate consumption and the other to be consumed 4 days later; the goal was to demonstrate that although the milk remained packaged, it did not require refrigeration. Milkpak was positioned as a pure dairy product; processed in a scientific, hygienic way; and consistent in quality throughout the year. (Exhibit 3.6 and Exhibit 3.7 show print advertisements for Milkpak brand UHT milk and butter. Sales promotion and advertising expenses for Milkpak are summarized in Exhibit 3.8.)

Milkpak's heavy users were "modern housewives," who were concerned about both convenience and product quality. Another target market was lower-income consumers, who were often sold relatively cheap adulterated milk by the traditional milkmen; Milkpak provided a higher-quality milk than they had previously purchased. (Exhibit 3.9 presents the results of a consumer survey sponsored by Milkpak.)

EXHIBIT 3.6   Print Advertisement for Milkpak Brand UHT Milk

Translation

Top Lines: Fresh, pure Milkpak milk—the best for the whole family.
Bottom Line: A product of Milkpak dairy. Pure, delicious, and fresh.

EXHIBIT 3.7 Print Advertisement for Milkpak Brand Butter

Translation

Top Lines: Prepared from fresh and pure milk. Milkpak butter—the best for the whole family.

Bottom Line: A product of Milkpak dairy. Pure, delicious, and fresh.

EXHIBIT 3.8	Milkpak Sales Promotion and Advertising Expenses	
Year	*Expenses (Rs)*	*% of sales*
1981	778,540[1]	8.2
1982	1,517,576	1.6
1983	1,158,329	0.8
1984	900,204	0.4
1985	1,728,077	0.7
1986	8,283,452[2]	2.4

[1]Sales promotion and advertising expenses of Rs 778,540 were incurred in 1981, but were written off in three equal yearly installments in 1982, 1983, and 1984.

[2]Increase in sales promotion expenses was required to launch new products and sustain market share.

Source: Company records.

Packaging

Milkpak brand UHT milk was initially sold in tetrahedron-shaped containers, in sizes of $\frac{1}{2}$ liter and $\frac{1}{5}$ liter. In 1984, a one-liter rectangular-shaped "brickpak" was introduced. The more conventionally shaped brickpak eliminated the need for special crates required to store Tetra Paks, but used more packaging material. In 1986, a quarter-liter brickpak was introduced.

EXHIBIT 3.9	Results of 1986 Milkpak Survey of Middle/High Income Urban Consumers on UHT Milk and Milk Powder

- Sixty-five percent of respondents used more than one source of milk (e.g., UHT milk, fresh milk, powdered milk).
- In Karachi, 9% of respondents bought UHT milk; in Lahore, 25% bought UHT milk.
- Forty percent of respondents had no brand preference in purchasing UHT milk, while 35% preferred Milkpak.
- Respondents' prompted recall of the Milkpak brand name was 86%. Unprompted recall was 29%.
- Fifty-six percent of UHT milk purchasers bought it in general stores, 25% in bakeries, and 16% in shops that were combined general stores/bakeries.
- Fifty-eight percent of respondents purchased UHT milk on a daily basis; 11% bought it three times a week; 18% purchased it twice a week; 13% purchased it less frequently.
- Respondents who did not purchase UHT milk cited the following reasons: It was too expensive (18%); they thought chemicals were added to the milk (12%); they were used to fresh milk (11%); and UHT milk contained no cream (10%).
- Consumers purchased family milk powder for several reasons: (1) to feed children (40%); (2) to make the following foods: tea (16%), desserts (11%), yogurt (11%), and drinks made from milk (10%); (3) and for drinking (11%).
- Respondents purchased milk powder from general stores (60%), combined general/medical stores (24%), and bakeries (10%).
- Seventy-four percent of respondents purchased milk powder once a month; 23% bought it twice a month; only 3% purchased powdered milk weekly.

Source: Company records.

Pricing

Table 3.1 shows the 1986 retail prices for Milkpak and other types of milk in two major cities in Pakistan. Milkpak competed with the traditional milk distribution system that supplied fresh, or "raw," milk to consumers each day. Milk powder competed with Milkpak as a convenience product.

Distribution

A key success factor in Milkpak's rapid growth was the expansion of its distribution network. In 1981, there were an estimated 1,000 retail outlets selling Milkpak; by 1986, the number had grown to 13,000. Milkpak was sold in grocery stores, bakeries, general stores, and supermarkets. The company had sales offices in Karachi, Lahore, and Islamabad, and had a nationwide network of distributors in all major cities and towns. For Milkpak brand milk, the margin to the distributor was between .2 and .25 rupees per liter, depending on the shipping distance. The retail margin was .52 rupees per liter. The UHT business was viewed as similar to the soft drink business, with high turnover and low margins, requiring flexibility and fast decision making.

Evolution of the UHT Milk Industry

Milkpak's success in developing a market for UHT milk spurred the entry of several other companies. By the end of 1986, eight plants owned by different companies could manufacture UHT milk. Total sales of UHT milk grew from 11.25 million liters in 1981 to approximately 80 million in 1986 (*Pakistan's Dairy Industry*, 1989). In 1986, Milkpak estimated that its share of the market was over 50%. Milkpak had a reputation for consistency and high quality, both with consumers and the trade.

Some of Milkpak's early competitors were short-lived. Milkpure and Purabrand, which entered the market in 1983, competed with Milkpak by offering consumer and trade promotions such as free tea bags and raffles for free air tickets. Milkpak did not offer similar promotions in response; management felt that profit margins on UHT milk did not allow such marketing investments. Both companies had financial problems and went out of business by the end of 1985.

Other more stable competitors included Milko, the UHT plant originally leased by Packages to test the market for UHT milk. Milko returned to its original owners after Milkpak's founding. By 1986, Milko had an estimated 10% share of the market. Pakistan Dairies, the country's first producer of cheese, started manufacturing UHT milk in

Table 3.1 Comparative Retail Prices of UHT Milk, Raw Milk, and Dried Milk Powder in Different Cities in Pakistan (rupees per liter)					
	Raw Milk		**Whole Milk Powder[1]**		
City	*Peri-Urban Producer*	*Milk Shop[2]*	*Tinned*	*Polythylene Bags*	*UHT Milk*
Lahore	5.00–6.00	4.50–5.50	7.50	6.00	7.50
Karachi	5.50–7.00	5.00–6.50	6.88	5.50	8.00

[1]In liquid milk equivalent terms, assuming a dried milk to liquid conversion ratio of 1:8.
[2]In general, the quality of milk sold by milk shops was poorer than that sold by peri-urban producers.
Source: Adapted from Table 2.5 in *Pakistan's Dairy Industry: Issues and Policy Alternatives* (1986).

1983. Because of its other dairy products, Pakistan Dairies had an extensive and effective system for milk collection and was regarded as a high-quality producer. In 1986, the company's share of the market was approximately 18% to 20%. A new competitor, Chaudhuri Dairies, entered the market in June 1986 and captured a share of 15% by year end. Chaudhuri introduced its brand Haleeb in rectangular brickpak packaging, which was more convenient to store and was considered a competitive advantage.

Although the sales of UHT milk grew rapidly, they still constituted a relatively small share of total consumption. It was estimated that by 1987, UHT accounted for approximately 2% of the milk consumed in Pakistan's urban areas.

The emergence of an industry to process UHT milk was fostered by government policy, notably duty exemptions on the import of machinery for dairy plants and the provision of low cost financing by government agencies. The government had sanctioned a number of additional plants that would be brought on line in coming years, and there was, therefore, concern that the industry would have substantial overcapacity (*Pakistan Dairy Industry,* 1989).

STRATEGIC OPTIONS FOR GROWTH

As Milkpak reviewed its growth options, management increasingly saw the development of a milk powder plant as a necessity. First, a powder plant would help smooth the seasonal mismatch between the supply of and demand for milk. During the summer (the time of peak demand), milk powder would be combined with liquid milk to extend the supplies of UHT milk. The growth potential for UHT milk had been limited by seasonality; Milkpak's marketing managers were reluctant to promote UHT milk heavily during the flush season because they felt they were creating demand that could not be satisfied in the lean season. Although Milkpak's managers were very committed to increasing UHT milk sales, they knew that the UHT business was inherently a high volume, low margin business. As a result, the company wanted to explore the possibility of producing other value-added foods, such as milk powder, cereal, and infant formula, among other products.

In addition to using milk powder as an ingredient in UHT milk, Milkpak could sell milk powder, which competed with UHT milk, as a convenience product. In 1986, 25,002 tons of milk powder, with a value of Rs 406 million, were imported. Only two domestic companies manufactured milk powder, one of which produced solely for the military. The other company, Noon Ltd., established with the technical assistance of Cow & Gate, a U.K. company, had an output of 600 tons per year. The Pakistan Dairy Association, chaired by Yawar Ali, argued that the government's low tariffs on milk powder imports (which historically had been subsidized by European producers) impeded the development of a domestic dairy industry. In 1986, the government imposed a 16% tax on imports of milk powder, which improved the viability of domestic production.

About 20% of milk powder imports were branded. The major brands, with estimated market shares, were NIDO, produced by Nestlé (24% market share); Red Cow, manufactured by Cow & Gate (25% of market); and Safety, manufactured by Friesland of the Netherlands (24% market share). NIDO's prices were the highest (Rs 107 per 1,800 gram tin), followed by Red Cow (Rs 92 to 102 per tin) and Safety (Rs 93 to 97 per tin.) The demand for branded milk powder was forecast to increase to 18,000 tons per year by 1996.

Milkpak's management had to decide whether to acquire foreign technology and management assistance to develop its own plant. Alternatively, Milkpak considered the possibility of finding a foreign joint venture partner.

Independent Study

Milkpak prepared a feasibility study for a milk powder plant. Exhibit 3.10 provides a summary of the project costs, financing sources, and projected profits. Milkpak estimated that by the third year of operation the plant would produce 2,400 tons of milk powder. A locally manufactured product could be competitively priced relative to imports. In addition, a Milkpak plant would use buffalo milk, a familiar taste for local consumers. A study of the

EXHIBIT 3.10 Milkpak Limited Milk Powder Plant Financial Feasibility Analysis			
			Rs 000
1. Cost of project and sources of finance			
1.1 Cost of project			
Building			2,640
Plant and machinery (including construction)			37,245
Trial-run cost and interest during construction			3,100
Contingencies			4,515
			47,500
Working capital			7,500
			55,000
	Foreign Currency	*Local Currency*	*Total*
1.2 Sources of finance			
Issue of preferential shares (one for every three shares)	—	11,667	11,667
Loan sanctioned by Agricultural Development Bank of Pakistan	16,000	2,000	18,000
New loan required	15,000	5,000	20,000
Bank overdraft	—	5,333	5,333
	31,000	24,000	55,000
	First Year	*Second Year*	*Third Year*
2. Profit and loss projections			
Sales 67,357	104,703	137,860	
Cost of sales	57,928	86,798	111,407
Operating profit	9,429	17,905	26,453
Financial cost/tax, etc.	6,259	6,024	12,140
Net profit	3,170	11,881	14,313
3. Payback period is 3 years and 2 months.			
4. Additional sales of UHT milk from increased availability of milk supplies as a result of project.	2,985	3,506	4,298

Source: Company records.

milk powder market commissioned by Milkpak recommended that Milkpak produce a branded product to capitalize on Milkpak's name and reputation. In addition to producing milk powder, the plant would also manufacture infant formula, butter oil, and butter.

Milkpak expected to hire an experienced expatriate production manager. Although Milkpak executives thought it was feasible for the company to develop a powder plant without a joint venture partner, they were concerned about the technical difficulties of doing so. For example, they felt that producing products such as infant formula required technical knowledge and expertise that the company did not have.

Joint Venture Partners

A joint venture partner could provide both the necessary technology and a reputable brand name that could be attached to locally manufactured, value-added products. Milkpak's managers debated the advantages and drawbacks of conducting a joint venture. Some thought Milkpak should seek out a joint venture partner that currently exported branded products to Pakistan and already had some brand recognition in Pakistan. Others were concerned that a company with established brands would expect high royalties that would leave too little profit for Milkpak to warrant the investment risk.

Another concern was that a large multinational joint venture partner might dominate Milkpak. Chairman Babar Ali, however, felt very comfortable with the prospect of a joint venture; Packages Limited, where he had worked for much of his career, was itself a joint venture.

A major challenge was to identify appropriate joint venture partners and find ways to approach them. Danish Turnkey Dairies and Tetra Pak, companies Milkpak and Packages already had ties with, could help in identifying and providing introductions to potential joint venture partners. As a result, Friesland and Nestlé emerged as particularly interesting prospects for a joint venture partnership.

Friesland

Friesland, established in 1913 as the "Cooperative Condensed Milkfactory Friesland," was founded by farmers in the Friesland province of Holland. Over 12,000 Dutch farmers supplied milk for the production of a variety of dairy products, including condensed and powdered milk and infant foods. In 1986, Friesland's net sales were 1,807 million guilders.[7]

Friesland's products were sold in 130 countries, primarily through exports. Friesland exported Safety brand milk powder and Omela brand condensed milk to Pakistan. The company also operated some manufacturing facilities and dairies overseas, usually in partnership with a local company. These included manufacturing plants in Guam, Indonesia, Lebanon, Malaysia, Nigeria, Taiwan, Thailand, Saudi Arabia, and Yemen. Friesland provided technical assistance to its affiliated companies as well as management assistance on a contract basis.

Nestlé S.A.

Nestlé was founded in 1867 by Henri Nestlé, a chemist who developed the first milk-based food for babies. In 1905, the company merged with the Anglo-Swiss Con-

---

[7]Exchange rate in 1986: 2.45 Guilders = $1.00.

densed Milk Company, a former competitor. From a base in dairy products, Nestlé's product line grew to encompass chocolate and confectionery, instant and roasted coffee, culinary products, frozen foods, and instant drinks. By 1986, Nestlé's consolidated sales were 38,050 million francs.[8]

Early in its development, Nestlé established production facilities outside of Switzerland. By 1986, Nestlé had plants in 60 countries. In determining whether to set up production facilities in a particular country, the company considered several factors, including the availability of raw materials, the overall economic climate, and consumer tastes and purchasing power. Nestlé's approach to foreign operations was summarized as follows: "The Company is guided in this respect by long-term goals and not by short-term objectives. It is essential for Nestlé that an industrial operation be in the reciprocal and lasting interests of both the Company and the host country" (Nestlé, S.A., 1991).

A hallmark of Nestlé was decentralization, which enabled the group's overseas subsidiaries to develop their own identity and the flexibility to respond to local market conditions. At the same time, Nestlé provided research, development, and technical assistance to these subsidiaries. This assistance could be used, for example, to develop products suited to local tastes and to improve the productivity of land and livestock.

Nestlé in Pakistan

Since 1974, Nestlé products had been imported and sold by the Burque Corporation, a small Pakistani distributor. In 1975, Burque decided to introduce Nestlé's NIDO brand of powdered milk, which accounted for an increasing share of Nestlé sales in Pakistan. Nestlé products were supported by an intensive distribution network and were also heavily advertised on television.

In 1983, Nestlé stationed a marketing advisor, Erwin Wermelinger, in Pakistan. Wermelinger's role was to investigate investment opportunities in addition to providing assistance to Nestlé's distributor. During the mid-1980s, Nestlé staff conducted a tour of the Punjab region of Pakistan to assess the potential for collecting milk to be used in local production of Nestlé products.

JOINT VENTURE NEGOTIATIONS

Discussions with Nestlé

Milkpak's management was aware of Nestlé's growing interest in the Pakistani market, as indicated by Wermelinger's presence in Pakistan. One of Milkpak's managers, formerly with Packages, knew Wermelinger from an earlier posting in Tanzania. As a result, there was an informal channel of communication between the two companies, which Milkpak viewed as a means of keeping Nestlé apprised of Milkpak's progress.

Milkpak approached Nestlé's senior management in 1986, when Babar Ali visited Nestlé's headquarters in Switzerland. During these conversations, Ali received the impression that Nestlé would want majority ownership in a joint venture and might also require sizable royalties and technical fees. In addition, Ali was concerned that Nestlé's attitude toward Milkpak seemed overbearing.

---

[8]Exchange rate in 1986: 1.80 Swiss Francs = $1.00.

Discussions with Friesland

Milkpak first approached Friesland in November 1985, through a mutual contact. Several factors made Friesland an attractive candidate for a joint venture, including extensive experience in the dairy industry and an established position in the Pakistani milk powder market. Milkpak's management also felt that a company of Friesland's size would be more responsive to Milkpak's concerns than a larger multinational.

An initial meeting between Babar Ali and a Friesland marketing director was followed by the visit of a three-member Friesland team to Pakistan in March 1986. The team included representatives from the marketing, finance, and technical areas. They spent 2 weeks studying both Milkpak and the Pakistani market. After the team's visit, Friesland made several requests for additional information. Company representatives next met in October 1986, when both Babar Ali and Yawar Ali visited the Friesland headquarters in Holland to meet the company's chairman and directors and tour the corporate plant and R&D facilities. Milkpak's executives were not shown the milk powder factory.

Friesland planned to follow the October meeting by sending a team to prepare a detailed feasibility study that would consider the milk powder project and other possible product introductions, such as cheese and ice cream. Friesland's tentative plans were to buy 25% of Milkpak's shares, obtain technical fees and royalties for their brands, and increase equity to 49% over a 5-year period. Friesland targeted the end of March 1987 as the date for making a final decision about the proposed joint venture.

A number of issues remained to be resolved. Milkpak needed to determine what government policies were with respect to technical fees and royalties on consumer products, assuming that Friesland made an initial equity investment of 25%. Friesland wanted to obtain royalties on its products in the range of 3% to 5%. In addition, for Friesland to be able to increase share holdings beyond 25%, changes in the ownership structure of Milkpak could be required, such as the divestment of some of the existing foreign shareholders.

Although Friesland was an attractive candidate for a joint venture, Milkpak had some reservations. Milkpak's executives were concerned that Friesland had not let them tour Friesland's milk powder factory on two separate occasions, which suggested that Friesland might be withholding certain information. Milkpak attributed Friesland's many requests to Milkpak for information to Friesland's relatively limited experience in establishing production facilities overseas. The time period within which Friesland expected to obtain a return on its investment was uncertain. Some managers at Milkpak also felt that, in light of Friesland's history as a dairy cooperative, the company would always be more interested in finding markets for products produced in Holland than in developing the Pakistani dairy industry.

Rudolf Tschan's Visit

In January 1987, Babar Ali was apprised of the forthcoming visit of Rudolf Tschan, Nestlé's new executive vice president for Asia Zone II, to Pakistan. According to Erwin Wermelinger, Nestlé's marketing representative in Pakistan, Tschan wanted to come to Lahore to meet Ali, tour Milkpak's Sheikhupura factory, and visit the company's milk collection centers.

On January 25, Yawar Ali led Rudolf Tschan and the Nestlé team on a tour of Milk-pak's plant and milk collection areas. Ali was struck by Tschan's quick assessment of the surroundings: "This side looks a lot like the other side [Indian Punjab], but your buffalo are better and your land is more fertile." As Tschan toured the milk plant, he noted that "we will have one milk powder plant here and one there [India]."

When Yawar Ali briefed Babar Ali about the Nestlé team's tour, he noted Tschan's evident interest in the Milkpak operation. Later in the day, top executives from Milk-pak and Packages were scheduled to meet with Tschan and Wermelinger to discuss the prospect of Nestlé and Milkpak working together. As Milkpak's team prepared for the meeting with Nestlé, they considered the major issues that would arise. In addition, they considered the benefits to each company of working together.

Assessing a Nestlé Joint Venture

For Milkpak, the possibility of a joint venture with Nestlé was appealing. The fact that Nestlé had a successful manufacturing operation, including a milk powder plant 80 miles across the border in Moga, India, gave Milkpak confidence that Nestlé knew how to operate in a very similar environment. Milkpak's management also believed that Nestlé typically took a long-term approach toward developing its operating companies. In addition, Milkpak might benefit from Nestlé training for its staff and from increased sales by other companies in the Ali Group. For example, Nestlé products could use packaging made by the group's companies.

At the same time, management felt that Milkpak offered a number of advantages as a joint venture partner. Milkpak knew that its extensive milk collection infrastructure provided access to a key raw material for Nestlé products. Milkpak's government contacts would facilitate obtaining the requisite licenses for establishing new production facilities. The Ali Group had a successful history of implementing other joint ventures. Through a joint venture with Milkpak, Nestlé would eliminate a potential future competitor that knew the Pakistani market. The fact that Tschan had come to Pakistan to see Milkpak's operations indicated that Nestlé already had a favorable impression of the company's capabilities.

Retaining majority ownership was important to Milkpak's management because Milkpak executives wanted to ensure that any joint venture partner paid attention to their ideas about the business. Babar Ali's earlier meeting with Nestlé management suggested that coming to mutually agreeable terms on topics such as majority ownership could present a challenge. However, Tschan seemed to be more flexible.

In addition to the question of ownership, both companies were likely to be concerned about management control of the operation. For example, Nestlé might want to appoint the milk powder plant manager. In addition, Nestlé already had an effective existing system for distributing its products in Pakistan, which would need to be integrated with Milkpak's marketing system.

Another agenda item concerned the products to be produced and sold by the joint venture and the location of their manufacture. Some Nestlé products currently imported could be manufactured locally in the new plant; others would continue to be imported. The new plant might also permit local manufacture of other Nestlé products not currently exported to Pakistan. Finally, there existed the possibility of introducing new products tailored more precisely to the consumption preferences of Pakistani consumers.

CONCLUSION

As Milkpak's management approached the meeting with Rudolf Tschan, they contemplated the key issues that would be addressed. Milkpak's objective was to increase its penetration of and success in the Pakistani market. The company was already involved in an extended negotiation with Friesland, a fact they would tell Nestlé, and one that gave Milkpak some additional leverage. At the same time, they needed to carefully evaluate what terms would make a joint venture with Nestlé more appealing than one with Friesland. The Milkpak executives had to decide what negotiating positions to adopt. Milkpak's executives were aware that, should they conduct a joint venture with Nestlé, today's meeting would set the foundation for a relationship that was likely to change and evolve over time.

References

Burki, Shahid Javed, *Pakistan: A Nation in the Making,* Boulder: Westview Press, 1986, p. 115.

Nestlé, S. A.. *Nestlé, The Story of an International Company,* Vevey: Nestlé, S.A., 1991, p. 10.

Pakistan Dairy Industry, 1989, p. 12.

Pakistan Dairy Industry, 1989, p. 16.

Pakistan Dairy Industry, 1989, p. 19.

CHAPTER

4

EXPLOITING MARKET LEADERSHIP

Koç Holding: Arçelik White Goods

In February, 1997, the top management team of Arçelik, the major appliance subsidiary of Koç Holding, Turkey's largest industrial conglomerate, assembled in Cologne, Germany, for the biannual Domotechnica, the world's largest major appliances trade show. The team was led by Hasan Subasi, president of Koç Holding's durables business unit, and Mehmet Ali Berkman, general manager of the Arçelik white goods operation, which accounted for two-thirds of the durables business unit's turnover.[1]

The Arçelik stand was in a prime location in Building 14; nearby were the booths of Bosch, Siemens, and Whirlpool. The Arçelik stand displayed 236 products carrying the Beko brand name, 35% of them refrigerators and freezers, 25% washing machines, 20% ovens, and 15% dishwashers.[2] Several innovative products were on display including washing machines that were more water and energy efficient than competitive products, as well as refrigerators made from materials that were 80% recyclable and incorporated special insulation panels for greater operational efficiency. In 1996, Arçelik's Beko brand had received a Green Dove award from the European Union (EU) for attention to the environment in design and production.[3]

The trade show exhibit, costing $1 million to organize, reflected Arçelik's determination to become a major player in the global white goods industry. There was, however, still debate in the company regarding how much emphasis to place on international sales; which geographical markets to concentrate on; and whether to focus on supplying appliances on an original equipment manufacturer (OEM) basis, building the company's own Beko brand, or both.[4]

---

[1]"White goods" was a term used to describe major kitchen appliances. The corresponding term, "brown goods," described major household appliances used outside the kitchen, such as televisions and stereo systems.
[2]Most Arçelik products sold outside Turkey carried the Beko brand name.
[3]In 1997, the European Union comprised 15 member countries with a combined population of around 350 million people.
[4]An OEM (original equipment manufacturer) sold products to other manufacturers, distributors, or retailers; these products typically carried brand names specified by the purchasing companies.

Research Associate Robin Root and Professor John Quelch prepared this case as the basis for class discussion rather than to illustrate either effective or ineffective handling of an administrative situation. Confidential data have been disguised.
Copyright © 1997 by the President and Fellows of Harvard College. Harvard Business School case 598-033.

COUNTRY AND COMPANY BACKGROUND

Turkey

In 1997, Turkey, a country of 63 million people, was positioned at the historical cross-roads between East and West, communism and capitalism, Islam and Christianity. Turkey bordered Eastern Europe, the Caucasus, the Balkans, North Africa, and Middle East—all regions in various states of political and economic flux in the 1990s. In this context, successive Turkish governments promoted domestic and foreign policies that would nurture its still modest private sector yet promote the pursuit of global competitiveness so that Turkey would be a credible candidate for entry into the European Union.

The establishment of the Republic of Turkey by Mustafa Kemal Ataturk as a secular nation state in 1923 marked the end of 600 years of sultan rule. Ataturk aimed to move Turkey quickly into the ranks of industrialized Western nations by anchoring the republic's constitution in a parliamentary democracy. From the start, a strict division between religion (Islam) and government was constitutionally guaranteed and backed by the Turkish military. To build the economy, Ataturk set up temporary state-run enterprises that would later be turned over to private sector management. Privatization, however, did not get fully underway until the mid-1980s, when the government also formally established the Istanbul Stock Exchange.

During the 1980s, the Turkish government established the convertibility of the Turkish lira, and promoted exports to improve its balance of payments. Turkey's rapid growth and relative economic stability, although the envy of other developing countries, was long overlooked by Western governments which focused instead on its strategic role as a NATO firewall against Soviet expansion. The possibility of membership in the European Union changed the business mentality within Turkey. Large family-run industrial conglomerates, the engines of Turkish modernization, started to emphasize professional management and to apply global manufacturing standards.

In 1990, the growth in Turkey's gross national product reached an all-time high of 9.2%, sparking the interest of investors from Europe and North America. After a slowdown to 0.9% growth in 1991, the Turkish government stimulated consumer demand and increased public investment; the economy grew 5.9% in 1992 and 7.5% in 1993. A major recession in 1994 that saw 5.0% negative growth was followed by 7.3% growth in 1995 and 7.1% in 1996. Despite the political uncertainties that accompanied Turkey's first Islamist government, sustained GNP growth of 8% was forecast for 1997. The country was, however, afflicted by high inflation (80% in 1996 and 75% forecast for 1997), high interest rates, depreciation of the lira, and a deepening budget deficit. Data on the Turkish economy between 1992 and 1996 are presented in Exhibit 4.1.

Koç Holding

Vehbi Koç began his business in 1917 with a $100 investment from his father, who was a shopkeeper. Seven decades later, he left behind one of the world's largest private fortunes and the most advanced industrial conglomerate in Turkey, Koç Holding, which was established in 1963. Until the death of Vehbi Koç in early 1996, at age 95, Koç Holding had been the only company on the Fortune 500 list of international businesses to still be owned and operated by its founder.

EXHIBIT 4.1 Turkish Economic Data: 1992–1996	*1992*	*1993*	*1994*	*1995*	*1996*
GDP growth rate (%)	6.4	8.1	−5.4	7.3	7.1
GDP per capita (US$ at PPP[1] rates)	4,991	5,562	5,271	5,411	5,634
Inflation (%)	70	66	106	94	80
Exchange rate (lira/US$)	8,555	14,458	38,418	59,501	81,995

[1]Purchasing Power Parity (PPP) refers to the rates of currency conversion that equalize the purchasing power of different currencies. The GDP and PPP per capita in Istanbul were thought to be double the national average.

Sources: Bank of America WIS Country Outlooks, November 1996; Union Bank of Switzerland New Horizon Economies, August 1995; Union Bank of Switzerland New Horizon Economies, April 1997; Statistical Yearbook of Turkey, 1996.

The legacy bequeathed by Vehbi Koç was as philosophical as it was financial. Shortly after Ataturk established the Republic of Turkey in 1923, Koç became the first Turk to challenge the trading power of the Republic's Greek, Armenian, and Jewish minorities. By age 22, he had discerned that the higher living standard enjoyed by these groups was a function of their dominance in commerce—a vocation that most Turks had been discouraged from entering. Koç went on to become one of the first Turkish businessmen to realize the benefits of foreign partnerships. In the late 1930s, he became a sales agent for companies such as Burroughs, Mobil Oil, and Ford, and in 1948 he built his first factory to manufacture light bulbs with General Electric. Half a century later, Koç Holding controlled close to 100 companies in nearly every sector of the Turkish economy, the total output of which accounted for approximately one-tenth of the country's GNP.

As a testament to the passions and principles he cultivated over his 7 decade reign, the Koç patriarch circulated a letter among his three grandsons just 3 months before he passed away in 1996. In it, he exhorted them to rise to the challenge faced by most third-generation managers in family businesses, namely, to single-mindedly focus on enhancing further the company's financial and social value.

In 1996, the 36,000 employees of Koç Holding generated $12 billion in revenues. Koç was a major player in the automotive industry, household appliances, consumer goods, energy, mining, construction, international trade, finance, tourism, and services sectors. The company grew three times faster than the Turkish economy between 1985 to 1995. Its corporate logo, a red ram's head (Koç means ram in Turkish), was visible on street corners, shops, and office buildings throughout Turkey. Koç Holding had a nationwide distribution network of 9,400 dealers, and 23 overseas offices responsible for achieving $884 million in foreign exchange earnings. As the leading taxpayer in Turkey, Koç Holding initiated and underwrote numerous philanthropic projects in the areas of education, health, cultural heritage, and environmental conservation.

Arçelik

Arçelik was established in 1955 to produce metal office furniture.[5] In 1959, the company began manufacturing washing machines. Arçelik subsequently began manufacturing refrigerators, dishwashers, air conditioners, and vacuum cleaners in five Turkish factories. Unit sales across these five categories reached 2,110,000 in 1995, making Arçelik the

---

[5]Arçelik (pronounced arch-e-lick) is a Turkish word meaning clean steel.

EXHIBIT 4.2 Arçelik's Sales and Earnings: 1990–1996							
U.S. $million	*1990*	*1991*	*1992*	*1993*	*1994*	*1995*	*1996*
Sales	765	1,001	1,060	1,150	859	982	1,241
EBIT	98	134	159	148	147	144	172
Net earnings	72	91	86	97	39	60	84

Source: Company records.

sixth largest European manufacturer of household appliances and the only significant white goods manufacturer between Italy and India. In addition, Arçelik sourced other appliances including ovens, televisions, water heaters, and space heaters from affiliated Koç companies. Unit sales of these products reached 900,000 in 1995. Arçelik owned 63% of Ardem, a Koç company that made cooking appliances, and 23% of Bekoteknik, which made televisions and other consumer electronic products. To round out its product line, Arçelik sourced small household appliances such as irons from other companies outside the Koç Group. By 1996, Arçelik was the largest company within Koç Holding. Sales and earnings data for 1990 to 1996 are reported in Exhibit 4.2. Key dates in Arçelik's history are summarized in Exhibit 4.3.

EXHIBIT 4.3 Key Dates in Arçelik's History	
Year	*Event*
1955	Arçelik is founded.
1959	Arçelik produces Turkey's first washing machine.
1960	Arçelik produces Turkey's first refrigerator.
1965	Joint venture with General Electric to produce electric motors and compressors. Bekoteknik is founded to operate in the "brown goods" electronics industry.
1966	Arçelik produces vacuum cleaners.
1974	Bekoteknik manufactures TV sets. Arçelik produces Turkey's first automatic washing machine.
1975	Arçelik receives General Electric technology licenses for white goods.
1977	Ardem joins the Koç group to produce kitchen ranges.
1980	Arçelik exports refrigerators.
1985	Arçelik licenses washing machine technology (two models) from Bosch-Siemens. (Production ceased in 1994.)
1986	Arçelik licenses dishwasher technology (one model) from Bosch-Siemens. No exports are permitted. (Still in production in 1996.)
1989	Arçelik establishes its Beko sales office in the United Kingdom.
1991	Bekoteknik and Arçelik receive ISO 9001 certification. Research and development center is established. Arçelik launches first toll-free customer call center in Turkey.
1993	Arçelik opens a new dishwasher plant in Ankara.
1994	Bekoteknik receives the EU Green Dove Award.
1996	Arçelik agrees to supply 100,000 OEM dishwashers to Whirlpool each year for 5 years. Çayirova, Eskirsehir, and Ankara plants receive ISO 14000 certification.

Source: Company records.

Arçelik manufacturing capacity, actual production, and unit sales for 1992 to 1996 in the three most important white goods categories are summarized in Exhibit 4.4. Arçelik's unit market shares in Turkey in 1996 were 57% in refrigerators, 60% in washing machines, and 70% in dishwashers. Competitive market share and market size data for each category of white goods are presented in Exhibits 4.5 and 4.6. Refrigerators accounted for 38% of Arçelik sales (by value), washing machines for 32%, dishwashers for 10%, and ovens for 15%.

In 1988, the Turkish government agreed to a phased program of tariff reductions with the European Union. With respect to white goods, Turkish tariffs on imports from the European Union, which ranged between 40% and 55%, would be reduced to zero between 1992 and January 1996, according to the schedule shown in Exhibit 4.7. A 5% Turkish tariff on imported components from the European Union would also be removed. As a result, exports into Turkey of Western European appliances would become progressively more price competitive (not least because white goods plants in Europe were operating at only 65% capacity utilization) and possibly challenge Arçelik's dominance of the Turkish market.

In preparation for the removal of import tariffs, Arçelik invested heavily in upgrading its manufacturing quality and productivity to world class standards. Between 1991 and 1996, capital expenditures totaled $247 million, approximately 6% of sales. By 1995, all Arçelik plants had received ISO 9001 quality certification. Through the incorporation of just-in-time and flexible manufacturing systems, Arçelik reduced raw material and labor costs, thereby increasing the productivity of its refrigerator production by 43%

EXHIBIT 4.4 Arçelik Capacity, Production, and Sales by Major Appliance: 1992–1996 (in thousands)				
	Capacity	*Production*	*% Change*	*% Capacity utilization*
Refrigerators				
1992	1,050	569.2	2.7	54
1993	1,050	709.6	24.6	67
1994	1,050	630.4	−11.1	60
1995	1,050	900.6	42.8	85
1996	1,050	990.8	10.1	94
Washing machines				
1992	760	551.8	−7.2	72
1993	800	653.7	18.4	81
1994	800	500.4	−23.4	62
1995	900	625.6	25.0	70
1996	1,100	750.8	20.0	68
Dishwashers				
1992	200	180.0	36.9	90
1993	300	244.5	35.8	81
1994	300	217.3	−11.1	72
1995	300	205.3	−5.5	68
1996	500	301.6	46.9	60

Source: Company records.

EXHIBIT 4.5 Turkish Market Share and Unit Sales for White Goods

	Refrigerators		Washing machines		Dishwashers		Ovens	
	1995	*1996*	*1995*	*1996*	*1995*	*1996*	*1995*	*1996*
Koç	54.6%	56.5%	64.2%	59.7%	75.8%	70.4%	68.0%	67.6%
Peg	38.2%	30.9%	23.5%	23.5%	17.0%	20.5%	25.9%	23.0%
Merloni	4.3%	4.1%	4.0%	5.5%	1.9%	2.6%	—	—
Others	2.9%	8.5%	8.3%	11.3%	5.3%	6.5%	6.1%	9.4%
Unit Sales[1]	868,197	1,039,519	856,890	1,135,669	263,570	331,030	446,591	509,493

[1]Unit sales include imports so Arçelik market shares reported here are lower than the company's share of domestic production.

Source: Company records.

EXHIBIT 4.6 Brand Share Breakdowns for Two Principal White Goods Marketers in Turkey: 1996

	Refrigerators (%)	Washing machines (%)	Dishwashers (%)	Ovens (%)
Koç Group				
Arçelik	39.2	39.9	53.7	44.4
Beko	17.3	19.8	16.7	22.9
Peg Group				
AEG	8.3	5.6	2.4	5.1
Profilo	18.9	10.6	2.8	13.1
Bosch	3.3	6.1	13.7	4.5
Siemens	0.4	1.2	1.6	0.4

Source: Company records.

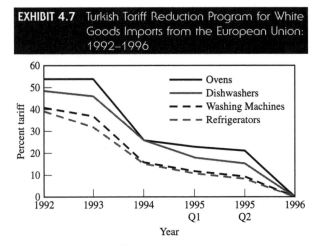

EXHIBIT 4.7 Turkish Tariff Reduction Program for White Goods Imports from the European Union: 1992–1996

Source: Company records.

between 1990 and 1995. The corresponding increases for washing machines and dishwashers were 50% and 20%. Arçelik had no manufacturing plants outside of Turkey.

In addition, Arçelik also invested heavily in R&D. During the 1970s and 1980s, Arçelik licensed technology from General Electric and Bosch-Siemens. Arçelik paid unit royalties but was only permitted to sell its production in Turkey. Over time, Arçelik developed its own appliance designs, often at lower cost than the licensed technologies. Starting in 1989, Arçelik transformed itself from a manufacturer that used licensed technologies to one of the leaders in white goods research and development. The company sponsored master's theses at Turkish engineering schools on subjects relevant to its research agenda, and secured World Bank funding to research how to eliminate CFCs from refrigerators. Between 1990 and 1995, $69 million or 1.5% of sales was allocated by Arçelik to R&D. The fruits of these investments were evident in the innovative technology-based features on display in the Arçelik booth at Domotechnica in 1997.

In the area of human resources, Arçelik prided itself on lean management with only four levels in the organization. The work force was highly educated and many Arçelik managers had attended business schools in North America and Europe.

WHITE GOODS MARKETING IN TURKEY

Demand

As of 1996, 99% of Turkey's 13 million households owned refrigerators, the same percentage as in the European Union. The corresponding percentages for other major appliances were 47% for automatic washing machines (90%), 15% for dishwashers (31%), and 56% for ovens (70%).

Demands for white goods in Turkey was influenced by the pace of household formations and urbanization, interest rates, retail price levels, and the rate of economic growth. Sensitivity analyses estimating the effects of changes in some of these variables on unit sales of appliances in Turkey are presented in Exhibit 4.8. Consumer purchases of appliances increased dramatically in the first half of 1996 as shown in Exhibit 4.9. Arçelik sales increased 21% in this period. Berkman commented:

> Domestic demand is strong and will remain so. Annual population growth is 1.7% and the number of households increases by 2.5% each year. Around 50% of the population is under 30 and an increasing percentage (currently 63%) live in cities and towns which makes it easier for us to reach them.

EXHIBIT 4.8 Impact of Changes in Interest Rates, Consumer Prices, and GNP Per Capita on Arçelik Sales and Profits			
Change in Arçelik's	*Interest rates increase by 10%*	*Consumer prices increase by 10%*	*GNP per capita increases by 10%*
Refrigerator unit sales	−12.5	−12.7	+1.3
Washing machine unit sales	−8.1	−7.1	+4.3
Dishwasher unit sales	−10.4	−10.1	+21.6
Total sales revenues	−6.9	−8.1	+3.7
Total profits	−13.3	−14.1	+11.5

Source: Adapted from a Schroeders investment report, 1996.

EXHIBIT 4.9 Percent Change in White Goods Retail Unit Sales in Turkey		
	January-April 1995	*January-April 1996*
Refrigerators	−8.6	+17.8
Washing machines	−36	+68
Dishwashers	−40	+56
Ovens	−15	+4.5

Source: Adapted from a Schroeders investment report, 1996.

Imports satisfied some of the increase in domestic demand, reaching 3% of white goods sales in Turkey in 1993. In 1994, when the Turkish lira devalued sharply and the economy went into recession, imports of white goods declined while exports increased. In January, 1996, with the import tariffs cut to zero and the economy strengthening, imports increased. For example, between January and July of 1996, 20% of dishwashers sold in Turkey were imported. Analysts estimated the sustainable import penetration rate at 5% for refrigerators, 10% for washing machines, and 15% for dishwashers.

Competition

Arçelik's principal white goods competitor was Peg Profilo. Facing increasing competition, Peg Profilo had been sold to Bosch-Siemens of Germany in 1995. Peg Profilo sold its products under the Profilo and AEG brand names.[6] Imports of premium-priced Bosch and Siemens appliances began in 1996. Although penetration was limited to date, Arçelik managers noted heavy advertising behind the Bosch name aimed at challenging Arçelik's dominance of the premium end of the white goods market. Several Bosch shops were opened to supplement the existing network of Peg Profilo dealers. There was some evidence of strained relations as Bosch-Siemens tried to impose formal contracts on dealers used to the handshake-style agreements of Peg Profilo.

Profilo's market shares in 1996 were 31% in refrigerators, 24% in washing machines, 23% in ovens, and 20% in dishwashers. Profilo capacity utilization was only 60%. Arçelik managers expected that Profilo would become more competitive in washing machines and dishwashers (in which the firm had not invested in new production technology) as a result of the acquisition. Units carrying the Profilo name could be imported from Bosch-Siemens' efficient German or low-cost Spanish plants. In addition, Profilo refrigerators, which were more up-to-date, were expected to be exported through Bosch-Siemens' overseas network.

The number three competitor, Merloni, was a joint venture between the Italian consumer durables producer and Pekel, the Turkish white goods company owned by Vestel, which was originally owned by Polly Peck International. Merloni had obtained majority control of the refrigerator factory in 1993. Arçelik managers believed that Merloni competed for market share with Peg Profilo's brand more than with the Arçelik and Beko brands.

---

[6]AEG was an Electrolux brand sold under license in Turkey by Peg Profilo. After the Bosch-Siemens acquisition, little effort was put into promoting the AEG brand.

Consumer Behavior

Relative to per capita income, the penetration of white goods in Turkish households was high. This was attributed to the desire of Turkish consumers to buy prestigious durables for their homes and to sustained marketing efforts on behalf of the Arçelik and Beko brands.

When buying a new or replacement appliance, 50% of consumers were believed to shop only one store; the remainder shopped around. Replacement purchasers were invariably triggered by the breakdown of an existing appliance and were therefore especially unlikely to shop around. High inflation also encouraged consumers to shorten their decision-making processes. In 1996, wage increases were outpacing inflation so demand for white goods was especially strong.

A consumer's perceived risk and brand sensitivity varied according to the white goods being purchased. As explained by Arçelik's marketing manager:

> Refrigerators are nothing more than boxes and consumers are familiar with them. There's little that can go wrong. Dishwashers, on the other hand, are more complex appliances and first-time dishwasher purchasers are more risk averse.

ARÇELIK MARKETING IN TURKEY

Brand Building

Arçelik sold white goods under two brand names, Arçelik and Beko. A third brand, Aygaz, that Arçelik had inherited through the acquisition of an oven manufacturer, was discontinued in 1995 and its product line absorbed into the Beko brand family.

In 1996, there were 33 million Koç white goods appliances in use in 13 million Turkish households. Arçelik was a trusted brand. However, some older consumers did not remember fondly the product quality of Arçelik's early appliances sold in the 1960s; to them, the quality of Turkish-made products was still doubtful. Though the product lines of both brands were similar, except for external design differences, Beko brand managers claimed their brand had a more "high tech" image that appealed to younger consumers. The strong penetration of Beko in brown goods (25% market share) was believed to reinforce this perception. Beko was also marketed in Turkey as a "world brand;" Beko retailers capitalized on the brand's penetration of export markets as a signal of quality to Turkish consumers.

In 1996, Arçelik and Beko advertising and promotion budgets accounted for 2% and 4%, respectively, of both brands' sales. Advertising included both television and print advertising. The print component included some cooperative advertising with the cost shared between Arçelik and its retailers on a 50/50 basis. Promotions included "trade-in" offers designed to accelerate consumers' repurchase cycles.

Pricing

Arçelik's product lines covered a full range of price points; the most expensive, fully featured item in a product line was typically double the price of the least expensive. With an inflation rate of 80% in 1996, Arçelik prices were increased that year by 9% every 2 months. Reductions in unit manufacturing costs, stemming from improved productivity and declines in world plastic and stainless steel prices, enabled Arçelik to take price increases below the rate of inflation. Doing so helped Arçelik retain market share.

EXHIBIT 4.10 Comparative Index of Retail Prices for Turkish White Goods Brands: 1996

Brand name	Refrigerators	Washing machines	Dishwashers	Ovens
Arçelik (Arçelik)	100	94	58	42
AEG (Peg)	91	89	64	38
Bosch (Peg)	112.5	102	87	—
Miele (import)	123	—	—	—
G.E. (import)	320	—	—	—
Westinghouse (import)	147.5	—	—	—
Electrolux (import)	116	127	90	—

Source: Company records.

Arçelik white goods were priced consistently nationwide. They were the highest priced among domestically manufactured white goods but retailed at prices lower than imported models. Exhibit 4.10 compares white goods retail prices (including 23% value-added tax) across a variety of brands.

As shown in Exhibit 4.11 Arçelik's average operating profit before interest and taxes was 13%. Arçelik's operating profit on exports was considerably lower. Although registering strong profits on refrigerators, Arçelik unit margins on washing machines and dishwashers in 1996 were lower than competitors' margins due to depreciation charges associated with Arçelik's heavy investments in plant modernization and the fact that several lines were still ramping up to efficient volumes of production.

EXHIBIT 4.11 Arçelik Cost and Price Structure in Turkey

Cost structure	
Retail selling price[1]	125
Wholesale price[2]	112
Advertising and promotion	3
Selling and distribution	5
Factory price	100
Variable costs	58
Direct materials	51
Direct labor	4
Variable overhead	3
Research and development	4
Depreciation	10
General and administrative expenses	15
Operating profit (before interest and taxes)	13

[1] The price at which exclusive Arçelik retailers sold to the end consumer excluding value-added tax. Retailers generally made 5% to 6% pretax profit.

[2] The price at which Atilim, Koç's captive marketing company, sold the product to the exclusive retail network in Turkey.

Source: Company records.

Distribution and Sales

Ninety-five percent of white goods were sold to individual consumers through retail stores; only 5% were sold by manufacturers direct to building contractors. Single brand retailers accounted for 60% of retail unit sales of white goods in Turkey; the remaining 40% were sold through multibrand outlets. In addition to traditional appliance specialty stores, new channels such as Carrefour and Metro hypermarkets were opening in greater Istanbul. Selected Beko products (but no Arçelik products) were sold through these outlets. Around 28% of Turkish white goods were sold in Istanbul.

Arçelik delivered products to the Turkish market through exclusive retailers. There were 1,650 outlets carrying only the Arçelik brand, of which 700 accounted for 70% of sales. Another 1,050 outlets carried only Beko products. Beko also reached consumers through a further 2,500 to 3,000 non-exclusive outlets, which accounted for 30% of Beko sales. Arçelik was not available in any multibrand outlets. Arçelik typically added 100 new outlets per year and discontinued 30. New outlets included existing multibrand appliance dealers who applied to become Arçelik dealers, stores established by the sons of existing Arçelik dealers, and stores started by sufficiently well-capitalized entrepreneurs. New outlets had to be established in new residential areas and in areas where appliance demand increased with disposable income. According to Arçelik's national sales manager:

> Being the Arçelik dealer in a community is a much sought after position of importance. We have many applicants to choose from. Our dealers are loyal because our brand pull results in inventory turns three times faster than for our nearest competitor. As a result, our unit margins at retail can be narrower.

The product mix varied according to the size of each store and the demographics of the neighborhood in which it was located. An Arçelik store manager commented:

> Consumer demand for appliances is strong. People are switching from semi-automatic to automatic washing machines. First-time purchases of dishwashers are strong. Consumers living in apartments often have big families and need large refrigerators.

One hundred salespeople visited the Arçelik dealers, typically once every 2 weeks. Beko sold through 150 salespeople. Sales force turnover was a modest 5% per year.

A strong Arçelik retailer might carry $100,000 worth of inventory in the store and $500,000 in a warehouse, all on 100-day payment terms from the manufacturer. Typically, 15 sales would be made each day including six washing machines, four refrigerators, and two dishwashers. An average dealer might make 5 sales per day and hold $50,000 in floor inventory.

Ninety percent of Arçelik white goods were sold to consumers on credit installment plans of between 3 and 15 months. In addition to factory-sourced finance, a newly established Koç finance company also offered credit, often at interest rates slightly below the rate of inflation.[7] Each Arçelik dealer was liable for payment on the units sold on installment. The bad debt rate was less than 1%. Arçelik's competitors such as Bosch

---

[7]Securitizing receivables and installment loans through Koç Finans reduced Arçelik's working capital needs and, therefore, its average cost of capital.

were obliged to offer the same terms. Carrefour stores in the major cities could only offer their consumers bank credit at rates significantly higher than Arçelik.

Service

With the average white goods appliance in use for 12 years, the quality and availability of after-sales service was important to Turkish consumers in influencing other brand purchase decisions. Service for Arçelik and Beko white goods was provided by 500 authorized dealers who serviced only these two brands. Another 450 dealers serviced the brown goods of the two brands. There was no joint ownership of sales outlets and service dealers, though informal ties were common. Forty percent of service dealer revenues was generated by installations of newly purchased appliances; delivery and installment costs were included in the retail prices. The service organization was especially challenged when there was a surge in consumer sales, as in 1996.

INTERNATIONAL EXPANSION

Opportunistic exports of Arçelik white goods began in the 1980s through Koç Holding's export company, principally to the geographically neighboring markets of the Middle East and North Africa. Arçelik models did not have to be adapted to local requirements. In 1983, an export department was established within Arçelik. One of its tasks was to develop bid proposals on foreign government tenders and for foreign contract builders of low income housing. In 1988, Arçelik's export department contracted to supply refrigerators on an OEM basis to Sears Roebuck for distribution in the Caribbean and Latin America under the Kenmore name. Though Arçelik's exports were a modest percentage of total sales during the 1980s, Arçelik was the largest exporter among Koç Holding companies.

In 1988, the Turkish government's tariff reduction agreement with the European Union prompted an increased interest in exports. Berkman explained:

> We needed to find out more about our likely future competitors. One way to do so was to sell Arçelik products in the tough developed markets. The Americas were too far away, in terms of both transportation costs, product adaptation requirements (for 110 volt current), and our ability to understand consumers. Western Europe was much closer. We thought we would learn a great deal by competing against the best in the world on their home turf and better prepare ourselves to defend our domestic market share against the likes of Bosch and Siemens.

As of 1996, almost half of the 990,000 Arçelik and Beko refrigerators produced were exported. In that year, 7.6% of Arçelik's total sales (by value) were exports, up from 2.4% in 1991. A breakdown of exports by destination is presented in Table 4.1. Arçelik exported to the countries listed in Exhibit 4.12, which reports 1996 unit sales of refrigerators and washing machines by market. Arçelik's most successful European market was the United Kingdom, where it had achieved 8% market penetration. In the Middle East and North Africa, Arçelik had achieved almost 20% market share in Tunisia. The firm held between 1% and 4% market share in most of the other product markets listed in Exhibit 4.12.

In 1996, Arçelik exports of white goods were principally refrigerators and washing machines, as shown in Table 4.2. Technology licensing agreements precluded exports of

TABLE 4.1 Value of Arçelik Exports, by Destination: 1996

Destination	Percentage	Destination	Percentage
United Kingdom	28	North Africa	17
France	18	Eastern Europe and Central Asia	6
Other European Union	14	Other	17

EXHIBIT 4.12 Total Refrigerator and Washing Machine Unit Sales in Arçelik Export Markets: 1996

	Refrigerators 1996 unit sales	Automatic washing machines 1996 unit sales
European Union		
France	2,500,000	1,600,000
Germany	3,600,000	2,600,000
United Kingdom	2,500,000	1,400,000
Benelux	1,200,000	600,000
Denmark	200,000	130,000
Spain/Portugal	2,000,000	1,300,000
Greece	NA	NA
Middle East & North Africa (MENA)		
Egypt	500,000	250,000
Lebanon	100,000	40,000
Syria	200,000	100,000
Iraq	400,000	200,000
Iran	1,000,000	250,000
Tunisia	120,000	25,000
Algeria	250,000	30,000
Morocco	110,000	20,000
Eastern & Central Europe & Central Asia		
Albania	NA	NA
Romania	300,000	150,000
Bulgaria	130,000	70,000
Russia	2,200,000	600,000
Malta	NA	NA
Turkmenistan	100,000	15,000
Uzbekistan	100,000	15,000
Kazakstan	100,000	15,000
Azerbaijan	NA	NA
Ukraine	300,000	50,000

Source: Company records.

TABLE 4.2 Arçelik White Goods Exports and Mix: 1996

	Export units	% Beko	% OEM
Refrigerators	430,000	70	30
Washing machines	55,000	50	50

most dishwashers. In 1996, Arçelik's refrigerator plants were operating at full capacity. By 1998, an extra 350,000 units of capacity were expected to come on line. Management expected to double exports of washing machines in 1997 without any addition of capacity. Dishwasher exports were expected to increase to 110,000 units in 1997 when Arçelik was to supply the first of five annual installments of at least 100,000 OEM units to Whirlpool for distribution in Europe. This was the first time Arçelik had agreed to an OEM contract with a global competitor; Arçelik was not permitted to sell similar models in Europe under its own brand names.

Arçelik in Western Europe

Starting in 1989, Arçelik opened sales offices in the United Kingdom, then France, then Germany, reasoning that, in these larger European markets, there might be more opportunity for a new brand to establish a sufficient volume of sales to be viable. At the same time, the export effort to other markets continued. In all export markets, Arçelik focused on building the Beko name (because it was easier to pronounce than Arçelik in a wide variety of languages).

United Kingdom

A sales office was established in the United Kingdom in 1989. The U.K. market was selected for this initial effort because it was price sensitive and not dominated by domestic brands. By 1997, there were one million Beko appliances in use in the United Kingdom, two-thirds of which were refrigerators and one-third televisions. Sales of 30,000 Beko refrigerators were expected in 1997, of which two-thirds would be tabletop-height refrigerators and one-third full-size refrigerators.[8]

In addition to refrigerators, Beko was beginning to sell dishwashers, washing machines, and ovens. Management had focused from the outset on building the Beko brand; only 10,000 of the units sold in 1996 were marketed on an OEM basis.

Melvyn Goodship, managing director, explained Beko's success in the United Kingdom:

> We exploited an underserved niche for tabletop refrigerators. Our factories in Turkey had spare capacity in the early nineties, so could promptly fill our orders and deliver consistent product quality. At first, we were accused of dumping but lower priced brands from Eastern and Central European countries are now criticized for that. Through patience and persistence, we have built our brand reputation and distribution.

By 1996, Beko had penetrated the three principal specialty appliance chains in the United Kingdom—Curry's, Comet, and Iceland. Beko appliances were also sold through the principal mail order catalogs—Empire and Littlewoods. Management believed Beko appliances were available through 65% of selling points in the United Kingdom. Beko maintained a warehouse in the United Kingdom to serve its retail accounts.

In 1996, the Beko brand was supported by £600,000 of advertising, including £100,000 to launch Beko washing machines and £150,000 of cooperative advertising.[9]

---

[8]In contrast, the market as a whole comprised 60% full-size refrigerators and 40% tabletop-height refrigerators.
[9]In 1996, one U.S. dollar was equivalent to 80,000 Turkish lira (June, 1996); one British pound was equivalent to U.S.$1.60; and one German mark was equivalent to U.S.$0.65.

The retail price of a typical Beko tabletop refrigerator was £150 including 17.5% value added tax and a 25% distribution margin. Comparable refrigerators of other brands would retail at £300 for Bosch, £200 for Hotpoint (the U.K. market share leader), and £160 for Indesit (an Italian manufacturer). Cheap brands of inconsistent quality from Eastern and Central European countries could be found for £120. Manufacturer prices of branded products were so competitive that large retailers saw no need to assume the inventory risk of contracting for OEM production.

France

Arçelik opened a French sales office in 1993. By 1996, annual sales were up to 75,000 units. However, according to the French sales manager:

> The French market is in a recession and is cluttered with competitors. It is hard for us to break into new accounts. 1997 will be a crucial year.

The French white goods market was highly competitive. Fifteen trade accounts controlled 75% of consumer sales. Thirty percent of white goods unit sales carried store brand names. Appliance specialty stores accounted for 45% of unit sales, hypermarkets for 30%, and mail order companies and department stores for 25%. There were no dominant national brands. The long-standing French brands, Thomson and Brandt, each accounting for 20% of unit sales were, by 1997, owned by Italian manufacturers.

Arçelik pursued a two brand strategy in France. Management believed that, if the Beko brand was launched at a low price, it would be impossible to raise it later. The Beko brand was therefore positioned and priced similarly to the mainstream Candy brand from Italy. The Beko brand accounted for 25% of the company's unit sales in France in 1996. Other Koç or OEM brands were priced lower than Beko to attract volume orders.

Of 75,000 units sold in France in 1996, 68,000 were refrigerators and 7,000 were washing machines and ovens. Of the 75,000, 15% were sold to kitchenette manufacturers and 15% were sold on an OEM basis to Frigidaire. Seventy percent of the remaining units were shipped to hypermarkets, notably LeClerc (the third largest hypermarket chain in France) and 30% to appliance specialty stores. The French sales office had not yet been able to break into any department stores or mail order accounts. A 2 year test, involving telemarketing Beko white goods to high street retailers, was currently underway. The only advertising for Beko in France appeared in the LeClerc catalog.

Germany

Arçelik opened a German sales office within an existing company called Interbrucke GmbH in 1994 under a general manager which had previously been an importer of Beko televisions.

Well-known, premium-priced German brands such as Bosch, Siemens, AEG, and Miele held a 60% unit market share of white goods. The remaining 40% was divided among numerous lower-priced Italian and East European manufacturers, none of whom held more than a 4% share.

About 60% of white goods were sold through traditional appliance retailers, almost all of whom were members of retail buying groups or served through regional wholesalers. Twenty percent of white goods were sold through mail order firms like Quelle, usually at prices below those in the specialty retailers. Of the remaining units, 10% were sold through mass merchandisers, 5% through hypermarkets, and 5% through traditional department stores.

In 1996, Beko sold 30,000 refrigerators in Germany, up from 10,000 in 1995, and 20,000 washing machines, up from 5,000 in the preceding year. Unit sales of refrigerators and washing machines in Germany in 1996 were 3,600,000 and 2,600,000 respectively. Management predicted sales of 70,000 and 30,000 for the two Beko lines in 1997. To date, 80% of Beko sales had been made to retail buying groups and regional wholesalers; the remaining 20% had been made to the manufacturers of prepackaged kitchenettes that were sold to home builders. By the end of 1996, Beko white goods were being bought by 12 accounts, in all cases on an OEM basis.

Beko white goods were imported from Turkey and stored in a rented warehouse in Germany. The average retail price of a Beko refrigerator was DM 399. Comparable Bosch and Siemens refrigerators sold for DM 499 to DM 599.

Beko had no resources for a consumer advertising campaign, though some funds were available to buy advertising space in retailer catalogs.

The general manager commented on Beko's prospects in Germany:

> The German economy is weak right now and population growth is flat. Demand for appliances is soft but fairly predictable. Consumers and, therefore, distributors are more price sensitive, especially in the former East Germany. This plays to our strength as a value brand. More retailers than ever before are scrambling to sell appliances, so that's putting further pressure on margins.
>
> In this price sensitive climate, I believe Beko's prospects are good. Germany is Turkey's largest trading partner. The challenge is to develop relationships with the big customers and persuade them to switch to Beko. If we can build unit volume by supplying OEM (or private label) product to these customers, we may be able to make enough money to invest in building the Beko brand.

Assessing Progress

Progress in Western Europe was slower than some executives expected, leading them to question the strategy. A senior manager at headquarters in Istanbul commented:

> We should not focus on breaking into Western Europe where growth is limited and where five companies control 75% of unit sales of white goods. Instead, we should focus on the emerging markets of Russia and Central Asia where foreign brand names are not yet entrenched in consumers' minds. We are geographically well-positioned to supply these markets. The fact that our products are made in Turkey will be a plus in those markets whereas, in Western Europe, we have to avoid mentioning it.

However, another supported the emphasis on Western Europe:

> The former communist markets of East and Central Europe will be important but, right now, they are too volatile. Tariff rates change overnight and we have no tariff advantage over Japanese and Korean competitors in these markets like we do in Western Europe. We would have to make risky investments in local manufacturing and distribution; finding the right local partners and

sufficiently skilled workers would be difficult. I would rather focus on Western Europe for the moment. The markets are tough to crack and our unit margins are lower than in Turkey but at least our goods enter duty free and demand is predictable.

CONCLUSION

In between hosting visitors to their Domotechnica booth in Cologne, Arçelik's managers continued to discuss informally whether or not they were placing the correct emphasis on international markets, and whether their brand-building and market selection strategies were appropriate. Some of the comments at the booth included:

In 1996, we showed we could hold our own in the Turkish market against the top brands in the world. In fact, our market share in refrigerators actually increased. This means we can now push our international exports more aggressively.

Wait a minute. Capacity is tight. If the Turkish market continues to grow at the current rate, we'll need most of our planned capacity for 1997 to meet domestic demand. And we know that we make at least twice as much unit margin if we sell an appliance in Turkey than if we export it.

The current rate of economic growth is not sustainable. The government, in anticipation of a general election, is pumping money into the economy. The economy will probably slow down, maybe even go into recession in 1997. I don't think we'll have a capacity problem.

We've got to emphasize building the Beko brand worldwide. We'll never make big money on OEM business, whether we are making to order for other manufacturers—who are, in fact, our competitors—or for retail chains. Special orders add to complexity costs in our plants and we lose our R&D edge when we simply follow the customers' blueprints. Occasionally, you can build up a long-term relationship with an OEM customer through consistent on-time deliveries but, more often than not, OEM orders are one-shot deals through which the customer is trying to exert leverage on his or her other suppliers or cover against a strike threat.

I'm not so sure. Selling OEM production is more profitable than selling the equivalent number of Beko branded units. Marketing costs per unit are lower and we don't have to invest in full advertising support through our national distributors.

You don't understand. We're making products of outstanding quality these days. Because Turkey's reputation for quality manufactures is not well-established, we've had to work doubly hard to achieve recognition. We shouldn't be wasting any more time doing OEM production of lower-priced, simple models when we have the quality to take on the best in the world at the premium end of the white goods market.

5 | ACHIEVING INTERNATIONAL EXPANSION

Hikma Pharmaceuticals

On May 19, 1996, Samih Darwazah, chairman of Hikma Investment, the holding company for Hikma Pharmaceuticals, proudly announced that the Jordanian company had begun exports of approved drugs to the United States:

> The shipment is of $100,000 worth of prescription drugs to four U.S. distributors. Hikma is the first Arab-owned drug company from the Middle East to obtain Food and Drug Administration (FDA) approval to sell to the U.S. market, following inspection of our plants in Jordan by an FDA team. This is a vote of confidence which will not only enable us to sell in the United States but also boost our sales in Jordan and the Arab world. It's the latest in a long series of marketing challenges that we've overcome.

Hikma was already selling drugs in the United States manufactured by its Westward subsidiary, acquired in 1991 and run by Said, Darwazah's son. Hikma's top management team was keenly debating the appropriate strategy for the company's U.S. operations, how they should fit with Hikma's other operations in Jordan and Portugal, and how important a role they should play in the company's overall growth.

COMPANY BACKGROUND

Samih Darwazah, Hikma's founder, was born in Palestine. He came to the United States in the late 1960s on a scholarship to the St. Louis College of Pharmacology, earned a master's degree in industrial pharmacy, and joined Eli Lilly on graduation. After 14 years in a variety of international marketing positions in Europe and the Middle East, Darwazah decided in 1977 to settle in Amman, Jordan. His objective, with the as-

Research Associate Robin Root and Professor John A. Quelch prepared this case as the basis for class discussion rather than to illustrate either effective or ineffective handling of an administrative situation. Confidential data have been disguised.

sistance of his two sons, was to create a pharmaceutical company to serve the Arab world. Darwazah explained:

> Jordan is a small country—only 4.3 million people—and a relatively poor country with per capita income of only $1,650. Yet the multinational pharmaceutical companies were already selling here, so we had to think internationally from the outset.

First, Darwazah established a joint venture in Amman with an Italian firm. The joint venture negotiated a license from Fujisawa Pharmaceutical Corp. of Japan to manufacture in Jordan and market in the Middle East cefazolin,[1] one of the world's top-selling injectable (rather than oral) cephalosporins (cephs).[2] In addition, the company manufactured and marketed its own formulation of another common, but less technically advanced, class of penicillin-based antibiotics called amoxicillin. However, because the Jordanian market was already well-served by multinational pharmaceutical firms, Darwazah knew he had to differentiate his new firm if he was to succeed. He built credibility among local physicians, who were skeptical of the quality of locally manufactured products, by emphasizing the company's commitment to research and new product development, by inviting them on plant tours, and by stressing added-value customer services delivered by highly trained salespeople, most of whom were former pharmacists. He identified three keys to the company's success: procure additional manufacturing licenses to expand the firm's product line; develop cutting-edge generics that were more than just "me-too" products; and market these product lines in ways that would make his firm an indispensable source to physicians in the Arab world.

Production began in 1978. Over time, manufacturing licenses were obtained from Fujisawa, Chugai, and Dainippon of Japan for a range of additional drugs including antirheumatics, cardiovascular drugs, tranquilizers, antidiabetics, antispasmodics, antiulcer medications and hormones. The factory was expanded in 1984 to include a sterile area for the production of injectables. To comply with best practices and avoid cross-contamination, a separate plant was set up in 1988 for production of cephalosporins and penicillins.

During the 1980s, Hikma supplemented the production of licensed products with branded generics to leverage further its sales and distribution organization.[3] Hikma became the first Arab drug company to perform bioequivalency studies. The company expanded the dosage forms for amoxicillin. First, Hikma developed a more convenient twice-a-day (as opposed to three times a day) dosage form of amoxicillin which resulted in higher patient compliance. Hikma also developed a chewable version of amoxicillin, previously unavailable even in the United States. As a result, Hikma enhanced its reputation as a quality company with a growing research and development capability.

Hikma gradually increased its focus on cephs. In 1985, the firm secured a second license from Fujisawa to manufacture Cefizox, another injectable ceph. Shortly thereafter, the company signed a manufacturing agreement with Smith, Kline, and French Laboratories for a third injectable ceph (which needed to be administered to a patient

---

[1]Lederle held the license from Fujisawa to market cefazolin in Europe.
[2]See page 89 for a full description of cephalosporins.
[3]In the United States, generic imitations of off-patent drugs did not usually carry brand names. In Europe and the Middle East, they often did and were, as a result, called branded generics.

only once a day). In return, Hikma furnished these multinationals with royalty payments on its sales.

As the focus on cephs increased, Darwazah decided that Hikma should backward integrate into the production of raw materials. Although supplies of the necessary raw materials were plentiful, he wanted to tighten quality control by backward integration and to ensure Hikma's independence from outside sources. In 1990, a sterile plant was established with an initial annual production capacity of 24 tons of bulk cephs but with expansion potential to 48 tons. Only a few plants in India could produce bulk cephs at lower cost.

By 1995, Hikma was making 40 drug products in Jordan. The top five sellers accounted for 50% of sales. Oral cephalosporins accounted for 30% of sales, drugs manufactured under license for 30%, and branded generics for 50%.[4]

INTERNATIONAL EXPANSION

By 1994, Hikma Investments included wholly owned manufacturing operations in Portugal and the United States as well as four plants in Jordan. Exhibit 5.1 details Hikma's sources of revenues between 1990 and 1996, while Exhibit 5.2 breaks down Hikma Jordan's sales by drug class in 1990 and 1996. In 1996, the proportion of total company profits generated by Hikma Jordan was 45% and its capacity utilization rate was 70%. The corresponding figures for Hikma Portugal were 10% and 30%, and for West-ward (the United States operation) the figures were 30% and 95%.

Hikma employed around 500 people in Jordan, 70% of them college graduates; many managerial positions were held by women. Hikma also owned Arab Medical Containers, a health care-related plastics manufacturing company that supplied Hikma and other companies with containers, tamper-resistant bottles, and other drug packaging. A manufacturing joint venture had been established in Tunisia in 1992 to produce cephs and penicillins under the Hikma name for supply to the French-speaking countries of North and West Africa. Through a second joint venture, Hikma provided technical support for the manufacture and marketing of products in Egypt, the largest pharmaceutical market in the Middle East. A third joint venture had been signed to build a $35 million plant in Saudi Arabia, completion of which was expected at the end of 1997. Hikma had marketing offices in 20 countries, including Russia, Slovakia, and China.

The pharmaceutical industry was the second most important exporter in Jordan. Hikma, as the largest pharmaceutical company in Jordan, was, therefore, one of the country's most significant exporters. In 1995, the Jordanian pharmaceutical industry produced $225 million worth of drugs of which $120 million worth were exported. Hikma exports in 1995 accounted for $50 million of the company's $60 million in sales. In contrast to exports, Hikma sales in Jordan were only $10 million in 1995. Despite Hikma's efforts, locally made drugs accounted for only 30% of Jordan's consumption. In 1996, Hikma was trying to persuade the Jordanian government to approve increases in local drug prices. Margins were so low that Hikma's ability to invest in research and development was limited. Hikma was contemplating curtailing the production of cer-

---

[4]Percentages do not total 100 because some of Hikma's oral cephs were made under license.

EXHIBIT 5.1 Sources of Hikma Sales ($000)[1]							
	1990	*1991*	*1992*	*1993*	*1994*	*1995*	*1996E*
Jordan (domestic)	2.8	5.2	6.5	10.6	3.3	7.8	8.2
Jordan (exports)	21.9	19.5	30.8	41.2	34.2	30.9	27.9
Portugal (domestic)	—	—	0.6[2]	2.6[2]	4.9[2]	1.6	2.6
Portugal (exports)						4.6	4.1
United States (domestic)	N/A	3.5[3]	5.9	9.6	11.9	12.7	14.4

[1]Internal transfer sales have been excluded.
[2]Portugal domestic and export sales combined.
[3]United States 1991 reflects 6 months of sales only.

EXHIBIT 5.2 Sources of Hikma Jordan Sales by Drug Class: 1990 and 1996E		
	Hikma Jordan	
	1990	*1996E*
Oral cephs	2.7	5.7
Injectable cephs	0.8	4.4[1]
Amoxicillins	4.0	4.2
Anti-inflammatories & antirheumatics	3.4	4.7
Cardiovasculars	2.0	1.0
Antidiabetics	1.9	0.6
Antispasmodics	1.6	0.4
Antiulcer	1.1	0.5
Tranquilizers	0.1	0.4

[1]Approximately 30% of Hikma Jordan's injectable cephs were exported.

tain drugs, which would leave only the more expensive imported substitutes available to the Jordanian consumer.

The Arab World

Darwazah's initial vision was to develop "an Arab company that serves the Arab world." In the early 1980s, he found markets for his joint venture's generic products in the Middle East and North Africa, winning government procurement contracts in Iraq, Syria, and Tunisia. The firm's growth was restricted, however, as Saudi Arabia, a key market in the region, only allowed originator manufacturers to sell their drugs in the market. Hikma was the first company to secure permission from Saudi Arabia to market generic drugs, but then faced the further obstacle that Saudi Arabia only provided tax exemptions to 100% Arab-owned firms. To achieve this exemption, Darwazah bought out his Italian partner in 1984, and then obtained permission from his licensors to expand distribution into Saudi Arabia, Syria, and Iraq. In 1986, Hikma, an Arabic word denoting wisdom and reason, was selected as the company's new name.

Over time, Darwazah concluded that his initial vision for Hikma was too limiting and that the company should diversify further its sales base. He commented:

> Increasingly Saudi Arabia, Syria, and other countries in the region decided to promote their own pharmaceutical industries and protect them against imports, even from an Arab neighbor. Spimaco, a $100 million Saudi pharmaceutical manufacturer has, for example, pressured the Saudi government to protect the large domestic market for its benefit. In addition, the disruption to regional trade caused by the Gulf War in 1991 convinced us that we had to diversify further afield—though we cemented our relationships with Iraq's doctors by keeping supply lines open to them during the crisis.

In selecting countries for international expansion beyond the Middle East, Hikma's initial impulse was to explore opportunities in other Muslim markets, such as Malaysia and Indonesia, in order to gain experience that would equip the company to take on the more competitive European and U.S. markets. Senior managers soon discovered, however, that the health services in these developing countries were not yet set up to accept imported generic drugs. Moreover, the predominantly European and North American (as opposed to Asian) experience of most of Hikma's senior managers justified an earlier-than-expected shift in the company's market focus towards Europe and the United States. Nevertheless, in 1996, 90% of Hikma exports from Jordan were still to the Middle East and North Africa.

Expansion Into Europe

Darwazah realized that the pharmaceutical industry was increasingly global, that there were no obvious reasons why generic drug manufacturers should not, like the research-based companies, sell internationally, and that Hikma could not survive merely as a regional player. The Jordanian market was becoming cluttered as Hikma's success prompted half-a-dozen new pharmaceutical manufacturing companies to be established by 1987. Meanwhile, discussion of European economic integration attracted Darwazah's attention. For a small pharmaceutical firm, the prospect of a single new drug registration filing in Brussels to secure access to the 330 million consumers of the European Union was especially appealing. Finally, Darwazah had been able to recruit high caliber scientists and managers into Hikma's Jordanian operations, many of whom had European education and/or experience; their continued motivation depended in part on sustained corporate growth.

Darwazah therefore began to explore the possibilities of establishing a manufacturing plant in Europe. He focused on Ireland and Portugal, both members of the European Union with access to some 330 million consumers. The national governments of both countries along with the European Union in Brussels offered attractive investment and tax incentives to foreign companies interested in establishing high technology manufacturing plants. Darwazah explained why Hikma settled on Portugal:

> There were three reasons. First, most of the major multinational pharmaceutical companies already had operations in Ireland. In Portugal, the pharmaceutical industry was less developed so we could offer something special by coming in. At the same time, our manufacturing processes were not that complicated so we didn't need a big pool of talented people to recruit from.

Second, the population of Portugal was 12 million versus 3 million in Ireland. Sales in the domestic market could justify the plant even if we didn't export that much.

Third, the multinational pharmaceutical companies were consolidating their Portuguese and Spanish operations in anticipation of the 1992 European Union market integration. This often resulted in the closure or downsizing of their Portuguese plants. As a result, there were many pharmaceutical managers and workers on the job market.

Jordanian banks that had already invested in Hikma's Jordanian operations were reluctant to loan Darwazah capital. However, the International Finance Corporation of the World Bank provided a $7 million loan commitment in 1988, and also purchased a 6% equity stake in Hikma Investments that owned 100% of Hikma Portugal.

The plant took 3 years to be completed. The fully automated 4,800 square meter plant outside Lisbon was designed to incorporate two separate operations that both met Food and Drug Administration standards:

- A filling plant for injectable cephalosporins with an annual capacity of 30 million vials.
- A liquid-filling plant for other chemical entities with an annual capacity of 42 million vials and ampoules.

By 1996, Hikma Farmaceutica, the Portuguese subsidiary, was generating sales of $10 million. All but 5% of these sales were of cephalosporins; 80% of the ceph sales were of injectables and 20% were of oral drugs. Sixty percent of ceph production was of cephs still under patent, manufacturing of which was licensed from Fujisawa, while 40% was of generic cephs. Some of the raw materials for ceph production were imported from Jordan. The non-ceph 5% of revenues came from sales of branded drugs including oral antibiotics and tranquilizers that Hikma manufactured under license in Jordan and for which the company was able to obtain Portuguese marketing licenses. Marketing of these drugs occupied the firm's 25 salespeople and provided cash flow while production of injectable cephs was coming on line and the relevant manufacturing approvals were being obtained from the Portuguese health authorities.

Seventy percent of Hikma Portugal's sales were exported. Of the exports, 20% were of generic cephs shipped to Germany, 10% were sent to China, and 70% were exported to the Middle East and North Africa. In effect, the role of the Portuguese operations was to produce injectable cephs for Hikma's worldwide marketing network.

Darwazah was concerned about Hikma Farmaceutica's marketing efforts in Europe. Although contracts with private hospital chains had been obtained, it was proving difficult to sell into the government agencies that dominated drug procurement for the national health care systems of many European countries. In particular, French manufacturers of injectable cephs defended their market shares vigorously. Another difficulty in Europe was that Brussels regulations (unlike U.S. regulations) precluded generic manufacturers from working on formulations of patented drugs until they actually came off patent. As a result, Darwazah was keenly waiting for FDA inspectors to visit the Portuguese plant in 1997 as part of the approval process that would permit Hikma to sell its generic injectable cephs in the United States. Darwazah believed U.S. demand could prompt a doubling of injectable ceph output within a year.

Entry Into the United States

In the late 1980s, Darwazah conceived a three-pronged geographical production strategy in the United States as well as in Europe and the Middle East. Darwazah explained:

> There were at least four reasons why I wanted to secure a foothold in the United States. First, the United States is the largest and most competitive pharmaceutical market in the world. If you can make it there, you can make it anywhere. Second, the prospects for generic drugs gaining a larger share of prescriptions were excellent as keeping health care costs under control became an ever more pressing political issue. Third, the United States is a well-organized and open market; the large Asian markets are not so straightforward. Fourth, I felt our manufacturing quality was up to U.S. standards. Finally I have to admit that cracking the U.S. market was an entrepreneurial challenge and, having studied in the States, I wanted the satisfaction of succeeding in the American market.

Hikma began, in 1989, to look for an acquisition candidate in the United States. The pharmaceutical manufacturing sector in the United States was consolidating; the pressure to control health costs put many small companies under margin pressure. Cost concerns were also increasing the penetration of generics and many managed care health providers were mandating substitution of generics for their patients. Moreover, numerous drugs were scheduled to come off patent and thereby become available to generic competition. Hikma identified the West-ward company of New Jersey as one of several possible acquisition candidates and, after negotiations and due diligence, a deal was struck in June 1991.

West-ward's founders were manufacturing entrepreneurs with high quality standards. In the late 1980s, West-ward had been an approved vendor to many large hospital chains. However, the West-ward manufacturing operation had been acquired by a large drug wholesaler in 1988, and within 2 years, the firm's quality control standards were challenged by the FDA. West-ward's 1990 sales of $12 million were primarily of off-patent drugs sold on contract. Convinced that Hikma technicians could bring West-ward's production facilities back into compliance with FDA standards, Darwazah decided to make an offer for the company. Following the acquisition, a team of managers and technicians from Jordan worked at the West-ward plant to secure FDA recertification.

As of 1996, West-ward had 83 tablet and capsule products in its line. Forty of these were based on Abbreviated New Drug Applications (ANDAs)[5] approved by the FDA, 35 of which had been approved since the Hikma acquisition. Forty percent of West-ward sales were private label products sold to several health maintenance organizations; 40% were tablets and caplets sold under the West-ward branded generic label to drug wholesalers; and 20% were products manufactured to the specifications of several major drug companies. Sales of $15 million in 1996 resulted in an $800,000 pretax profit. According to Said Darwazah, the West-ward operation had recovered to 80% of its peak performance in the 1980s.

---

[5]Once the FDA approved an ANDA, the new drug could de facto be sold almost anywhere in the world except Canada, Japan, and Western Europe which had their own approval procedures.

HIKMA'S STRATEGIC FOCUS

By 1996, it was clear that Hikma's growth had stemmed from two key judgments Darwazah had made a decade earlier: the decision to focus on cephalosporins and the decision to focus on the manufacture of added value generics. Darwazah believed that continuation of these two strategies would enable Hikma to expand significantly its business in the United States. The proportions of Hikma sales that were cephs and generics in 1996 are shown in Table 5.1.

Cephalosporins

Cephalosporins were a class of anti-infective drugs with similar uses to penicillins. They were deployed against a broad array of bacteria-induced infections, especially those that occurred during or as a result of surgery. Most were used in hospitals rather than for out-patient treatment. In 1995, the value of all drugs sold worldwide at the dose form level was $270 billion. Of this, anti-infectives accounted for $23 billion, of which cephs, often described as "workhorse" antibiotics, accounted for 45% (or $10.2 billion), penicillins for 15%, and quinolones for 11%. Cephs were the eighth most frequently prescribed category of drugs in the United States (60 million prescriptions in 1995).

Oral cephs accounted for approximately 70% of total doses taken but for only 50% of sales value. The best-known oral cephs were Eli Lilly's Ceclor and Ceflex holding approximately 43% of the oral ceph market. Ceclor went off patent in December 1994. Injectable cephs, accounting for 25% of total doses, were more effective than oral cephs and were used more heavily in hospitals to treat acutely sick patients.

By 1995, there were several generations of cephs on the market. The first and second generation cephs were largely off patent, and therefore subject to competition from generics, while newer, third- and fourth-generation cephs had been developed, either to combat more virulent infections or to address more finely targeted indications. As shown in Exhibit 5.3, these cephs commanded higher margins than earlier generations. There were around 50 ceph products on the market; the cephalosporin molecule lent itself more readily than penicillin to line extensions because there were three places at which new chains could be attached. The frequency with which new versions of cephs were introduced led some physicians to refer semi-facetiously to the latest ceph discovery as the "ceph du jour."

The market share leaders in cephs were Eli Lilly (16% of doses worldwide in 1995), Glaxo Wellcome (15%), and Fujisawa (10%). Bristol Myers Squibb and Upjohn were

TABLE 5.1 Hikma Sales of Cephs and Generics: 1996E		
	% Cephs[1]	*% Generics*
Jordan (domestic)	25	50
Jordan (export)	20	50
Portugal (domestic)	50	30
Portugal (export)	100	60
United States	0	100

[1]Approximately 50% of ceph sales were of generics.

EXHIBIT 5.3 Index of Cephalosporin Prices: 1996			
Generation of cephs	**Middle East**	**Europe**	**United States**
Generic			
First	100	160	90
Second	200	250	N/A
Branded			
First	150	200	120
Second	300	400	400
Third	500	500	600

developing and launching fourth-generation cephs. Fujisawa had already licensed marketing of its fourth-generation injectable ceph to Johnson & Johnson. Approximately one-third of cephs were sold in North America, one-third in Europe, and one-third in Asia, principally Japan.

Bulk cephs, from which doses of cephs were made, were produced and marketed by a variety of companies, including companies in India and Taiwan. In 1995, 4,700 metric tons of bulk cephs were sold at prices ranging from $400 to $6,000 per kilo.

GENERIC VERSIONS OF PATENTED PRODUCTS

Darwazah recognized in the 1980s that demand for generic drugs was increasing and was likely to continue. Generic drugs, called by their basic chemical names, had the same active ingredients, strength, dosage form, and medical effects as their brand name counterparts. As patents on brand name drugs expired, there was an opportunity for lower priced generic manufacturers to capture market share.

In most Middle Eastern countries, drug patents were recognized for 10 years (as opposed to 20 years in the United States) and slight variations in manufacturing processes permitted generic equivalents to be registered under new names. Although generic versions of patented products could not be marketed in countries where the patents on the brand name drug were still in force, they could be sold in many developing countries where patent enforcement was not as tight. Hikma increasingly focused on the manufacture of generic cephs. Given the extra lead time and the opportunity to manufacture patented drugs under license, the company could perfect their production before they came off patent in the United States. Comparative cost and price structures for generic and branded injectable cephs are shown in Exhibit 5.4.

In the United States, where health care costs accounted for 15% of the gross national product, there was significant political pressure on the drug companies, even though pharmaceuticals represented only 7% of the total health care burden. Between 1985 and 1995, generics more than doubled their volume share of U.S. prescription drug sales to 43% but their share of the $50 billion U.S. prescription market was only 12% in value terms. Sales of generics were boosted in 1991 by the so-called "drug product selection law" that permitted pharmacists to substitute cheaper generics in place of brand name drugs when filling prescriptions and required that health

EXHIBIT 5.4 Comparative Cost and Price Structures for Hikma Injectable Cephs: 1996[1]

	Generic	*Branded*
Raw material cost ($ per gram)[2]	$0.50	$2.00
Vial & label	$0.50	$0.50
Quality control	$0.20	$0.20
Variable manufacturing cost	$1.20	$2.20
Clinical trials		$0.20
Sales & marketing	$0.10	$1.00
Total cost	$1.30	$3.40
Avg. manufacturer selling price	$1.90	$5.00
Profit margin	$0.60 (32%)	$1.60 (32%)

[1]Prices of injectable cephs (including those produced by Hikma) varied widely depending on the sophistication of the drug. Some third-generation cephs sold for $36 or more per gram.

[2]A gram was a typical patient dosage.

care providers charge the government-run Medicaid and Medicare the lowest possible drug prices.[6]

Price-sensitive consumers paying health care insurance through managed care companies and health maintenance organizations fueled demand for lower priced generics. The FDA set up a special office to handle ANDAS applications from generic drug manufacturers; these applications, of which 250 were approved in 1995 alone, could be filed before a brand name drug's patent expired, required bioequivalency studies and took, on average, 18 months to process.

Adding further to the potential for generic drug sales to increase in the United States was the fact that, between 1995 and 2005, 60 major brand name drugs, representing $40 billion in annual sales, would come off patent. Between 1995 and 2000, five major cephs were due to come off patent; as a result, Hikma was especially keen to file ANDAs applications for its generic equivalents, and obtain approval for them as soon as possible.

The large, research-based drug companies reacted to the advent of generic competition in several ways. In some cases, successful generic manufacturers were acquired. In other cases, the research-based drug companies fought generic competition claiming that the generic differed in some key way (for example, a binding or dispersing ingredient or chemical delivery variation). A third approach was to offer special long-term pricing contracts to the large managed care organizations while a drug was still covered by patent to insulate against share erosion when it expired. A fourth approach was to sign an agreement with a generic drug manufacturer ahead of patent expiration to try to influence the pricing of both the generic and the brand name versions. Eli Lilly signed such an agreement with Mylan Pharmaceuticals on Ceclor, its leading ceph, a year before the U.S. patent expired in 1994. By 1995, Ceclor's market share had, nevertheless, dropped from 36% to 14%.

---

[6]Although generic purchases by pharmacies represented 12% of total prescription dollars, the same generics accounted for 30% of pharmacy dispensing revenues, indicating higher markups than on brand name drugs.

Cephalexin was, in 1995, the tenth most frequently prescribed generic drug in the United States, accounting for 2.8% of generic prescriptions. Amoxicillin, which Hikma also produced in a generic version, accounted for 17% of generic prescriptions.

Because of the size of the ceph market, there were not so many generic competitors as in some of the more heavily prescribed drug categories. However, Hikma was far from being the only small pharmaceutical company interested in producing and marketing generic cephs. Marsam of the United States and Rambaxy of India were well-known in the field. Another competitor, Lupin Laboratories of India, signed an agreement with Merck Generics in 1995 to manufacture and market a line of injectable cephs.

U.S. GROWTH OPTIONS

Having established a U.S. foothold by purchasing West-ward, Said Darwazah was keen to grow Hikma's sales in the United States. His ambition was to achieve $30 million in sales of West-ward manufactured drugs by 2000 with another $70 million coming from sales of cutting-edge injectable cephs made in Portugal. These drugs would not be subject to import tariffs and transportation costs would be minimal. Hikma Portugal was not finding it easy to make sales in other European countries so capacity to supply the U.S. market was likely to be available. West-ward would continue to manufacture tablets and capsules; the plant could not be upgraded to produce injectable cephs. However, sales and distribution of these highly technical drugs from Portugal would add to West-ward's reputation and help boost sales of its branded generics.

Two large firms had approached Hikma offering quantity purchase deals on the firm's injectable cephs. The first option was to sell injectable cephs to Northaid[7], which was the fifth largest manufacturer of ethical pharmaceuticals in the United States in 1995 and a division of a giant consumer goods company. West-ward had manufactured orally administered drugs for Northaid for several years through a joint venture in which both parties shared the profits equally. Northaid purchases accounted for 10% of West-ward's sales in 1995. Said Darwazah commented on Northaid's proposal:

> They have indicated an interest in buying $60 million worth of injectable cephs from us by 2000 plus $30 million worth of generic drugs manufactured by West-ward. Northaid wants a U.S. exclusive on our injectable cephs.

A second option was to suppy Sanitas[7], a large managed care organization that had distribution contracts to supply drugs to over 1,000 hospitals throughout the United States. Sanitas sales represented about 20% of 1995 hospital purchases of drugs through managed care organizations. Darwazah commented on the Sanitas opportunity:

> Sanitas have told us they can take all the injectable cephs we can supply. They say they'll need to procure $200 million worth of injectable cephs by 2000. We would have to double the capacity of our plant in Portugal to supply them at this level. Of course, they want rock-bottom prices, guaranteed delivery dates, and an exclusive on sales of our injectable cephs in the United States. They would put the Sanitas name on the product label; West-ward would not be mentioned.

---

[7]Disguised name.

Sanitas would not normally be talking to a company of our size, but we have the range and quality of injectable cephs they need. They gave West-ward a 1-year contract to supply them with some generic drugs to check out our quality control and customer service. That worked well but, unlike Northaid, they really don't want West-ward's branded generics. But, like Northaid, they want to sign a deal with a supplier soon, and we're not the only game in town.

Said Darwazah was attracted by the high volume purchase commitments these companies were prepared to make. Agreeing to one of these deals would, however, re-duce Hikma's independence and practically turn it into a captive OEM supplier. Said wondered if he could develop a strong enough sales and distribution system in the United States with the necessary breadth and depth of hospital contacts to go it alone and promote the West-ward brand. Alternatively, a 2- or 3-year agreement with Northaid or Sanitas would give Hikma time and cash to establish its reputation in the U.S. market and then sell direct with branded generics.

CHAPTER

6

DEVELOPING THE MARKETING PLAN

Gillette Indonesia

In October 1995, Chester Allan, Gillette's country manager in Indonesia, was developing his unit's 1996 marketing plan. Once completed, it would be forwarded to Rigoberto Effio, business director in Gillete's Asia-Pacific group based in Singapore. Each year Effio received and approved marketing plans for the 12 countries in his region, which reached from Australia to China. Once approved by Ian Jackson, Asia-Pacific group vice president, the overall marketing plan for the region would be reviewed subsequently, along with other regional plans, by Robert King, executive vice president of Gillette's International Group.

Allan's plan projected a 19% increase in blade sales in Indonesia in 1996 from 115 million to 136 million. This seemed reasonable given a 17% increase in 1995 over the previous year. With a population of almost 200 million, Indonesia represented an important country in the portfolio of markets for which Effio and Jackson were responsible. Effio wondered whether investment spending in marketing beyond the 1995 level of 12% of sales might further accelerate market development. Given the growth rates of Gillette's business in other Asia-Pacific countries, Effio believed that a 25% to 30% increase in blade sales could be achieved in Indonesia in 1996.

THE COMPANY

Founded in 1901, Boston-based Gillette was the world leader in blades and razors and in nine other consumer product categories—writing instruments (Paper Mate, Parker, and Waterman), correction products (Liquid Paper), men's electric razors (Braun), toothbrushes (Oral-B), shaving preparations, oral care appliances (Braun, Oral-B plaque remover), pistol-grip hair dryers (Braun), hair epilators (Braun), and hand blenders (Braun).

Gillette manufacturing operations were conducted at 50 facilities in 24 countries. A London office had been opened in 1905, and a blade factory opened in Paris the fol-

---

Research Associate Diane E. Long prepared this case under the supervision of Professor John Quelch as the basis for class discussion rather than to illustrate either effective or ineffective handling of an administrative situation. Confidential data have been disguised.
Copyright © 1996 by the President and Fellows of Harvard College. Harvard Business School case 597-009.

lowing year. The company's products were distributed through wholesalers, retailers, and agents in over 200 countries and territories.

Gillette managed its worldwide business through a combination of business and regional operational units. The North Atlantic Group manufactured and marketed Gillette's shaving and personal care products in North America and Western Europe. The Stationery Products Group, part of the Diversified Group, produced and sold Gillette's stationery products in North America and Western Europe. The Diversified Group also included Braun, Oral-B, and Jafra, each managed by a worldwide unit. The International Group, headed by Robert King, produced and marketed the shaving, stationery, and personal care products everywhere, except for North America and Western Europe. The International Group comprised three geographic divisions: Latin America; Africa, Middle East and Eastern Europe; and Asia-Pacific. Ian Jackson, group vice president based in Singapore, oversaw operations in 12 Asia-Pacific countries.

Of Gillette's 1995 sales of $6.8 billion, blades and razors accounted for $2.6 billion (40%). Blade and razor sales in the Asia-Pacific region were more than $600 million. The company had consistently maintained profitable growth over the previous 5 years. Between 1990 and 1995, sales grew by 9% annually, net income by 17%, and earnings per share by 18%. Gillette's mission was to achieve worldwide leadership in its core product categories. In 1995, three-quarters of sales came from product categories in which Gillette held worldwide share leadership. The company emphasized geographic expansion along with research and development, advertising, and capital spending as drivers of growth. New-product activity and entry into and development of new markets were considered essential.

Geographic expansion required the company management to "think global, act local." Eduardo Kello, International Group business manager, explained:

> Headquarters develops new products. They are usually launched first in the U.S. or Western European markets, but quickly introduced in every market worldwide. We start in a new emerging market with simple blades, we introduce the shaving concept. Later, we upgrade the market to higher value products and shaving systems. The country management in each market usually decides the mix of products to push and how to allocate marketing resources against them.

Robert King further emphasized the importance of persuading Gillette's country managers to take initiative:

> Trying to drive new product activity from headquarters is like pushing on a string. The string moves much more easily if a country manager is pulling on it than if headquarters is pushing on it.

Although headquarters in Boston emphasized increasing worldwide sales and distribution of higher-margin shaving systems such as Sensor, this was not feasible in many Asian markets. Only a few consumers were sophisticated and wealthy enough to be potential customers for the Sensor. In Indonesia, for example, the focus was still on introducing the concept of shaving with basic Gillette products.

INDONESIA IN 1996

The Republic of Indonesia was an archipelago of more than 15,000 islands and 196 million people who spoke over 250 regional languages and dialects. (See Exhibit 6.1 for a

EXHIBIT 6.1 Map of Indonesia[1]

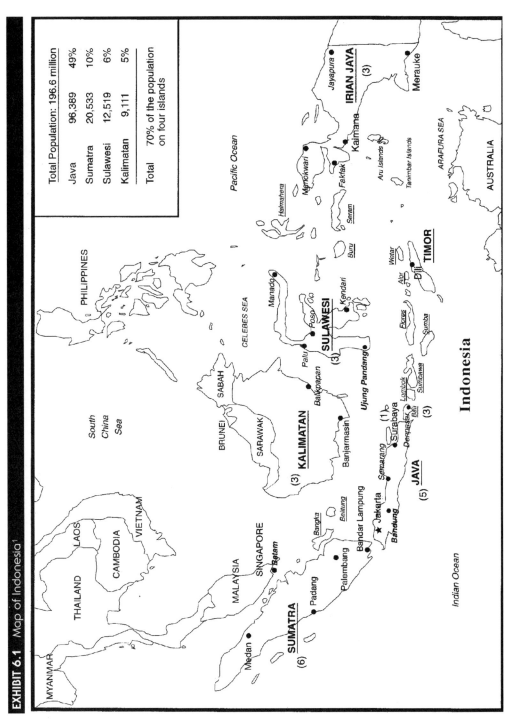

Total Population: 196.6 million		
Java	96,389	49%
Sumatra	20,533	10%
Sulawesi	12,519	6%
Kalimatan	9,111	5%
Total	70% of the population on four islands	

Indonesia

[1]Numbers in parentheses indicate number of Gillette distributors in a particular region.

map of the country.) Approximately 3,000 miles separated Sigli on Sumatra to the west from Sarmi on Irian Jaya to the east. President Suharto had led the country since 1965 and provided continuity and stability. Major economic development programs, legal reforms, and changes in domestic policies could be enacted only if supported by the president. Although rumors of his pending retirement circulated, there was no sign of any change in the political power structure in 1996.

By 1995, Indonesia's population had reached 196 million, with 35% living in towns and 65% in rural areas. Indonesia had averaged annual GDP growth of over 7% for more than 20 years. The country traditionally exported agricultural and oil petroleum products, but economic development plans since the oil crisis of 1988 had encouraged growth in nonoil-related industries. Economic policy was laid out in 5-year plans known as *Replita*.[1] The goals of Replita VI, applicable in 1996, were to maintain annual GDP growth of 6.2%, expand the manufacturing sector by 9.4% a year, and expand the nonoil/gas component of manufacturing by 10.3% a year. Inflation in 1996 was expected to be 12%. Over the years, the liberalization of foreign investment policy had increased private sector involvement in the economy; the central government focused on developing infrastructure in the poorer regions and on human resources.

Economic progress was manifested in increased per-capita incomes and improved standards of living for most of the population. The government stressed export-oriented industrialization to fuel growth and a demand for labor that would keep pace with population growth. During Replita VI, it was expected that more than two million Indonesians would enter the workforce each year. The rupiah[2] had depreciated in order to maintain Indonesia's export competitiveness. The value of committed foreign investment reportedly increased from $826 million in 1986 to $10.3 billion in 1992 and to $23.7 billion by June 1994 (*EIU Country Profile 1995*). In 1996, Indonesia was expected to have the highest foreign direct investment/export ratio (74%) of any major emerging market. However, only about one-half of approved foreign direct investment projects had been implemented.

Economic growth had not been consistent throughout the archipelago. Java and Bali had grown much faster than poorer regions such as Irian Jaya and East Timor; contribution of these poorer regions to the country's economy was minimal. Java and Bali accounted for 7% of the land, 60% of the population, and 75% of the gross domestic product. Four of the five major urban centers (Jakarta, Bandung, Surabaya, and Semarang) were on Java.

The average standard of living on Java and Bali was much higher than in the rest of Indonesia. An improving education system ensured that foreign companies would be attracted to the major urban areas, fueling further growth. Market research showed that consumer marketers launched their campaigns in and expected most of their sales from the top five cities (the four in Java plus Medan on Sumatra) that together accounted for 35 million of the population. About 60% of Gillette's 1995 sales were made in these five metropolitan areas.

Table 6.1 shows the percentages of households falling into each of several income classes in 1995 and projections for 2000. Also shown is the percentage of each income group who shopped regularly in supermarkets in 1995.

---

[1]*Replita* was the shortened form for the Indonesian name *Rencana pembangunan lima tahun,* which meant 5-year development plans.
[2]Rupiah exchange rate in 1995 was US$1 = 2,200 rupiah.

TABLE 6.1 Percentages of Households by Income Sector and Supermarket Shopping Incidence: 1995 and 2000E

Income segment ($)	Percentage of population		Percentage shopping in supermarkets: 1995
	1995	2000	
>10,000	15.9	20.6	40
5,000–10,000	17.0	19.6	25
2,000–5,000	32.7	33.8	10
<2,000	34.4	25.9	2

INDONESIAN SHAVING PRACTICES

Gillette traditionally entered a market with the basic double-edge blade. Effio explained, "We lead with our strength—the shaving business. Later we leverage the distribution established for our blades on behalf of our other product lines."

Shaving was still underdeveloped in Indonesia, but the incidence of shaving was increasing. A 1995 survey of urban men over 18 years (of whom there were 40 million) indicated that 80% shaved. Those who did, shaved on average 5.5 times per month, compared with 12 times per month in Hong Kong and 26 times per month in the United States. Tracking data indicated that, in 1993, 66% of urban adult men had been shaving with an average incidence of 4.5 times per month.

Shaving incidence was influenced by several factors. There was increasing awareness of Western grooming practices, especially in urban areas, as a result of exposure to foreign media and the increasing presence of multinational companies and their overseas personnel. College students and graduates entering the workforce were especially important trendsetters. On the other hand, grooming products were still regarded as luxury items by many. In addition, Asian beards did not grow as fast as Caucasian or Latino beards, so shaving incidence would be lower, even in a fully developed market.

Forty percent of men who shaved used store-bought blades all or part of the time. The remainder used dry or wet knives. The average number of blades used in a year by the 20% of shavers who always used blades was 15. The average number of blades used by occasional users was 4. Only 4% of men used shaving foam or lotion, 25% used soap and water, 12% used water alone, and 58% shaved dry.

TABLE 6.2 Shaving Incidence per Month

Shaving incidence per month	Percentage of surveyed
10 times or more	15
5 to 9 times	34
4 times	26
3 times	10
2 times	7
1 time	8

GILLETTE'S OPERATION

Gillette entered Indonesia in 1971 with majority ownership of a joint venture with a local company. Gillette's razor blade plant, built in 1972, was located about one hour from Jakarta. Gillette manufactured 75 stockkeeping units in the factory, of which 65 were shaving items. The major product was the double-edge blade for razors and cartridges. Double-edge blades accounted for 60% of the value of products manufactured. Oral-B products were a small portion of the plant's operations; the plant had just begun to "tuft" or put the bristles on the brush handles. The plant was highly automated and run by 68 full-time employees. In addition, 75 casual workers were employed on one- to two-year contracts. In 1995, the plant produced 150 million blades, of which 46 million were exported. The 1996 production plan called for output of 168 million blades, of which 50 million would be exported. Production manager Eko Margo Suhartono said:

> We are looking to import new equipment and expand the line capacity to 230 million double-edge blades per year which we hope will be sufficient to meet demand for the next 5 years. We needed this extra capacity by 1996 but implementation has been delayed to 1997. This means, in 1996 we will have more overtime and must continue to improve plant productivity.

The manufacturing team had improved business processes as well as production efficiencies. They cut the cycle time from placement of order to product out the door from 50 to 43 days. Effio explained, "Before it would take us 7 days to make almost three million blades; now we only need 3 days on the floor. This is an incredible response to sales demand." Due to the demand of other multinational corporations (MNCs) for experienced workers, there was a need for continuous staff recruiting and training and increasingly upward pressure on worker wages.

In addition, the production team carefully planned the timing of materials inputs. Because of distribution and transportation inefficiencies, the need for buffer inventories was substantial. Cartridges and handles for the razors were imported. Gillette's women's razor was launched in 1995. The razor was imported, but packaged in the country. Problems with customs clearances could impact the entire manufacturing cycle.

The plant obtained electricity from the local grid, supplemented by two backup generators. Water was drawn from a well on the property. Gillette purchased ammonia and other basic raw materials from local suppliers.

Gillette and Competitive Product Lines

The Gillette brand name was synonymous with high-quality double-edge blades. In fact, the Bahasa Indonesian word for blade sounded similar to the name *Gillette*. In 1993 Gillette held 28% of the blade market by volume. By 1995 Gillette's unit share had grown to 48% and was expected to increase to 50% in 1996.

Gillette's policy was to make all of its products available to all of its country subsidiaries. Headquarters persuasion and successful launches of new products in other countries were often helpful in motivating country managers to adopt new products.

Gillette's product line in Indonesia included:

- Double-edge blades. The three types included the basic Gillette blue stainless blade, a premium double-edge blade (Gillette Goal Red), and an improved blue blade (Gillette Goal Blue).
- Disposables. In the United States and Europe, Bic dominated the market for disposable razors with plastic handles as a result of aggressive pricing. In other markets, Gillette had been able to position its disposable as a system, rather than a low-priced convenience product. In Indonesia, Gillette sold two types of disposables, the Goal II and the more advanced Blue II.
- GII. Named the Trac II in the United States, it was the earliest shaving system from Gillette to incorporate twin blade technology, whereby the first blade lifted the hair out of the follicle for the second blade to then cut it off.
- Contour. The Contour system (named Atra in the United States) added a pivoting head (as opposed to the fixed head on the GII) that enabled the twin blades to stay on the face more consistently.
- Sensor. The Sensor system added an improved pivoting action and independently sprung twin blades.

Exhibit 6.2 provides a detailed breakdown of Gillette sales by product. Information on Gillette's gross margin as well as manufacturer, distributor, and retailer selling prices by product line is also provided. Gillette sold 115 million blades in Indonesia in 1995, of which 100 million (87%) were double edge. In contrast, double-edge blades accounted for 70% of sales in Malaysia and only 20% in Australia. Sales of systems and disposables accounted for 30% and 50% of units sold in Australia and 25% and 5% of units sold in Malaysia. The share of Gillette Indonesia sales accounted for by the higher-margin disposables and systems was projected to increase in 1996 to around 20% of units.

As indicated in Exhibit 6.3, Gillette Indonesia's 1995 sales from shaving products were valued at $19.6 million. Through a combination of volume increases (19%) and price increases (20%), Gillette Indonesia management projected that this number would increase to $27.6 million in 1996. Gillette's overall gross margin on shaving products was 46% of gross revenues (or 55% of net revenues after discounts). An income statement for Gillette Indonesia's shaving products business is presented in Exhibit 6.4.

Gillette's main competitors were imported, low-end, double-edge blades from Eastern Europe and China. Based on market research conducted in the four major cities, Tatra, Super Nacet, and Tiger were the most often mentioned competing brands on the market. Gillette's retail prices were sometimes four times those of competitive products. Chester Allan in Jakarta explained, "Currently most of the poorer rural shavers cannot afford Gillette products and buy low-price, low-quality brands such as Tiger and Tatra. However, with rising incomes and improved Gillette distribution and display, consumers are moving to Gillette."

Gillette's disposables faced two competitors: Bic, from the United States, and Bagus, a locally manufactured brand. Neither of these sold in high volumes, so the competition was not keen. The Schick division of Warner Lambert imported its higher-end products, but sales were minimal. According to Allan, "Gillette has 90% of the premium-priced segment of the market which we developed."

Gillette-brand blades commanded high awareness in the Indonesian market. Market research conducted in 1995 among Indonesian male shavers, reported in Exhibit 6.5, showed 97% brand awareness and 55% brand used most often ratings for Gillette's Goal Red blade.

EXHIBIT 6.2 — Gillette Indonesia Product Line and Margin Structure: 1995

Products	Unit sales (millions)		% of units sold made locally	Manufacturer selling price/unit[1]	Manufacturer gross margin %	Distributor selling price/unit[2]	Retail selling price/unit
	1995	1996E					
A. Double-edge blades	**100**	**108**					
Gillette Blue Blade	5	5	100	0.06	47	0.08	0.11
Gillette Goal Red	80	90	100	0.11	50	0.15	0.20
Gillette Goal Blue	15	13	100	0.08	48	0.11	0.15
B. Disposables	**5**	**10**					
Goal II	4	8	100	0.21	32	0.31	0.40
Blue II	1	2	0	0.35	52[3]	0.49	0.64
C. Systems blades	**10**	**18**					
Gillette GII	2	3	20	0.45	52	0.68	0.82
Gillette Contour	5	7	20	0.55	52	0.77	1.00
Gillette Sensor	3	8	0	0.65	40[3]	0.91	1.19

[1]In U.S. dollar equivalent.

[2]Distributors often sold (at an average 8% markup) to subdistributors or wholesalers who in turn (at an average 12% markup) sold to mom-and-pop retailers who took, on average, a further 20% markup.

[3]Represents, in the case of imported products, the difference between Gillette Indonesia's selling price and the landed transfer price.

EXHIBIT 6.3 Gillette Indonesia Sales Breakdowns: 1995 and 1996

Sales revenues in 1995	1995 ($)	1996E ($)
1995 Total revenues	23.00	32.20
Revenues from export sales	1.40	2.30
Revenues from in-country sales	21.60	29.90
In-country sales:		
a. Shaving products total sales	19.60	27.60
Blades	10.30	11.20
Disposables	1.20	2.50
Sensor	5.60	10.40
Razors	2.00	3.00
Prep products	0.50	0.50
b. Nonshave products	2.00	2.30

Distribution and Sales

Indonesian regulations prohibited a foreign company from directly importing or distributing its products. These regulations protected Indonesian distributors and resulted in inefficiencies. The American Chamber of Commerce in Jakarta estimated that 45% of retail prices in Indonesia covered distribution services.

To ensure distribution of products in the face of weak communications, poor traffic conditions, and lack of distribution service technology, Gillette managers and those in other MNCs had to focus on the basics of distribution over which they had little control and from which they extracted no direct profit.

Gillette had originally appointed a single national distributor, but by 1993 it was apparent the arrangement was not working satisfactorily. No single distributor could provide an even depth of coverage in every district throughout the entire country. Mohammad Slamet, Gillette's national sales manager in the early 1990s, explained:

> There are many distribution issues which require on-the-spot responses. A distributor who is headquartered hundreds of miles away cannot provide a quick enough response. In addition, there often arise sensitive, purely local,

EXHIBIT 6.4 Gillette Indonesia: Percentage Income Statement for Shaving Products, 1995

Gross revenues from shaving products	100%
Trade discounts	− 10
Net revenues	90%
Variable manufacturing costs	− 36%
Variable selling costs (sales commissions)	− 2
Variable distribution costs	− 6
Gross margin	46%
Advertising	− 9%
Consumer promotions and merchandising	− 3
General sales and administrative costs	− 14
Profit from operations	20%

EXHIBIT 6.5 Indonesian Male Consumer Awareness and Usage of Blades: 1995[1]

Products in survey	Brand awareness	Ever used	Brand used most often
A. Double-edge			
Gillette			
Gillette Goal Red	97	85	55
Gillette Goal Blue	49	18	5
Gillette Blue Blade	14	5	1
Competitors			
Tatra	42	21	4
Super Nacet	16	4	—
Tiger/Cap Macan	59	44	11
B. Disposable			
Goal II	41	16	4
Blue II	9	3	—
C. System blades			
Gillette GII	12	4	1
Gillette Contour	9	4	3
Gillette Sensor	12	4	1

[1]Based on a sample of 300 male adult consumers.

Source: Company records.

issues which can only be resolved by someone familiar with the relationships, customs, and dialects of each area.

In 1993, Gillette appointed 23 distributors dispersed across the country. The new distributors were previously known to Slamet or were identified through referrals. In the year following implementation of the new system, sales rose by 60%.

A good distributor had the working capital and/or bank credit line to stock sufficient inventory and to bridge the time gap between paying Gillette and receiving payments from its customers. Second, a good distributor also had sufficient salespeople, warehouses, and reliable transportation equipment. Third, strong local connections with government officials and the trade were critical to success.

A typical distributor represented different manufacturers and product lines. Gillette's distributors were encouraged to hire people to handle only the Gillette business in the belief that such focus would result in the greater push. Gillette itself expanded its internal sales and trade relations staff to work with the new distributors.

In 1995, Nyoman Samsu Prabata was Gillette's national sales manager. Nyoman's organization comprised three regional managers (covering western, central, and eastern Indonesia) who supervised a total of 12 area managers and supervisors. These managers were well compensated but were often tempted away by better offers from other multinationals, because of the shortage of general management talent in Indonesia. Nyoman's group coordinated the efforts of 23 geographically based independent distributors and their 260 salespeople. Although Gillette's distributors hired many of the sales staff and paid their base salaries, Gillette covered their commissions and other incentives for reaching targets, which averaged 20% of their total compensation.

Nyoman explained:

> The number one job of the Gillette sales team is educating the distributors
> and their salespeople. We have to train them how our products work, so they
> can demonstrate the products on their own. We have to educate them on the
> benefits of our products compared to both traditional shaving methods and
> to competitive products. We also educate them on warehousing and handling
> methods to reduce damage to the product.

For example, one distributor's warehouse was located in an area of Jakarta with
poor transportation and prone to flooding. "A few days ago, the warehouse roof fell in
under pressure from the rain. The actual damage was minimal but the operation had to
stop for a day. He just would not listen to us," explained Nyoman.

In Indonesia, direct verbal confrontation was socially unacceptable. This sometimes
resulted in strained relations between a distributor and an area manager festering for
months without being solved. Another challenge was the different degree to which employees and consumers observed Muslim religious practices. Nyoman commented:

> In Jakarta, while people are faithful followers, the attitude is a bit more ca-
> sual and there is an understanding that not everyone is practicing to the same
> degree. However, outside Jakarta, religious practices are more closely ob-
> served. In Aceh on Sumatra it would be an insult to wave good-bye with your
> left hand. In Bali, the Hindu religion is dominant so, for the "Galungan" holi-
> day, Hindus fast for 2 days. For Nyepi, complete silence must be observed for
> 1 day, so any devout Hindu stays home and does not even turn on the elec-
> tricity. Not only does this affect our business but I must plan ahead for holi-
> day staffing.

Gillette gave its distributors 45 days' credit. In return, the distributors would give
their customers anywhere from 30 to 60 days' credit. Nyoman said:

> While we try to insist on timely payments via bank transfer, there are many
> times when receivables are overdue. Though the sales staff and area man-
> agers are responsible for receivables, I often have to get involved and it is im-
> portant to be tough on the issue. As you move further away from Jakarta, the
> legal system does not provide much support, so ensuring distributors have the
> working capital to cover the spread between payables and receivables is criti-
> cal to their selection.

In addition to the distributors who supplied wholesalers and, in turn, the extensive
network of small retailers in Indonesia, Nyoman also supervised a national accounts
team who negotiated sales to the major Indonesia supermarket chains, often shipping
to them direct. Supermarket chains included Hero that had 54 outlets, Metro with 5 outlets, and others located in the large urban centers. These chains purchased directly from
manufacturers and could handle products efficiently. In 1995, supermarkets accounted
for 5% of Gillette's shaving products sales in units and 8% in value; corresponding 1993
figures were 2% and 4%. Market research showed that higher-income, urban consumers were increasingly shopping in supermarkets. Most sales of Gillette's higher-
priced shaving products were through these outlets. Competition for shelf space was

intensifying. Some supermarkets were imposing slotting allowances on suppliers of up to 80% of a new product's cost to provide shelf space.

Traditional wholesalers and distributors came under pressure as a result of these trends. Many wholesalers had poor facilities, traditional goods-handling methods, and antiquated accounting—some still used an abacus to track the business. They tended to focus on turnover alone rather than in conjunction with profit margin. They were also slow to see the potential of upgrading their customers to higher unit-margin products.

Distribution coverage in Indonesia required consumer goods manufacturers like Gillette to reach more than 60,000 small kiosks and mom-and-pop shops. Gillette did not distribute through the many itinerant salespeople who traveled with their wares on bicycles from village to village. The entrepreneurial owners of the small retail outlets would respond to requests from consumers and, in turn, demand the product from their wholesalers. "Pull marketing can be effective," Slamet said. "Once the mom-and-pops start getting requests for a new product, they are willing to stock it. This is how marketing testing takes place," Effio explained.

Communications

As indicated in Exhibit 6.4, Gillette Indonesia spent 9% of gross sales on advertising and 3% on consumer promotions and merchandising. Ten percent of gross sales was accounted for by off-invoice allowances to the trade and other forms of trade deals. The advertising budget for shaving products in 1995 was around $2 million.

Media advertising was targeted principally at urban male consumers. About half the advertising budget was spent on television (there were five private channels and one government-owned) and half on print. Television advertising included some program sponsorships. The adult literacy rate in Indonesia was 77%, and half of Indonesian adult males read a newspaper at least once a week. The allocation of Gillette advertising was weighted towards systems and disposables to encourage consumers to trade up.

Gillette headquarters developed television advertisements for use worldwide, with the intent that local voiceovers and local package shots would be superimposed. (A sample Gillette print leaflet, with translation, is shown in Exhibit 6.6). Gillette Indonesia's marketing manager explained:

> We are still in the early stages of educating consumers about shaving. An ad made in Boston for the U.S. market may not have sufficient details about the basics. Nothing can be taken for granted here, especially when it comes to advertising the entry-level products, the double-edge blades.

Gillette Indonesia managers differed over the relative emphasis that advertising should place on persuading consumers to shave for the first time, increasing the incidence of shaving among existing shavers, and trading existing shavers up to higher-margin, more sophisticated shaving systems. As a compromise, the 1995 advertising budget was split equally among these three objectives. One-third of the total budget was allocated to advertising Sensor.

Special promotions were run in 1995 on the Sensor and Contour systems. Gift-with-purchase promotions (involving an Oral-B travel toothbrush, a toilet bag, or a trial sample of Foamy shaving cream) were targeted at upper- to middle-income urban males. Promotional efforts were sometimes focused on the members of executive clubs, attendees at golf tournaments, or workers in specific office buildings.

EXHIBIT 6.6 Gillette Indonesia Print Leaflet

Tahukah Anda ?

- Jumlah rambut yang tumbuh di wajah pria bisa mencapai 30.000 helai.
- Pertumbuhan rambut tersebut per hari rata-rata 0,38 milimeter.
- Panjang maksimum yang bisa dicapai seumur hidup sekitar **80 sentimeter**.
- Dalam keadaan kering, janggut sama kakunya dengan serat lembaga yang berdiameter sama.

● **18.000 SEBELUM MASEHI** Manusia primitif mengerik rambut pada wajah mereka dengan batu dan tulang yang dipertajam, sebagaimana tergambar pada lukisan-lukisan di gua purba.

● **336 SEBELUM MASEHI** Iskandar Zulkarnaen menitahkan para prajuritnya untuk bercukur, sehingga tentara Persia tak dapat menjambak janggut mereka dalam pertempuran.

● **1698**. Kaisar Rusia, Peter Yang Agung, mengenakan Pajak atas janggut, untuk membiasakan rakyatnya mengikuti tradisi bercukur yang dilakukan masyarakat Barat.

● **1895**. King C. Gillette, asal Amerika, menemukan pisau cukur moderen yang mengubah total kebiasaan bercukur pria di seluruh dunia. Dimana-mano orang meninggalkan pisau cukur tradisional dan menggantinya dengan pisau cukur bermata ganda yang dapat diganti-ganti.

ENAM LANGKAH MENCUKUR LEBIH LICIN, LEBIH LEMBUT DAN LEBIH NYAMAN

1. Bersihkan Wajah

Cucilah muka dengan air hangat dan sabun, lalu bilas hingga bersih. Tak perlu dikeringkan, biarkan kulit wajah dan rambut dalam keadaan basah.

2. Usapkan Gillette Foamy

Usapkan Gillette Foamy secara merata di atas permukaan yang akan dicukur.

Mencegah penguapan air dan mengurangi gesekan antara kulit dengan mata pisau. Sekaligus melembutkan kumis atau janggut yang akan dicukur.

3. Mulailah dari tempat yang Tepat.

Cukur rambut cambang, pipi, dan leher terlebih dulu. Rambut yang paling kaku tumbuh di dagu dan sekeliling bibir dan memerlukan waktu lebih lama untuk menyerap air untuk menjadi lembut.

4. Bercukurlah Secara Benar.

Bercukurlah dengan tarikan yang lembut dan ringan. Usahakan untuk sesedikit mungkin melakukan tarikan. Pisau cukur Gillette dirancang untuk menghasilkan cukuran yang lebih licin, lebih lembut dan nyaman.

5. Bilaslah Mata Pisau

Di tengah kegiatan mencukur, sesekali bilaslah mata pisau cukur dengan air yang deras (misalnya dari keran) guna membuang limbah cukuran. Usai bercukur, mata pisau harus langsung dibilas dan dihentak - hentakkan sampai airnya kering.

6. Jangan Mengusap Mata Pisau.

Jangan sekali-kali mengusap mata pisau dengan apa pun, karena akan merusak ketajamannya.

Gunakan cartridge yang sesuai dengan pisau cukur Gillette Anda.

Do you know?

- Up to 30,000 hairs can grow on a man's face.
- The hairs grow at an average rate of 0.38 millimeters per day.
- They can reach a maximum length of approximately 80 centimeters (32") over a lifetime.
- When it is dry, a beard is as stiff as copper fibers of the same diameter.

- **18,000** B.C. Primitive men scraped the hair off their faces with sharpened stones and bones, as depicted in drawings in ancient caves.

- **336 B.C.** Alexander the Great ordered his soldiers to shave so that the Persian army would not be able to grab their beards in battle.

- **1698.** Peter the Great, Czar of Russia, imposed a tax on beards to get his people used to following the shaving practices of Western societies.

- **King C. Gillette**, an American, invented the modern razor, which totally changed men's shaving habits all over the world. People everywhere gave up traditional razors and replaced them with replaceable double-edged razors.

SIX STEPS TO A SMOOTHER, GENTLER AND MORE COMFORTABLE SHAVE

1. *Clean your face*

Wash your face with hot water and soap, then rinse it until it is clean. You don't have to dry it, leave your face and hair wet.

2. *Apply Gillette Foamy*

Apply Gillette Foamy evenly over the surface to be shaved. It prevents water evaporation and reduces friction between the skin and the razor blade. At the same time it softens the mustache or beard which you are going to shave.

3. *Start at the Right Place*

First shave the sideburns, cheeks and neck. The stiffest hairs grow on the chin and around the lips and need more time to absorb water in order to become soft.

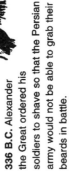

4. *Shave Correctly*

Shave with gentle and light strokes. Try to make as few strokes as possible. The Gillette razor is designed to produce a smoother, gentler, more comfortable shave.

5. *Rinse the Razor Blade*

While shaving, rinse the razor blade once in a while under running water (for example from the tap) to get rid of the whiskers. After shaving, the razor blade must be rinsed right away and shaken until dry.

6. *Don't Wipe the Razor Blade*

Don't ever wipe the razor blade with anything, because it will destroy its sharpness. *Use the cartridge that is right for your Gillette razor.*

Coupons were not used in Indonesia; redemption systems through retailers were not yet in place. However, Gillette found that lucky draws with entry forms inside product packages worked well; consumers had to mail in entry forms to be included in the draws.

Gillette used similar packaging in Indonesia as in the United States for its more expensive systems products. The Goal II, the cheaper of Gillette's disposables, was advertised on radio. The number of blades per pack varied by outlet; twice as many were included in the pack for supermarkets as in the pack for mom-and-pop stores.

CONCLUSION

As Allan reviewed his initial projections for 1996 (see Exhibit 6.3), he wondered how rapidly the Indonesian market for blades and razors could or would expand. Should the Indonesian market be allowed to just move along at its own pace? If so, what would that pace be? Alternatively, should Gillette Indonesia invest additional resources either in advertising and promotion or in sales and distribution, to accelerate the process of market development? If so, which products should be emphasized? Would further investment be wasted if it was based on concepts and products that were beyond consumers' understanding or willingness to pay?

Allan resolved to set out his objectives for Gillette Indonesia in 1996 and to develop a detailed marketing plan including an income statement projection. He knew his plan would have to satisfy Effio's objectives for Gillette's growth in the Asia-Pacific region.

Reference

Economist Intelligence Unit (EIU) Country Profile 1995, p. 19.

7 || PRODUCT LINE PLANNING

SADAFCO

In presenting his 1998 plan at the marketing meeting, Khalid Tahir, senior group product manager in the Saudi and Dairy Foodstuff Company Limited (SADAFCO), wanted to leave his colleagues in no doubt about the seriousness of the threat to the company's ice cream business:

> In the last few years, Nestlé, Unilever, and Mars have all stepped up their efforts to dominate Saudi Arabia as a keystone market in the region. We could not face any tougher competition: They have deep pockets, internationally proven brands, and confidence. Against this, we have market leadership and our local brand strength. The 1997 figures I am about to present show clearly the pressure on our profits and our distribution presence. The actions we take in the near future will determine our fate in this battle.

This challenge came at a critical point in SADAFCO's development. Having enjoyed 20 years of successful expansion, the company's core recombined milk business was experiencing its first volume losses, mostly to local competitors. At the same time, the company was nurturing a number of new product lines, such as tomato paste, hummus, mineral water, and snacks, and was considering a major drive into international markets in the region. As reported by the company's general manager, Bill Pace, SADAFCO's vision was to be "the Nestlé of the Middle East," the dominant foods company in the region. Ironically, that vision was threatened by a group of multinationals, including the very company SADAFCO sought to emulate.

SADAFCO—COMPANY BACKGROUND

SADAFCO, headquartered in Jeddah, Kingdom of Saudi Arabia (KSA), had evolved from a company formed in 1976 as the Danish Saudi Dairy Co., Ltd. This was one of a number of companies formed in the Kingdom of Saudi Arabia by Danish Turnkey Dairies, a firm based in Denmark that specialized in building and operating recombined milk

Professor David Arnold prepared this case as the basis for class discussion rather than to illustrate either effective or ineffective handling of an administrative situation.
Copyright © 1998 by the President and Fellows of Harvard College. Harvard Business School case 599-021.

plants.[1] Over the years, some of these plants had diversified into other businesses that required related production capabilities, such as ice cream, soft cheese, and tomato paste. SADAFCO was formed in 1990 by combining the Jeddah company with other separate but related recombined milk companies in Riyadh, Dammam, and Medina (see Exhibit 7.1 for a map of Saudi Arabia). Production was reallocated to permit specialization and improve scale economies, so that by 1996, Jeddah produced most of the recombined milk and snacks, Riyadh produced all of the company's ice cream, and Dammam produced tomato paste products and other foods. From October 1997, a new reporting structure separated manufacturing from sales and marketing, with new transfer prices in place between the factories and the sales and distribution operations. For the first time, profitability could be measured at the factory and product line level.

SADAFCO was a subsidiary of United Industries Company (UIC), a holding company with diverse interests based in the neighboring state of Kuwait. UIC, along with its own parent, the Kuwait Investment Projects Company (KIPCO), had been involved with Danish partners in establishing the Middle East's first dairy in 1970 in Kuwait. In 1997, SADAFCO's general manager, Bill Pace, was relocated to the Kuwait office (see Exhibit 7.2 for SADAFCO organization chart). Pace, an American with 30 years' experience of working in emerging markets in Africa, Asia, and the Middle East, attributed SADAFCO's success to its managerial capability.

> The company has never rested content with having overcome the technical challenges of the dairy industry in this part of the world, considerable though they have been, but has also long been one of the most forward-thinking local *marketing* companies, aware of the importance of brand building. We are proud of the brand strength that we have built up, and continue to innovate in all our product lines.

Much of this innovation had occurred since a 1995 decision to diversify the product line in order to maintain growth, as the core milk business achieved near-saturation distribution levels and matured. By 1997, SADAFCO achieved sales revenues of SR 818 million, with a trading profit of SR 81 million[2], and its Saudia brand, under which most of its products were marketed, enjoyed high awareness and trust throughout the country.

THE KINGDOM OF SAUDI ARABIA

Founded in 1932, the Kingdom of Saudi Arabia was an absolute monarchy that had been ruled by King Fahd bin Abdel-Aziz-al-Saud since 1982. With a land area approximately equal to that of Western Europe, much of it desert, the Kingdom of Saudi Arabia had a population of 18.5 million, about 75% of whom lived in urban centers, the two largest being the capital Riyadh, with 1.85 million people, and the main commercial center Jeddah, with 1.55 million. The country contained a quarter of the world's known reserves of oil, the basis for the rapid modernization of the Saudi economy from the 1960s

---

[1]The major raw materials used for the production of recombined milk were skimmed milk powder, milk fat, and water. Recombined milk producers claimed that this produced a better tasting milk than the simpler drying and rehydration process that produced reconstituted milk.
[2]Reported in Saudi riyals. In June 1998, US$1 = SR 3.75.

EXHIBIT 7.1 Map of the Arabian Peninsula

The Arabian Peninsula

THE EIGHT NATIONS OF THE ARABIAN PENINSULA: BAHRAIN, KUWAIT, OMAN, QATAR, SAUDI ARABIA, UNITED ARAB EMIRATES, YEMEN ARAB REPUBLIC, PEOPLE'S DEMOCRATIC REPUBLIC OF YEMEN.

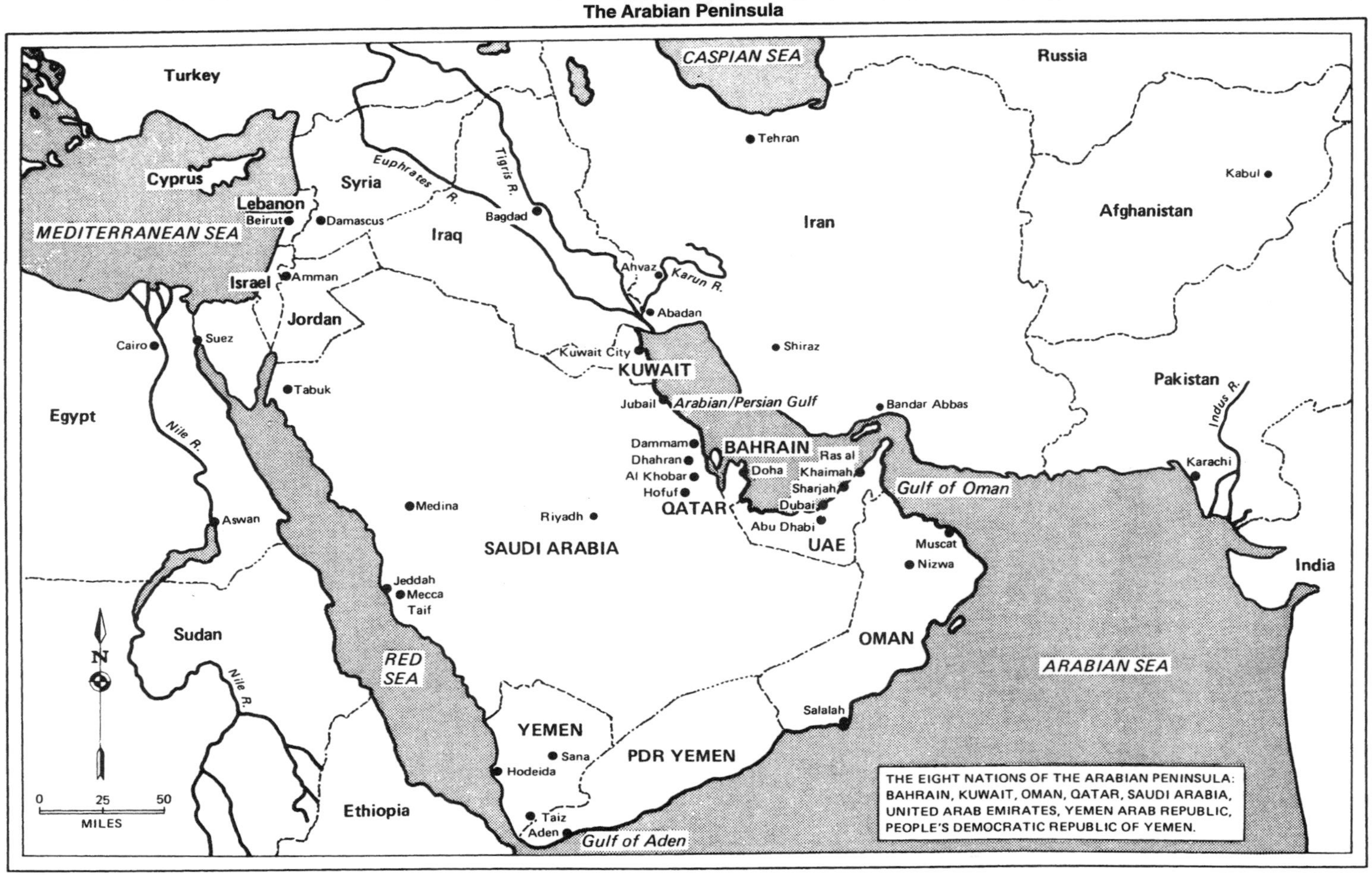

Source: Quentin W. Fleming, *A Guide to Doing Business on the Arabian Peninsula*, New York: AMACOM, 1981.

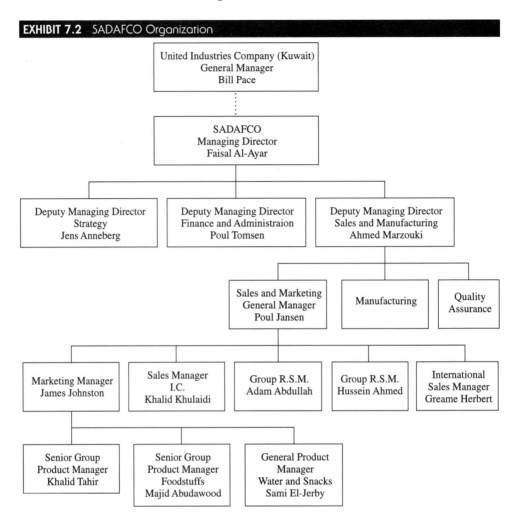

EXHIBIT 7.2 SADAFCO Organization

onwards. By 1998, almost all households owned at least one car, a refrigerator and freezer, washing machine, television, and video and audio equipment. This level of affluence also reflected the absence of income tax and extensive government subsidies in education, health care, utilities, and transport. Because the oil industry accounted for almost 40% of GDP and 90% of export earnings, the economy was sensitive to changes in the world price of oil: For example, per capita GDP was $1,200 in 1972, $16,650 in 1981, and $7,420 in 1996. The government's sixth 5-year economic plan (1995 to 1999) called for the development of private sector and non-oil-related sectors, and raised the possibility of privatization of the government's extensive holdings in all parts of the economy. Progress, however, toward these goals remained below published targets. In 1998, with world oil prices at their lowest in decades, the government was facing a record budget deficit and the possibility of economic recession. Investment regulations required foreign companies wishing to operate in the Kingdom of Saudi Arabia to have a local agent as a joint-venture partner, with strong financial incentives to partnerships with a majority Saudi ownership position.

Culturally, the dominant influence on Saudi society was the Muslim religion. As the homeland of the prophet Mohammed, the Kingdom of Saudi Arabia welcomed over two million pilgrims a year, most of them congregating in the holy city of Mecca during the month-long pilgrimage season of *haj*. The Islamic *sharia* (holy law) shaped daily life. For example, women could not appear in public unveiled and could not obtain driving licenses; alcohol was prohibited; expatriate workers were required to live in self-contained residential compounds; and non-Muslims were prohibited from entering the holy cities of Mecca and Medina. Foreigners were only issued visas for pilgrimages or business visits. Although the Kingdom of Saudi Arabia remained a conservative society, in 1998 the population was exposed to increasing Western influence via satellite TV broadcasts and an increasing number of international brands, manufacturers, and retailers.

The population of Saudi Arabia was young, with over 60% under age 25. Moreover, the fast growth rate ensured that the younger age groups would grow as a proportion of the total population until at least 2020. These demographics had led to some concern for the employment prospects of the Saudi population. Like many of its neighboring Gulf states, the Kingdom of Saudi Arabia had coped with its rapid economic growth by absorbing a high proportion of expatriate workers at all levels, from high-paid technical and managerial personnel, to construction workers and domestic servants (see Exhibit 7.3 for data on countries in the region). By the mid-1990s, the government had instituted a "Saudi-ization" program, which raised the cost of employing expatriate staff and imposed targets on companies to employ increasing proportions of Saudi nationals. The government also encouraged its brightest young students to obtain advanced degrees abroad; in SADAFCO, most senior Saudi nationals in the company were graduates of American universities.

Marketing in Saudi Arabia

The 1990s had seen substantial change in the marketing landscape of the country, stimulated by the entry into the market of a number of multinationals. Coca-Cola, which entered Saudi Arabia in 1995, was an archetypal instance. Long absent from the Middle East in the face of Arab boycotts for doing business in Israel and seizure of some of its operations in the region, Coca-Cola encountered a more favorable climate in the 1990s, as the Arab boycott slackened after the Gulf War. With its hot climate, young population, and lack of alcoholic drinks, the Middle East represented a very attractive market for Coca-Cola, which was reported to be investing over $500 million in entering the

EXHIBIT 7.3 Selected Data on Middle East Countries

	Saudi Arabia	*Kuwait*	*Bahrain*	*United Arab Emirates*	*Oman*	*Qatar*	*Yemen*	*Lebanon*
Population (thousands)	18,500	1,690	568	2,530	2,102	350	16,500	4,000
% expatriate	25	59	37	78	25	60	5	18
% under age 25	58	49	47	36	53	45	65	38
GNP per capita 1997 (US$)	7,110	17,440	7,890	17,900	4,840	11,660	270	2,680

market and competing with the already present PepsiCo. Its co-promotions with Mc-Donald's characterized the new commercial landscape.

Consumer marketing was also enhanced by the growing number of media available to advertisers. Saudi television had historically been restricted to two government-controlled channels, which carried only a limited amount of advertising that had to conform to the sharia. All the advertising permitted in one day was shown together at nighttime after the day's last program finished and before the channel closed. By 1998, not only had these restrictions been relaxed, but a number of international channels were available by satellite or cable. Subscriptions to these new TV services, initially stimulated by coverage of the Gulf War on international channels such as CNN, was growing rapidly, especially among the young population.

The level of change in consumption patterns could be deceptive, however. Comparing the Kingdom of Saudi Arabia with other markets in which he had worked, SADAFCO's marketing manager, James Johnston, commented that "it's very easy to get trial here, because people are willing to experiment and new brands have some novelty value. But changing the underlying purchase habits is much more difficult, because tastes remain the same. Often you see an initial sales surge, with an easing off after a month or two."

Shopping habits were strongly influenced by the Islamic culture. In all types of retail outlets, at least half the shoppers were men shopping alone, in some cases the household's driver. The remainder were couples shopping together, or women shopping alone, most of whom were domestic servants. Senior Group Product Manager Majid Dawood reported that "for the most part, women write a shopping list which is then taken to the store by the man or a domestic servant. More couples are shopping together, especially in supermarkets for the major weekly shop, but for the most part it's the women back in the home who make the decisions, and so they remain the main target of our advertising."

Price points were unusually strong in Saudi Arabia because most people did not carry coins, and dealt only in bills, the smallest of which was one riyal. Prices in whole riyal multiples were therefore much more acceptable, especially in consumer packaged goods, and there were numerous examples of products priced differently failing to gain consumer acceptance. When prices were set between price points, as was the case in categories such as produce or bread, retailers often gave change in the form of small items such as chewing gum, rather than in coins. Johnston commented that "strong price points can be a severe constraint in marketing, because they restrict the ability to make minor price adjustments and remove one element from the positioning equation by which different brands compete." Particularly affected were items bought singly rather than in supermarket baskets, such as ice creams.

Distribution

The retail sector was experiencing considerable change in Saudi Arabia. The number of outlets in all categories of retail was increasing with the liberalization and growth of the market for consumer goods, but a number of new supermarket chains were expanding at the expense of the traditional small store, the *bagalla*. SADAFCO's sales through the supermarket channel in 1998 were running 50% higher than the previous year. Exhibit 7.4 shows the composition of the retail sector.

Bagallas remained important, their traditional place in the commercial culture reinforced by the fact that women could not drive. Although most bagallas had tradition-

EXHIBIT 7.4 Saudi Arabia Retail Development		
	1992	*1996*
Supermarkets (500 sq. m +)	207	239
Self service (100–499 sq. m)	2,234	3,442
Large grocery (40–99 sq. m)	8,354	12,218
Small grocery (<40 sq. m)	16,892	24,773
Pharmacy	2,070	2,912
Catering	10,046	18,719
Perfumeries	2,237	3,147
Total	42,040	65,450

Source: SADAFCO research

ally visited wholesalers for supplies, an increasing number were supplied by vans belonging either to a major vendor or a wholesaler. SADAFCO had its own fleet of 290 vans. Van drivers would call on an individual bagalla frequently, because most had no warehouse or other storage, and replenish the store's shelves with small consignments of product. With the large number of bagallas and the small size of the orders, SADAFCO marketing executives did not receive sales by outlet in this sector. Although van drivers were asked to provide lists of all the outlets they visited and submit copies of all invoices, they were generally more oriented toward their relationships with their customers than toward the administrative requirements of the company, and data was usually both incomplete and unreliable. In some cases, for example, drivers would take orders from wholesalers who served bagallas, rather than from the retailers themselves.

Supermarkets had been introduced to the Kingdom of Saudi Arabia in the mid-1980s, and by 1998 represented 15% to 20% of sales. The largest chain in 1998, Panda, operated 13 outlets nationally, with two to three new stores opened annually. Although Saudi owned, a large proportion of Panda's executives were American, and they had introduced up-to-date retailing practices and technology, such as shelf-edge bar codes for inventory management and pricing. Although supermarkets were the fastest-growing sector, many observers thought that their growth prospects were limited by the fact that women could not drive. Cash-and-carry (discount) formats were proven more successful in the Kingdom of Saudi Arabia than high-service value-added formats. Other leading supermarket operators were Watani (a warehouse club), Star, Bin-Dawood (a Saudi-owned low price group in Jeddah), Al-Uthaim in Riyadh, and Giant stores in Dammam. SADAFCO had established a new key accounts team to manage supermarket sales. Headed by Scott Saul, the team negotiated annual contracts, volume targets, and merchandising with 60 key accounts, with dedicated sales and promotions staff to service the accounts.

Competition for shelf space in the growing supermarket sector had intensified in the 1990s as many international brands entered the market. This had led to a situation in which Saudi supermarkets not only demanded slotting allowances for new products, as in other countries, but also extracted annual space rental fees based upon the amount of shelf space occupied by a vendor. Saul commented:

> This is something I've never seen anywhere else. It originated in the last few years, largely from vendors coming into the market and competing for scarce shelf space. It has some strange results. For example, you will see all Nestlé's

brands together in one area, and all Kraft's in another, so that the alternative brands of, say, tinned tomatoes, will not be side-by-side, but each in their company's piece of real estate. The amount of space you get reflects the rental fee, rather than the brand's market share or profitability. Even though it's out of line with the trend towards category management in other countries, this practice is intensifying for the moment. Of my SR 3 million promotion budget last year, I had to use up two-thirds just on shelf rental.

Supermarkets in the Kingdom of Saudi Arabia averaged 15% to 20% gross margin and benefited from generous terms when opening new stores, such as free first orders and higher space rental fees as brands competed for preferential placement.

Medium-sized stores were generally either self-serve outlets, modeled on supermarkets, or more traditional wholesalers. Wholesalers not only supplied smaller outlets, but also sold direct to consumers eager to take advantage of the bulk discounts available. Wholesalers offered only large packs or multipacks, because they did not break bulk, and there was no merchandising in their outlets, which resembled a warehouse format.

SADAFCO PRODUCT LINES

Building on the new products introduced by the dairy companies from which it was formed, SADAFCO had undertaken a number of new product launches to diversify its product portfolio around the core milk business. Exhibit 7.5 shows profitability by product line.

Ice Cream

SADAFCO had entered the ice cream business in the 1970s, and by 1998 had an established portfolio of its own brands plus the Mövenpick Swiss Premium ice cream, for which it acted as a regional licensee. The SADAFCO portfolio of ice cream products encompassed eight brands: Sandwich, Choco, UFO, More, Saudia Premium, Primo, Baboo, Chew-Top, and Saudia Take-Home Tubs. Baboo was the largest brand, with SR 20 million sales, while all others were in the SR 3 to 5 million range. All ice cream production had been centralized in the Riyadh plant in 1996.

Although ice cream was a recent and culturally novel product in the Kingdom of Saudi Arabia, the market potential was viewed as significant because of the youth of the population and the hot climate. By 1997, the market had grown to 37 million liters, equivalent to $106 million at retail, with continuing growth forecast at 5% for the next 5 years on the grounds that per capita consumption remained low (see Exhibits 7.6 and 7.7). However, a number of factors made ice cream a difficult business to operate profitably, in particular the high capital costs of the freezers customarily installed in retail outlets, and the high distribution and merchandising costs resulting from the large distance between urban centers and the harsh climate. In addition, SADAFCO was still carrying the reorganization costs incurred by the reallocation of its production to the Riyadh plant.

The market could be categorized according to product type and sales channel. Product types were milk based or water based, and were produced in tubs or as handheld items. Product forms included bars, sandwiches, cones, and lollies.[3] Sales channels

---

[3]"Lollies" described all products on sticks, including the type generically known as "popsicles" in North America.

EXHIBIT 7.5 SADAFCO Brand Profitabilit—1997 (in SR thousands)

Description	Saudia milk	Saudia flavored milk	Saudia ice cream	Mövenpick ice cream	Saudia juices	Ribena juices	Saudia cheese	Tomato products	Yogurt & laban	Snack products	Water products	Total
Gross sales value	**527,464**	**20,166**	**58,679**	**12,161**	**37,041**	**2,806**	**40,448**	**78,331**	**15,454**	**25,393**	**448**	**818,391**
Sales volume: cartons (000)	17,698	870	3,529	157	1,937	125	386	1,496	1,073	628	40	27,939
Sales volume: liters (000)	127,896	4,439	5,998	736	11,088	884	3,163	9,645	2,771	1,084	599	168,305
Net sales revenue	**481,868**	**16,837**	**50,806**	**10,501**	**28,672**	**2,506**	**35,767**	**68,910**	**12,744**	**21,761**	**381**	**730,753**
Cost of sales, raw materials, and packaging	210,490	9,910	22,886	5,703	17,823	1,698	31,569	35,378	7,061	14,077	208	356,803
Gross margin	**271,378**	**6,927**	**27,920**	**4,798**	**10,849**	**808**	**4,198**	**33,532**	**5,683**	**7,684**	**173**	**373,950**
Manufacturing	50,639	2,948	12,795	1,291	6,669	328	0	5,381	3,664	2,415	113	86,243
Unapplied manufacturing expense	11,481	440	1,321	275	807	61	0	1,707	337	714	10	17,152
Sales	50,811	1,942	11,864	2,471	3,567	258	3,896	7,544	1,488	2,223	43	86,108
Transport & distribution	10,619	522	2,117	94	1,162	75	241	898	644	377	24	16,774
Total variable cost	**334,040**	**15,762**	**50,983**	**9,834**	**30,029**	**2,420**	**35,706**	**50,908**	**13,194**	**19,806**	**398**	**563,080**
Gross contribution	**147,828**	**1,075**	**-177**	**667**	**-1,357**	**86**	**61**	**18,002**	**-450**	**1,955**	**-17**	**167,673**
Marketing	13,310	753	2,869	410	185	341	909	4,186	0	2,247	957	31,074
Net contribution	**134,518**	**322**	**-3,046**	**257**	**-1,542**	**-256**	**-848**	**13,816**	**-450**	**-292**	**-974**	**136,598**
Overheads	33,247	1,271	5,247	1,088	2,335	177	2,550	4,937	974	3,018	28	54,872
Trading profit	**101,271**	**-949**	**-8,294**	**-830**	**-3,877**	**-432**	**-3,397**	**8,878**	**-1,424**	**-3,310**	**-1,002**	**81,726**
Gross margin/sales (%)	51	34	48	39	29	29	10	43	37	30	39	46
Gross contribution/sales (%)	28	5	0	5	-4	3	0	23	-3	8	-4	20
Marketing/sales (%)	3	4	5	3	0	12	2	5	0	9	214	4
Net contribution/sales (%)	26	2	-5	2	-4	-9	-2	18	-3	-1	-217	17
Trading profit/sales (%)	19	-5	-14	-7	-10	-15	-8	11	-9	-13	-244	10

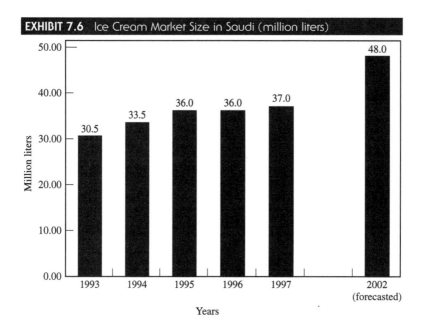

EXHIBIT 7.6 Ice Cream Market Size in Saudi (million liters)

Years

EXHIBIT 7.7 Per Capita Consumption of Ice Cream—IMES 1998

Country	Per capita consumption of ice cream in 1997 (liters)
United States	20.43
Australia	18.56
Sweden	15.84
Canada	9.19
Germany	5.90
Japan	4.92
Saudi Arabia	1.95

included bagallas and supermarkets and also a number of dedicated outlets or parlors (see Exhibit 7.8).

Ice cream was consumed mostly outside the home, mostly in the form of hand-held novelty products, and mostly by children; the 5 to 15 years age group accounted for 30% of the population but 55% of ice cream consumption. There was no tradition of eating ice cream in the home as a dessert. Cultural barriers included a bias against eating in public, especially restrictive for women, and a view of ice cream as a children's product comparable to candy with possible negative health consequences; in the winter months, the government ran public health campaigns urging children not to eat ice cream because of the possibility of throat illnesses caused by the cold temperature.

Competition had intensified in the mid-1990s with significant investments in the ice cream market by Unilever, Nestlé (both of whom were already present in the Kingdom

EXHIBIT 7.8 Estimated Breakdown of Ice Cream Market by Product Type

Product type	1997 Volume (millions of liters)	1997 Retail value ($ millions)	1997 Volume share (%)	1998 Volume (millions of liters)	1998 Volume share (%)
Parlor hard ice cream	2.50	13	7	2.50	6
Take-home hard ice cream	4.80	12	13	4.50	11
Hand-held products	29.70	81	80	33.50	83
—Water-based lollies	9.55	21	26	8.40	21
—Cups	6.80	18	18	7.75	19
—Cones	5.50	16	15	7.70	19
—Ice cream sticks	4.35	14	12	4.20	11
—Bar/sandwiches	2.90	11	8	3.00	8
—Other novelties	0.60	<1	<2	2.00	5
Total	37.00	106		40.5	

of Saudi Arabia in other categories), and Mars. Unilever's ice cream business was known as Wall's, and Nestlé marketed its products under the Kimo brand name. Initially all three had imported product from Europe via frozen facilities in Bahrain. This meant that these players were offering European brands in European sizes, often too large for the hand-held market for children. Magnum, one of Wall's leading brands, was initially offered at SR 6, but soon reduced to SR 4. In 1993, Unilever had opened an ice cream factory in Dammamm, modeled on an established plant in India.

EXHIBIT 7.8 *(continued)*

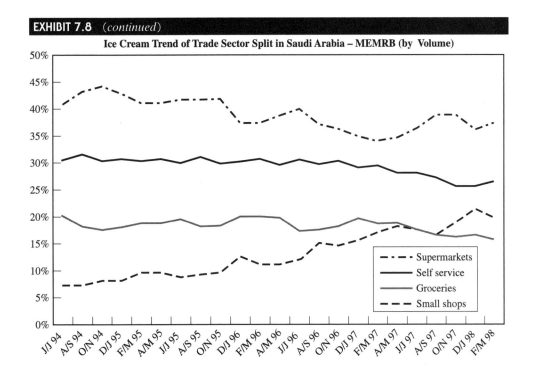

Ice Cream Trend of Trade Sector Split in Saudi Arabia – MEMRB (by Volume)

SADAFCO remained the market leader, followed by its traditional competitor, Kwality, a Saudi-based company with some Indian investment and management. However, in 1997, there were clear signs of share gains by Wall's and Nestlé in particular (see Exhibit 7.9 for market shares and trends). These gains appeared to be led by attacks in distribution.

The key issue in distribution was freezer placement. Retailers were generally provided with display freezers by vendors, on the condition that only the vendor's brands would be placed in the freezer. Bagallas and other small outlets only had room for one ice cream freezer, whereas supermarkets accommodated several, in which case vendors competed for the best position. SADAFCO had approximately 13,000 freezers placed in market, the most of any vendor. Each had cost on average SR 2,000 to 3,000 and was depreciated over 5 years. Their closest competitor, Kwality, was estimated to have 8,000, with Wall's and Nestlé placing approximately 4,000 each. Vendors filled their freezers directly, and wholesalers and other intermediaries played no part in ice cream distribution because of the need for freezer trucks. SADAFCO's specialist ice cream distribution operation consisted of 110 trucks and a separate sales force. They called on accounts to replenish stock at least once weekly.

Both Wall's and Nestlé had adopted a top-down entry strategy, focusing on the emerging supermarket sector and raising the investments required for preferred freezer positions within supermarkets. Contracts averaged SR 35,000 floor rental fees per supermarket in 1998; in the largest supermarkets, Wall's and Nestlé both adopted a multiple-freezer policy, with two to three freezers in the largest outlets. When a new supermarket opened, it was becoming increasingly common for vendors to provide the first order (i.e., fill the freezer) for free. Exhibit 7.10 shows distribution achieved by the main players by channel.

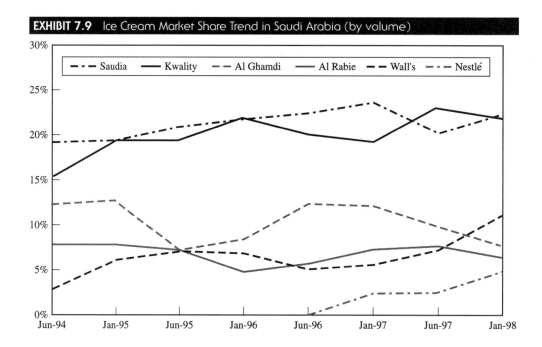

EXHIBIT 7.9   Ice Cream Market Share Trend in Saudi Arabia (by volume)

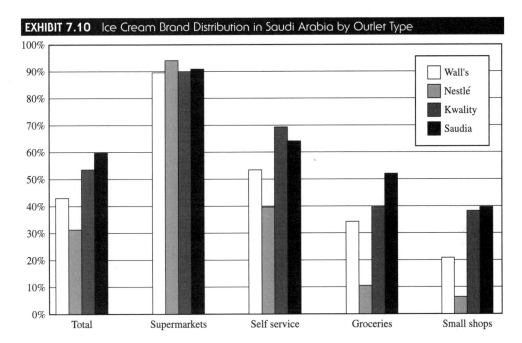

EXHIBIT 7.10 Ice Cream Brand Distribution in Saudi Arabia by Outlet Type

Tahir pointed out that by concentrating their efforts on supermarkets, the multinationals were accepting restricted distribution levels, when compared to the national coverage of SADAFCO, but were well positioned in the channels that were capturing ever-greater shares of the market. Their products were also coming into line with the tastes of the Saudi market (see Exhibit 7.11 for samples of product portfolios from SADAFCO, Wall's, and Nestlé).

In presenting his 1997 report at the marketing meeting, Tahir outlined a number of key learning points from the competitive activity of the previous year:

- SADAFCO's portfolio of ice cream brands was too diverse to allow for continuous marketing support for all brands. TV support could only be funded for the larger brands such as Baboo, and smaller brands suffered from limited exposure in media advertising.
- SADAFCO had been overtaken by Kwality in the take-home tub and cup segment. Kwality derived half its sales revenues from this sector, which accounted for almost half the ice cream market.
- Nestlé and Wall's were outperforming SADAFCO in supermarkets, due to their policy of paying higher space rental fees to obtain prime positions near check-out cashiers, and due to their policy of having multiple freezers in a single store.
- Multinationals were becoming an increasing threat because they were learning fast about the local market. For example, when Wall's first entered the Saudi market, they were promoting European products positioned as indulgences and suitable for adults, but now they were promoting a different type of product more suitable for the local market ("Max" range for children).
- In-store checks had indicated a possible weakness in the quality of merchandising in Saudia freezers in stores, both in terms of product assortment and presentation.

EXHIBIT 7.11 Examples of Competitive Products (Wall's)

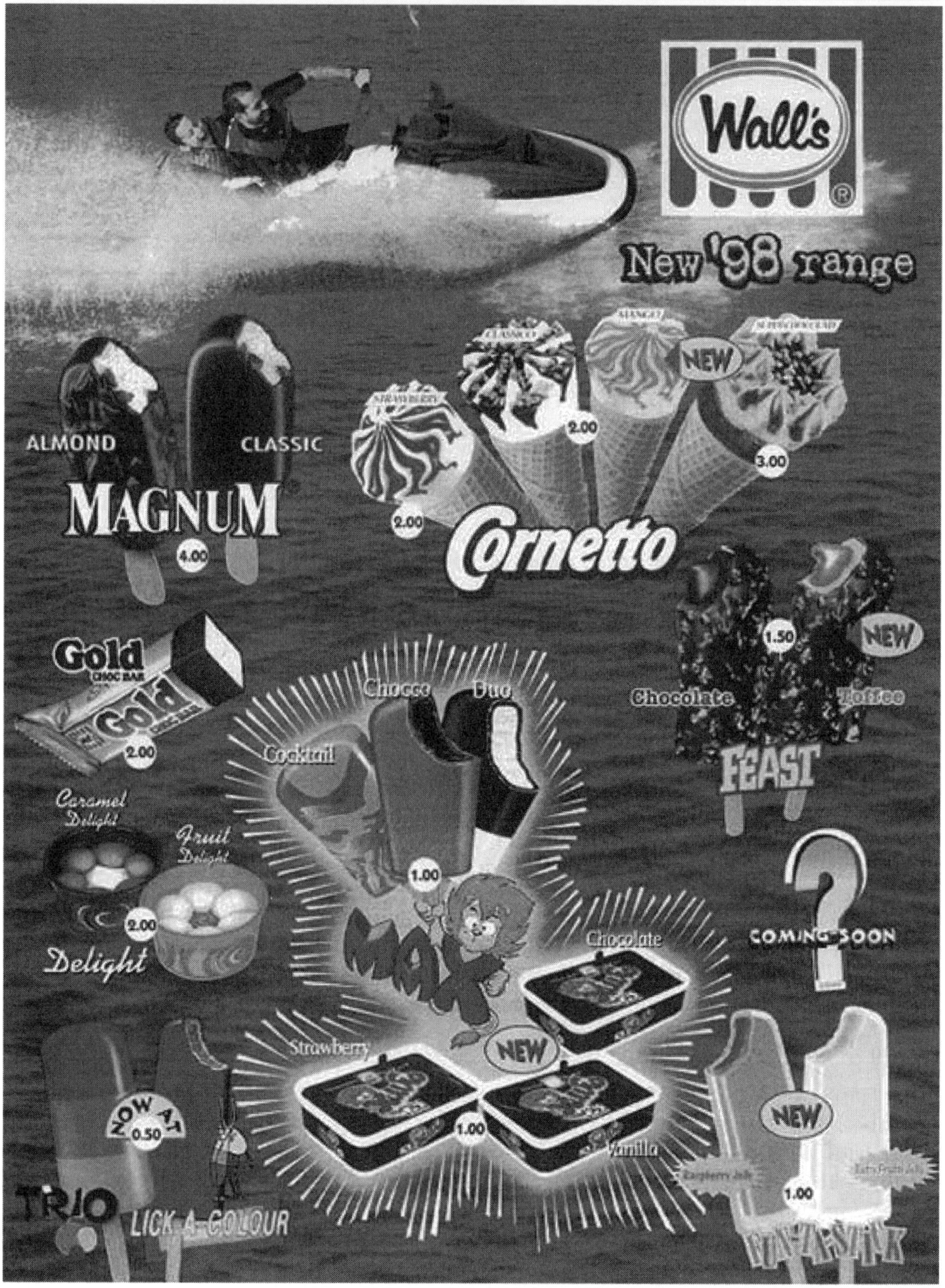

EXHIBIT 7.11 (*continued*)

EXHIBIT 7.11 (*continued*)

124

- Mövenpick ice cream awareness and trial levels were very low, at 16% and 9% respectively.
- The Mövenpick product line may be hindering sales, as it was built around the 1-liter tub. This cost SR 21, compared with SR 10 for the same size Saudia Premium tub. In Europe, the 500 ml size had proven much more successful for Mövenpick.
- Mövenpick's presence in supermarkets was weak, because its hand-held products were displayed in Saudia freezers.
- Certain Mövenpick flavors introduced recently, such as apricot and creme mandarin, had proved to be unappealing to local tastes.

Exhibit 7.12 shows SADAFCO's 1997 ice cream sales and marketing expenditures. It was estimated that Nestlé supported its ice cream business with a marketing budget of some SR 12, and Wall's, SR 16 million.

Milk

SADAFCO's core product had recently experienced its first declines in sales volumes as a result of increased competition. There were three main sectors in the Saudi milk market (see Exhibit 7.13). Powdered milk, the form in which milk was traditionally sold in the Middle East, was used extensively in cooking as well as to make drinks. Its use for drinking milk had declined from 60% of Saudi households in 1995 to 40% in 1998.

EXHIBIT 7.12 SADAFCO Ice Cream Marketing Expenditure 1997 (in SR thousands)

	Saudia	Mövenpick
Advertising		
TV production	0	0
TV media	0	0
Outdoor	302	45
Print	264	35
Soccer stadium	100	0
Promotion		
Indirect brand support		
Packaging	145	52
Research	65	0
Point-of-sale material	67	140
Other	107	0
Total	2,150	400

SADAFCO Ice Cream Gross Sales ($ millions)—Index vs. 1994

	Saudia ice cream			Mövenpick ice cream		
Year	Total	Saudi	Export	Total	Saudi	Export
1994	12.45	11.43	1.02	2.58	1.99	0.59
1995	13.19 (106)	12.23 (107)	0.96 (95)	3.36 (130)	2.39 (120)	0.97 (164)
1996	14.81 (112)	13.71 (112)	1.10 (114)	3.38 (100)	2.80 (117)	0.57 (59)
1997	15.57 (105)	14.48 (105)	1.07 (97)	3.19 (94)	2.66 (95)	0.52 (91)

EXHIBIT 7.13 Saudi White Milk Gross Sales					
	1993	*1994*	*1995*	*1996*	*1997*
$	117.6	126.4	132.2	133.5	140.5
% change		7.5%	4.6%	1.0%	5.2%
Tons	115,807	123,026	122,653	118,940	127,896
% change		6.2%	−0.3%	−3.0%	7.5%

Laban, a form of buttermilk, was predominantly drunk by Saudi men. The recent development in the liquid milk sector, in which SADAFCO's Saudia brand of recombined product competed, was the emergence of a number of fresh milk producers. A number of dairy farms had been established in Saudi Arabia from the 1970s onward with the strategic goal of making the country self-sufficient in milk, and by 1998 the country boasted the world's largest dairy farm. Even though they were located in the less arid regions of the country, these dairy farms still had to contend with challenging environments. Pace commented:

> There is now a lobby in the Kingdom, which we obviously support, arguing that the environmental and economic cost of these farms outweighs their strategic importance. For example, in irrigating the land and keeping the cows hydrated, these farms use over 1,000 liters of water to produce 1 liter of milk, compared with 5 liters of water in our recombination plant in Jeddah. The politics of this issue are complex, however, and while these debates continue our market share is coming under pressure.

The marketing problem facing Saudia milk was not one of product quality, according to James Johnston, marketing manager:

> In fact, Saudia recombined milk regularly wins in blind product tastings, probably because the conditions under which the fresh producers operate result in milk which is relatively low in solids, and hence rather thin in taste. Perception is another matter, though, and the fact that their milk is fresh appeals to many consumers. Our situation could become worse because of some pending Gulf Cooperation Council legislation requiring us to state on the package that our product is made from powder.

The other key element of competition was price, and the fresh producers could produce UHT milk at a price point 20% lower than Saudia in the critical winter months. Saudia first suffered share loss in 1995 after a price rise intended to reflect increases in raw material prices. A recovery followed in 1997, with volume rising from 173,000 to 181,000 tons, and share increasing from 47.4% to 49.7%. Most analysts expected fresh to continue its share increase at the expanse of recombined, but SADAFCO was intending to defend its position aggressively, with a planned increase in 1998 marketing expenditures to SR 16 million. The Saudia brand was to be positioned as the "best-tasting milk available," a claim supported by blind tasting test results, and would also focus on the brand's track record of innovation: It has been the first brand to introduce one-liter Tetra Slim packs with open and close tops; the first available in 500 ml size, which now accounted for more volume than the 1 liter pack; the first to launch skimmed milk in

Saudi Arabia; the first to launch a specially formulated milk for children, Junior; and was planning to launch a decholesterol milk in 1998.

Tomato Products

SADAFCO's second-biggest product line was tomato products, the bulk of which was the Saudia brand of tomato paste, which had been the success story of the category since its original launch in Tetra Pak cartons in 1989. Based upon limited experience in other countries, Tetra Pak had worked with SADAFCO in developing the production process for this innovative product form, which it claimed produced a product with better taste and better quality retention after opening. The acceptance of the Tetra Pak paste in the Kingdom of Saudi Arabia was boosted by the influx of Kuwaitis during the Gulf War of 1991 to 1992, as the product had previously been manufactured in this form in Kuwait by the Kuwaiti Danish Dairy Company. By 1997, Saudia tomato paste had risen to $21 million in sales revenues (compared with $9.5 million in 1993) and a market leadership share of 24.7% (16% in 1993), with 85% and only one competitor in the Tetra Pak sector. This growth reflected both an expanding market and share gains over tinned product. Majid Dawood, senior group product manager responsible for this product line, believed that further innovation would be necessary to maintain growth:

> It is questionable how much more share can be taken from tinned products, much of which is used in catering operations. The other sizable sector of this category is tinned whole tomatoes, about half the size of paste, but we are turning our attention to cooking sauces, currently a very small category consumed mostly by expatriates. We expect this to take off slowly, because it does not fit very well with local cuisine, and because convenience foods like this are somewhat scorned. The cooks employed by many families are expected to use basic fresh ingredients. Nevertheless, we regard it as vital for the brand to remain at the forefront of the category, and we will be formulating the product to meet local cuisine and tastes.

Saudia was positioned as the "best tomato paste consumers can buy," supported by its bright red color and the fresher and more natural taste. Tomato paste was bought on the spot market, and originated mostly from Turkey, Portugal, or California. The Tetra Pak cartons required lower levels of the heat treatment, which sometimes produced darkened product in tins, and guaranteed no unpleasant "tin taste" of which consumers complained. The Saudia brand was also regarded as more local, and therefore fresher, compared with the mostly imported tinned products. In 1997, export sales accounted for 12.5% of sales revenues and 29.6% of tonnage, reflecting a penetration strategy in markets where the brand received little promotional support.

Hummus

The year 1998 was also to see the launch of a new Saudia brand of hummus in Tetra Pak. Hummus was a dip of Lebanese origin made from chickpeas, salt, lemon juice, oil, garlic, and tahini (a sesame seed paste). Of the 50,000 tons estimated to be consumed annually in the Kingdom of Saudi Arabia, all but 400 tons were made fresh in restaurants, as an eat-in or take-out product, or in the home. The remaining tinned product, which was imported from Lebanon, was regarded as inferior in quality due to its lack of freshness, and required the addition and blending of lemon juice, tahini, and oil at the time of serving. Saudia hummus was to be the first ever in the world presented in Tetra Pak, the result of collaboration between SADAFCO and Tetra Pak. The new product promised the same quality as fresh hummus, but with greater convenience and a six-month shelf-life without refrigeration, compared to a one-week refrigerated shelf life for fresh hummus bought from restaurants. Majid Dawood commented:

> This is a relatively high-risk launch because it is a new product form which re-quires changes in consumer behavior and perception. The forecasting has to be discounted for this uncertainty and we cannot expect rapid success. Never-theless, there are real consumer benefits available and, for us, a potentially large market in the long run, since hummus is eaten in quantity throughout the region and is also available at delicatessen counters throughout the world. There is considerable pride at the company that we are at the leading edge with this innovation.

Saudia hummus was to be launched in March 1998, priced at SR 3.5 for 400 gm—compared with approximately SR 2.5 for the same sized tinned product, and would also be available in a smaller 135 gm size, priced at SR 1.5. Fresh hummus purchased in restaurants for home use generally cost SR 5 to SR 6 for 200 gm. Assuming a 5% share of a 45,000 ton market, budgeted first-year revenues were SR 12 million. The launch budget was SR 2.8 million, with 67% allocated to advertising, 13% to promotions, 3% to in-store sampling, and 8% to retail space rental. Promotions included joint offers with olive oil and Saudia tomato paste, and free dishes suitable for in-home serving of hum-mus offered with eight-pack purchases.

SADAFCO management had identified hummus as a potential spearhead for in-ternational marketing. The regional consumption of hummus was considerable—in Lebanon alone, the tinned market was some 11,000 tons annually and the fresh market approximately the same size. In addition, Pace wondered whether the pioneer advan-tage enjoyed by Saudia hummus in this packaging could be exploited in developed mar-kets in Europe or America, especially those with Middle Eastern communities. The TV advertising planned for Saudia hummus in August 1998 would reach audiences through-out the region.

Snacks, Water, and Other Product Lines

SADAFCO's snack business, with production based in Jeddah, had been growing at 10% annually to reach SR 40 million, approximately 40% share by value. Products were marketed under the Crispy and Baboo brands, and approximately half the volume came from potato chips. Some 70% of consumption was accounted for by the 5 to 15 years-age group, and so schools were an important outlet, with 28% of industry volume. Prospects for 1998 were uncertain because of the threat of a government ban on the sale of packaged snack foods in schools on nutritional grounds. Only 18% of sales were di-rect to large retailers, with the remainder going through wholesalers.

SADAFCO had converted its milk factory in Medina to produce bottled water in 1997, and marketed its mineral water under the Saudia brand name. In 1998, SADAFCO was planning to add a new water brand, Viviere, to its portfolio to boost margins in this product line. Total market size was estimated at 710 million liters, or SR 360 million at retail value, almost all of it still water. There was little or no promotion activity.

SADAFCO was considering the introduction of juice drinks in PET bottles, a category in which it already carried a minor product line, accounting for SR 35 million in 1997. The sale of carbonated drinks in schools had recently been banned by the government.

SADAFCO also competed in feta cheese and cheese in jars, with total 1997 revenues of SR 30 million.

EXPORT SALES

SADAFCO had achieved export sales in regional markets for some years, but with what it viewed as varying success. See Exhibit 7.14 for a summary of international sales.

The largest commitment to international activity was a recent one: purchase of a slightly used dairy factory in Egypt that would require substantial rehabilitation and equipment additions to produce UHT milk. This followed a smaller investment in 1995 in Egypt to construct a small ice cream factory, mainly to produce the premium quality Mövenpick brand for selling to top class hotels and tourist resorts.

The ice cream factory investment had been initiated by pressure from Mövenpick-Zurich, who wanted to have their specialty ice cream available for their expanding chain of tourist hotels in Egypt. It also represented for SADAFCO a significant step toward the option for more focus on the product-differentiated high-margin Mövenpick Swiss Premium Ice Cream that was outside the main stream of competition with Unilever (Wall's brand) and Nestlé. This strategy was proving to be reasonably successful in Egypt.

The larger factory, now being rehabilitated for UHT milk, juices, and tomato paste, was intended to capitalize on the fast growing market for safe, well-packaged foods in Egypt. To sell the product from this factory, SADAFCO had to cope with the challenge of mass distribution of low-margin products in highly congested distribution conditions. In addition, the Saudia brand was not appropriate. Although the lure of an undeveloped food market in a nation of some 65 million people experiencing rapid-economic growth was a powerful motivation, it was recognized that success was not certain. Correct decisions on branding and management appointments were considered to be crucial.

The rest of SADAFCO's international business was all exported by truck and handled by national distributors in a number of Gulf markets. The largest current export market was the United Arab Emirates (UAE), where the bulk of the sales had been the black currant concentrate drink, Ribena, for which SADAFCO had the regional license from the owner, SmithKline Beecham. A staple drink for British children, this found a receptive market in the former British colonies of the United Arab Emirates, Bahrain, and Qatar. However, SmithKline Beecham was introducing product formulation changes, and there was also uncertainty in the distributor relationship, raising the strong possibility that this line of business would terminate in 1998.

EXHIBIT 7.14 SADAFCO Export Sales 1995–1997 (in SR thousands)								
Year	*Lebanon*	*Oman*	*United Arab Emirates*	*Yemen*	*Jordan*	*Egypt*	*Canada*	*Total*
1994							150	150
1995	133	207						340
1996	76		809	160	96	176		1,317
1997	120		768	390	36	208		1,522

In Lebanon, SADAFCO was in partnership with its third distributor. The first partnership had been terminated when SADAFCO established a subsidiary in the country, but when this decision was reversed, a new distributor was found. In 1997, with the country emerging from war, SADAFCO already had a backlog of orders as it waited for a license to be granted to its new distributor. Although a small population, Lebanon was regarded as a cosmopolitan and sophisticated market and Lebanese were present throughout the Gulf states in commercial and trading positions.

Across other markets in the region, SADAFCO's export business varied considerably across product lines. There were significant differences between the Gulf states in terms of pricing structures, expectations of trading relationships, and in consumer preferences for tastes and package sizes. Bill Pace observed that "we have been more opportunistic than strategic in our approach, and as a result have not really achieved anything close to our potential in markets outside Saudi Arabia. A lot of us feel that we have to boost international business to become a regional player with the strength to hold our own against encroaching competition from the multinationals."

CONCLUSION

The marketing meeting in Jeddah had begun with Pace and Johnston outlining the broad challenge to SADAFCO in terms of finding new growth markets at a time when competition was intensifying. When Tahir introduced his report on the ice cream business, everyone present recognized it as a key battle. Johnston remarked that "we have to find out how a local player can compete with these giants. Although they are to some extent fighting against each other, they all know that the first battle is to establish themselves against the current market leader." Those at the meeting had to decide in which sectors SADAFCO should concentrate its resources, and what advantages would enable it to retain its position.

CHAPTER

8

LAUNCHING A NEW IDENTITY

Project Blue

In late November 1995, Pepsi-Cola International's (PCI) beverage division announced the global launch of a new brand identity and logo for Pepsi soft drinks. Plans called for a $500 million investment to update the look of Pepsi cans and bottles, point-of-sale signage, trucks, and vending machines worldwide. The redesign effort, known as Project Blue, aimed at rejuvenating the Pepsi image by associating the brand with the color blue in contrast to Coca-Cola's long-standing association with the color red.

COMPANY BACKGROUND

With 1995 revenues of $30.4 billion, PepsiCo was a worldwide food and beverage marketer that was ranked number 20 in the Fortune 500 and number 30 in market value among all companies in the world. Of total revenues, 35% were accounted for by beverages, 37% by restaurants (including KFC, Pizza Hut, and Taco Bell) and 28% by snack foods (including Lay's, Ruffles, and Doritos).

PepsiCo beverages included soft drinks (such as Pepsi, Diet Pepsi, Pepsi Max, 7-Up, Slice, and Mountain Dew), teas, bottled water, and juices. Package pictures of PepsiCo beverages are presented in Exhibit 8.1. In several noncarbonated beverage categories PepsiCo had formed alliances to distribute the ready-to-drink tea products of Thomas J. Lipton Co. and Ocean Spray fruit juices.

In 1995, PepsiCo's dollar beverage sales in the United States rose 7%. Volume growth accounted for one-quarter of this increase. Retail case sales grew faster than sales through fountains and restaurants (which included the many chains in PepsiCo's restaurant division). Dollar beverage sales outside the United States rose 14% in 1995. Volume growth accounted for 45% of this increase, the remainder stemming from acquisitions and price increases.

In the United States in 1995, PepsiCo accounted for 27% of the retail value of carbonated soft drink sales and held a 23% volume share. The corresponding figures for

Professor John A. Quelch prepared this case from published sources as the basis for class discussion rather than to illustrate either effective or ineffective handling of an administrative situation.

EXHIBIT 8.1 Chronology of Pepsi-Cola Logos

Coca-Cola were 35% and 30%. Coca-Cola's share lead in the United States was greater in vending machines and restaurants than in retail stores. Both companies had been subject to share pressure from lower priced own-label carbonated beverages in 1993 to 1995 but had been able to recover short-term share losses through new products, new packaging, and stepped-up advertising and promotion.

Around 29% of PepsiCo's 1995 beverage revenues and 18% of beverage operating profits were derived from international operations. The three Pepsi brands (Pepsi, Diet Pepsi, and Pepsi Max) accounted for 40% of PepsiCo's U.S. beverage dollar sales (with four billion cases of 24 8-oz. cans). Outside the United States, two billion cases of the three Pepsi brands were sold in 1995, accounting for 70% of PepsiCo's international beverage sales.

The marketplace rivalry between Pepsi and Coca-Cola was decades old. Pepsi had established itself in the 1930s as Coca-Cola's main rival with the price-oriented campaign, "Twice as much for a nickel, too." In the 1970s, Pepsi gained ground on Coca-Cola by focusing on taste superiority through the Pepsi Challenge. Some 20 million people took the Pepsi Challenge, of whom 60% chose Pepsi over Coca-Cola. In the 1980s, both brands invested heavily in image advertising and celebrity endorsements. Pepsi's tagline, "The choice of a new generation," positioned it squarely against a teenage target. Coca-Cola had typically followed a broader and more traditional positioning and, in 1993, reintroduced its classic contour bottle. The classic bottle, when surrounded by the red circle icon, was launched worldwide as the new Coca-Cola logo in conjunction with the "Always Coca-Cola" advertising tagline. Despite exploiting its classic heritage, Coca-Cola was able to successfully target some teenagers with innovative advertising, sport event sponsorships, and celebrity endorsements. Some analysts believed Pepsi was losing its edge over Coca-Cola in the youth market.

Outside the United States, the share gap between Coca-Cola and Pepsi was greater than in the domestic market. Pepsi exceeded Coca-Cola in market share in only 5 of the top 50 country markets. PepsiCo spent $500 million on advertising carbonated beverages in the United States in 1995 and $200 million internationally, up 3% and 7% respectively over 1994. Corresponding Coca-Cola expenditures in 1995 were $1.2 billion and $600 million.

The Pepsi system's two most important new product launches in 1993 were Crystal Pepsi and Pepsi Max. Crystal Pepsi, a clear rather than colored version of the classic Pepsi formula, was launched in the United States but failed to achieve more than 2% volume share of carbonated beverage sales. On the other hand, Pepsi Max, a "no sugar, maximum taste" cola targeted at 16- to 29-year-olds in a redesigned blue can and supported by television advertising featuring tennis star Andre Agassi quickly gained a 5% volume share in its launch market, the United Kingdom.[1] Pepsi Max was the first PepsiCo soft drink launched first outside the United States. It accounted for 20% of Pepsi sales volume in the United Kingdom by the end of 1995. During 1995, Pepsi Max international sales increased 70% over 1994 as the brand was rolled out in 50 countries. Pepsi Max accounted for one-third of all PCI soft drink volume growth in 1995. Even though it was not yet distributed in the United States, worldwide retail sales of Pepsi Max were expected to reach $450 million in 1995.[2]

[1]The United Kingdom was chosen in part because acceptance of sugar-free colas (17% market share) was among the highest in the world.
[2]Pepsi Max employed an artificial sweetener not yet approved by the Food and Drug Administration for use in the United States.

In addition to new product launches, PepsiCo achieved sales growth through several other strategies. First, PepsiCo continued its strong record of packaging innovation. In the United States, the launch of the Cube, an easy-to-store 24-can pack, was credited with increasing Pepsi volume 7% in supermarkets, compared to an overall 4% growth in soft drink volume through this channel. In the impulse-driven convenience/gas store channel, Pepsi-Cola became the share leader thanks to its Big Slam (a one-liter, single-serve bottle) and Quick Slam (20-ounce bottle) packaging innovations. In 1995, PepsiCo also pioneered the concept of freshness dating on soft drinks in the United States.

Overseas, PepsiCo continued to invest in acquisitions and joint ventures in emerging markets to try to close the share gap with Coca-Cola. In most emerging markets, teens—Pepsi's core target—accounted for a much higher proportion of the population than in the United States, yet per capita consumption of soft drinks was much lower.[3] Between 1993 and 1995, over $500 million was invested in beverage acquisitions and joint ventures. In Hungary and Poland, Pepsi acquired cola market share leadership. In India, Pepsi's market share rose to nearly 40%. Almost 40% of PCI's 1995 international soft drink volume growth came from emerging markets.

In addition to forging new alliances, PepsiCo continued to use surplus cash to purchase partial or total control of its independent bottlers around the world. Between 1990 and 1995, PCI refranchised, consolidated, or restructured almost 60% of its business. By the end of 1995, PepsiCo had outright ownership or shared equity in bottling operations accounting for 55% of international beverage volume, up from 20% in 1995, and for 70% of United States volume. Corresponding figures for Coca-Cola were 80% and 70%.

THE PRESENCE AUDIT

The visibility and impact of the Pepsi brand name and logo at the point-of-purchase were considered especially important to sales success in the impulse purchase-driven soft drink category. Consumers were exposed to the Pepsi name on signs outside of points-of-sale, on trucks, on vending machines, on "wraparounds" at the bottom of in-store displays, and on packages.

By the middle of 1994, there was increasing concern within PCI about inconsistent presentation of the Pepsi brand to consumers. Pepsi had only changed its brand identity seven times in the company's history, most recently in 1991. However, in many markets, old signs were still being used alongside new ones. In addition, each brand logo had been interpreted slightly differently by Pepsi's independent bottlers. Although Pepsi and the bottlers shared the cost of point-of-purchase signage and materials on a 50/50 basis, the bottlers decided what was used.

As shown in Exhibit 8.1, Pepsi's first official logo was created in 1898 when the pharmacist Caleb Bradham changed the name of the original formula, developed as a cure for dyspepsia, from Brad's Drink to Pepsi-Cola. The first Pepsi-Cola logo was red. This was dropped for red, white, and blue in 1941 as Pepsi gave its support to the World War II effort. A "bottle cap" logo was launched in 1950, evolving into the bull's-eye "swish" logo in 1973.

---

[3]For example, per capita soft drink consumption in the United States of 51 gallons per year compared to 20 gallons in Argentina, 15 gallons in Saudi Arabia, and 5 gallons in Thailand.

In late 1994, PCI commissioned Landor Associates, a corporate identity consultancy, to evaluate the point-of-sale presence of the Pepsi family of brands. After interviews with PCI executives in seven countries, Landor organized a worldwide photographic audit of Pepsi's brand presence. About 2,000 photographs were assembled from 34 countries. They showed inconsistencies and lack of integration in the presentation of the Pepsi logo and graphics both within countries as well as across countries. In addition, the photos showed that Pepsi owned no particular color except perhaps white. Pepsi graphics often looked weak, flat, and washed out when compared to Coke's bold red decal. The graphics did not express the energy and core essence of Pepsi. The long red pedestal and Pepsi ball did not work well on the sides of trucks or vending machines. In the view of some, cans of Pepsi looked like motor oil.

A team of consultants and PCI executives set out to develop an improved look for Pepsi graphics in merchandising materials around the world. The team identified blue as a much stronger color than white that Pepsi could own in contrast to Coke's dominance of red. Consumers viewed blue as modern and cool, exciting and dynamic, and a color that communicated refreshment. The team began to think of blue as a key component of Pepsi's brand equity. Only then did the team begin to do exploratory work on redesigning Pepsi packaging. At that point, the project needed top management approval. PCI's president saw Project Blue as a big idea that could galvanize the Pepsi system worldwide and refocus managers around the world on restoring Pepsi's marketing edge.

The original mission set out for the design team was to develop a graphics treatment and product line look that would strengthen the Pepsi brand identity and deliver higher impact in-market presence for the Pepsi brand. The team set out to:

1. Develop a flexible design (that could be used effectively on displays and trucks and in a variety of other media).
2. Establish blue as Pepsi's dominant color.
3. Develop a mnemonic device.
4. Create a modern, even futuristic, look and image to contrast with Coke's traditional positioning.

The project team first worked on developing a two-dimensional icon that retained some of the equity of the current brand identity—principally the Pepsi ball. Exhibit 8.2 shows the winning design from this phase of the project. The designers noted that the unitalicized logotype added boldness and stature. Spelling Pepsi in white on a blue-and-red background reversed the color architecture of the previous logo and ended up doing the same. The traditional Pepsi ball became a globe. Showing only a quarter of the ball enhanced its larger-than-life personality and effectively transformed it from a ball into a three-dimensional, futuristic globe.

The next challenge for the design team was to translate the off-pack design into an execution that would work equally well on three-dimensional cans and bottles. Although bottle volume exceeded can volume in many markets, the design team focused first on cans because they dominated away-from-home consumption and were therefore more often used and seen in public. By combining the toolbox of graphics they had already developed with a grid background on the can surface, the designers were able to produce in June 1995 the final can designs for the Pepsi family of brands shown in Exhibit 8.2.

EXHIBIT 8.2 Winning Logo Design and Final Can Designs

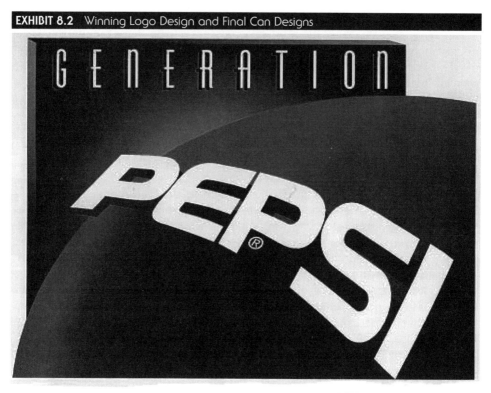

The final design, following the exploration of over 3,000 design approaches, featured a striking blue "grid" background; bold, vertical typography; and a three-dimensional globe that evoked Pepsi's well-known "ball" icon. The blue graphics would be carried on all packages of Pepsi-Cola, Pepsi Max, and Diet Pepsi.

THE HONG KONG BOTTLER MEETING: MAY 1995

PCI's president elected to announce Project Blue at the company's annual bottler meeting in Hong Kong in May 1995, a meeting attended by all company-owned and franchised bottlers worldwide.

The buzz in the corridors after the speech ranged from enthusiasm to concern. The PCI vice president in charge of Eastern Europe was bullish: "Maybe I can finally paint Red Square blue!" Others, including several franchisee bottlers, were concerned about the expense and management time that the rollout would require and whether Pepsi management would support the rollout of Project Blue in the United States. The PCI president followed up with a series of internal memos that ensured that Project Blue would be a focus of every country manager's and bottler's thinking as their 1996 business plans and budgets were developed and finalized during the period from September to November 1995.

THE BAHRAIN TEST: OCTOBER 1995

At the May meeting, it was announced that Project Blue would be launched initially in Bahrain in October. The selection of Bahrain was based on four factors. First, PCI regional management in the Middle East had already been experimenting with blue backgrounds in point-of-sale materials because the standard white background caused the logo to be washed out in the bright sunlight common to the region. Second, the Bahrain market was served by a single franchisee bottler who had, on occasion, been critical of PCI headquarters. The credibility of Project Blue would be enhanced if he could be convinced. Third, as in other Middle Eastern markets, Pepsi sales dominated Coke's by three to one, so any negative reaction towards Project Blue among existing Pepsi consumers used to the current logo and signage would surface in the test. Fourth, Bahrain was a small market of one million people who lived on two islands connected by a bridge; this enabled PCI to conduct a controlled field test to measure the impact of Project Blue.

A Blue Fund was established at PCI headquarters to cover the cost of the market test and a PCI task force was appointed to spearhead its implementation. The Bahrain bottler's marketing managers and sales force were also heavily involved in local execution. However, because the bottler had recently invested heavily in installing new production lines to increase capacity, he was not pressed to cover the cost of production line changes, the new signage and point-of-sale displays.

The PCI task force developed and executed a rollout of Project Blue in 12 weeks. Newly designed cans and bottles for all Pepsi brands were distributed throughout Bahrain. The entire Project Blue program, including signage and point-of-sale materials, was implemented in one-half of the city (around 500 of the 1,000 retail outlets). Implementation included both converting existing signage and adding new signage. A new advertising slogan, "New look. Same great taste," was appended to existing television and print advertising executions. Spending on advertising and promotion during the test was sustained at previously planned levels.

Tracking research was conducted before, during, and after the test. Measures of brand attitudes improved, as did sales volume and market share. Around 70% of consumers believed that there was no change in Pepsi's taste, 30% thought there was a taste change and, of these, 70% thought the perceived taste change was positive.

THE NOVEMBER MEETING

With the benefit of the positive results from Bahrain, PCI executives were convinced that their enthusiasm for Project Blue was well-founded. They were asked to present their recommendations for a worldwide rollout of Project Blue at a meeting at PCI headquarters in late November. Their recommendations covered the speed of the worldwide rollout and the sequence of countries in which Project Blue should be launched. In addition, they proposed a creative and expensive communications program to support the worldwide launch.

First, PCI executives recommended that Project Blue be rolled out in markets accounting for half of Pepsi's international sales volume by July 1996. By the end of the year, they expected more than 20 billion cans and bottles would reach store shelves. However, several executives were unconvinced that the Bahrain execution or results could be replicated on a worldwide basis. They pointed to Pepsi's unusually high share in Bahrain and the fact that it was a developing rather than mature market. These executives argued for a slower rollout on a region-by-region basis. A second group of executives advocated launching Project Blue first in a lead market in each region; success in each lead market would then motivate the other bottlers in the region to follow. PCI European executives, for example, argued that the United Kingdom should be a regional lead market for Project Blue because of the successful launch of Pepsi Max; because Pepsi's soft drink market share in the United Kingdom trailed CocaCola brands 19% to 50%; and because Pepsi brands were losing share to own labels marketed in red cans by the United Kingdom's powerful supermarket chains and also to the recently launched Virgin Cola.

PCI's Latin American executives pointed out that the bottlers in their region, especially in Mexico, had made significant capital investments in their infrastructure in the last 4 years. It would be difficult to demand that they change their signs again so soon. Hence, the Latin American launch would have to be postponed until 1997.

Other executives argued that a simultaneous worldwide launch of Project Blue would be a logistical nightmare. Some preferred to wait until each bottler was totally committed than risk half-hearted support from bottlers who might be pushed into going with Project Blue before they were ready, just for the sake of a global launch.

There was skepticism at the meeting about the U.S. organization's willingness to adopt recommendations from the international side of the business due to the not-invented-here syndrome. The U.S. organization was working on its own package redesign which, though similar, was not the same. The question was raised as to whether bottlers around the world would adopt the PIC plan if the U.S. organization was going in another direction.

PCI executives recommended a $500 million marketing program to support the worldwide launch. This investment, to be spent in 1996, included the systemwide conversion of bottles and cans, coolers and vending machines, and trucks. Advertising spending for 1996, originally set at $200 million for Pepsi brand beverages outside the United States, would be increased to $300 million and support a new advertising campaign that targeted younger consumers with the tagline, "Change the Script." This new tagline, which would replace "The Choice of a New Generation" introduced in 1984, would be launched in early April 1996 in Project Blue lead markets including the United Kingdom; a tentative media schedule called for the advertising to be seen by 300 million people in 20 countries in the first 4 weeks. The new campaign would include five television spots featuring, among other celebrities, Cindy Crawford (for 5 years a Pepsi spokesperson), Claudia Schiffer, and Andre Agassi.

Several public relations initiatives were planned to coincide with the launch of the advertising campaign. These included a 10-city tour of Europe and the Middle East by a Concorde jet adorned with Pepsi's new colors;[4] sponsorship of the Russian Mir Space Station that would permit the advertising tag line "Even in Space—Pepsi is Changing the Script"; and a 3-year alliance with Viacom's MTV Network to include cosponsorship in July 1996 of the Global Dance Connection, Europe's largest-ever interactive dance party to be held simultaneously in three European cities.

Executives at the November meeting were impressed but, in some cases, awed by the magnitude of the proposed worldwide communications campaign to launch Project Blue. Some argued that spending the money to support tactical marketing efforts, sales promotion, and additional sales coverage worldwide might be less glamorous but would be more effective and less controversial.

Others worried that funds might be diverted from the faster growing non-Pepsi brands to support the weaker links in the brand portfolio. Pepsi Max executives were concerned that extending the Project Blue idea to the main Pepsi brand would dilute its impact on their sales.

A third group acknowledged that Project Blue represented a huge bet on the future but, they argued, the sales and share trends versus Coke gave Pepsi no choice. For them, Project Blue represented the long-needed big, new idea.

References

de Jonquières, Guy, "Clash of the cans," *Financial Times,* March 4, 1993, p. 14.

Gleason, M., and D. Britt, "Pepsi to be Soft Drinks' Big Blue," *Advertising Age,* March 18, 1996, p. 4.

Marshall, Sharon, "Will Revamp Put the Fizz Back into Pepsi?," *Marketing,* March 14, 1996, p. 10.

Martin, Peter, "Back to Business as Usual," *Financial Times,* April 6, 1996, p. 12.

PepsiCo press release, "Pepsi-Cola Eyes Millennium with Launch of Revolutionary Blue Look," April 2, 1996.

PepsiCo press release, "Project Blue Fact Sheet," April 2, 1996.

Sellers, Patricia, "How Coke is Kicking Pepsi's Can," *Fortune,* October 28, 1996, pp. 70–81.

"Turning Pepsi Blue," *The Economist,* April 13, 1996, p. 15.

---

[4]According to PepsiCo public relations, the Concorde "changed the script" of air travel over 20 years ago.

CHAPTER

9 ‖ SECURING DISTRIBUTION

Disney Consumer Products in Lebanon

In March 1994, Jeremy Carter, Disney Consumer Products' (DCP) vice president and managing director for Disney Consumer Products Europe and Middle East (DCPEME), sat at his desk in his Paris office pondering expansion opportunities. DCPEME, a business unit of The Walt Disney Company, hoped to maintain its position as the fastest-growing division within the company. One growth possibility was in the Middle East. Penetrating Middle Eastern countries was attractive given their favorable demographics and discretionary spending patterns. The company could also receive additional royalties from its licensees' sales of Disney-related merchandise. At the same time, DCP executives were concerned that successful entry into Middle Eastern markets could encourage unauthorized imitations or pirate versions of Disney products to be introduced; these, in turn, might be difficult to control.

In 1993, DCPEME signed a joint venture agreement with a Saudi partner, making Saudi Arabia the first country to be penetrated in the area. Did Lebanon, Carter wondered, represent a logical second step? Carter reviewed the market research DCPEME had undertaken in Lebanon and the sales potential of various Disney-licensed products, and was assessing the pros and cons of several distribution options. If he recommended that DCPEME enter the Lebanese market, he would have to explain how it could be accomplished to Dennis Hightower, DCPEME president for Europe and the Middle East.

THE WALT DISNEY COMPANY

In 1923, brothers Walt and Roy Disney founded The Walt Disney Company (WDC) as an animated film business. By 1994, the company had become an entertainment giant comprising three major businesses (see Exhibit 9.1):

Theme parks and resorts included major facilities in Anaheim, California; Orlando, Florida; Tokyo, Japan; and Marne La Vallee, France (near Paris).

Filmed entertainment comprised the Walt Disney Studios, which produced live action films under the Touchstone, Hollywood Pictures, Miramax, and Caravan Pictures labels and animated films under the Walt Disney Pictures label. This subsidiary also pro-

Professor John A. Quelch prepared this case as the basis for class discussion rather than to illustrate either effective or ineffective handling of an administrative situation. Jean-Marc Ingea and Barbara Feinberg also contributed to the development of this case.
Copyright © 1995 by the President and Fellows of Harvard College. Harvard Business School case 596-060.

EXHIBIT 9.1 The Walt Disney Company: Key Financial Data, 1991–1993 ($ millions)

Year ending September 30	*1991*	*1992*	*1993*
Revenues	$6,112	$7,504	$8,529
Theme parks and resorts	2,794	3,307	3,441
Filmed entertainment	2,594	3,115	3,673
Consumer products	724	1,082	1,415
Operating income	1,095	1,435	1,734
Theme parks and resorts	547	644	747
Filmed entertainment	318	508	632
Consumer products	230	283	355
Net income	637	817	300[1]

[1]After loss from Euro Disney investment ($515 million) and accounting changes ($371 million).
Source: Company records.

vided programming for pay-per-view, network, and cable (including the Disney Channel) television and handled sales of videotapes.

DCP was responsible for all marketing and licensing activities and sales of Disney products through mail-order operations and retail outlets, including company-owned Disney Stores. Products consisted of publications, computer software, videogames, toys, personal care products, school supplies, party goods, watches, apparel, home furnishings, and food. DCP licensed the Disney characters, songs and music, and visual and literary properties.

WDC's objective was to remain the world's premier entertainment company. Adhering to Walt Disney's dream to "make people happy," the company's products were associated with such values as quality, integrity, and imagination. The company believed future growth lay in the worldwide character licensing business; more Disney stores, theme parks, and resorts; accelerated output of feature-length animated films; and increased demand for motion picture software and TV programming. In addition, the video market was considered significant, as household VCR penetration worldwide began approaching that of the United States.

Disney Consumer Products

Of DCP's 1993 $1.4 billion in revenues, 1.3% came from Greece and the Middle East, and 23% from Europe (excluding Greece). Table 9.1 summarizes DCPEME revenues

TABLE 9.1 Percent DCPEME Revenues by Product Category, 1993

Publications[1]	61
Merchandise	25
Music	6
Computer software	4
Other	4

[1]Revenues for publications (80% magazines, 20% books) represent sales rather than royalties. Royalty revenues from publications approximated merchandise revenues.

TABLE 9.2 Percent Breakdown of DCPEME Merchandise Revenues, 1993	
Apparel	31
Toys	24
Food	12
Home furnishings	12
Stationery	9
Gifts	8
Personal care	4

by product category, while Table 9.2 provides more detail on DCPEME merchandise revenues.

DCP tightly controlled its licensees to ensure a high level of design and creative integrity, and although royalties for product categories varied, they averaged about 9%. Among the characters DCP licensed were "classics" like Mickey and Minnie Mouse, Donald and Daisy Duck, Goofy, Peter Pan, and Pinocchio, along with the characters from more recent Disney animated films as *The Little Mermaid, Beauty and the Beast,* and *Aladdin.* Characters from *The Lion King,* opening in summer 1994, were also expected to be popular. Mattel, DCP's principal licensee, planned its largest-ever selection of toys for a Disney film. More than 100 Lion King publications—from coloring books to videogames—were also planned. Donald Duck would turn 60 on June 6, and special promotions, books, and other licensed merchandise would be launched to celebrate that event.

Licenses were usually granted for a specific territory, although worldwide or regional licenses were held by a few licensees—for example, Mattel (for infant and preschool toys); Nestlé (for food products); and Seiko (for watches). In 1993, there were about 1,000 licensees for Disney products in Europe and the Middle East—a number that might decrease as more multiterritory deals were signed.

Disney stores showcased the activities and products of the company's divisions via promotions and in-store videos. By early 1994, over 300 (26 in Europe) operated worldwide, 80% of which were in the United States; by late 1994, the company hoped to add 100 more. Given high startup costs, the European stores had not yet turned a profit.

THE LEBANESE MARKET

In March 1993, DCPEME signed a 50/50 joint venture with a Saudi partner. The joint venture company became the legal entity that would manage Disney's Consumer Products' business interests in Middle Eastern countries, excluding Turkey and Israel. Saudi Arabia was the first country in which this joint venture would operate. The next step might be to extend distribution to Lebanon. Exhibit 9.2 compares DCPEME's operations in Saudi Arabia, France, and Lebanon.

Founded in 1943, the independent Republic of Lebanon, bordered by Israel to the south and Syria to the east and north, was roughly the size of Connecticut. During the ensuing 3 decades, the country prospered, with especially dramatic growth in the service sector, particularly tourism, financial services, and port-related activities; per capita

EXHIBIT 9.2 DCPEME Operations in Saudi Arabia, France, and Lebanon, 1993			
	Saudia Arabia	*France*	*Lebanon*
Disney royalty revenues (Year 1)	$ 800,000[1]	$28,000,000[2]	$105,000
Disney royalty revenues (Year 5)	$5,200,000[3]		(uncollected)
Merchandise	87%	69%	65%
Publishing	12%	19%	35%
Music	1%	12%	0%
Profit margin	30% to 75%	80%	NA
Distribution	Exclusive and nonexclusive nondistributors	Licensees' direct sales force and exclusive distributors	Not authorized except for worldwide licensees
Piracy	Exclusively on videotapes	Minimal	Exclusively on videotapes

[1]Objective for the first full year of operations.
[2]Revenues include fully integrated businesses and have been restated on a royalty basis for comparison purposes.
[3]Objective for the fifth year of operation.

gross domestic product was estimated at $1,070 in 1974. At that point, however, the country plunged into a civil war that lasted until 1990. According to United Nations' estimates, the resulting cost in damage to property and infrastructure was $25 billion. Nevertheless, the Lebanese economy subsequently displayed remarkable resilience. In 1991, GDP grew at 50% from the depressed 1990 level, and the World Bank forecast that real GDP would increase at 68% per year until 1999, as the infrastructure was restored. By early 1993, the economy was characterized by free market pricing for most goods and services, and by an unrestricted exchange and trade system. After years of devaluation, the Lebanese pound had stabilized (US$1 = 1,700 Lebanese pounds). Most consumer products were priced in dollars. Exhibit 9.3 summarizes key demographic and economic data on Lebanon.

Although the Lebanese market was small, it offered several advantages. First, its population was much more literate than the populations of neighboring Arab states, and it was also more familiar with Western products, including those of Disney. Second, Lebanese distributors, many of whom occupied important positions in companies throughout the Middle East, might help DCPEME penetrate other Arab markets. Third, because Lebanese society was comparatively liberal, all Disney products could readily be sold.

In 1993, Disney products were distributed in Lebanon through one of three channels:

- Worldwide licensees, e.g., Mattel, that legitimately distributed Disney products through their Lebanese distributors.
- Non-worldwide licensees that distributed Disney products through Lebanese distributors even though they did not hold Disney licenses for Lebanon.
- Non-worldwide licensees unaware that several of their wholesalers were selling Disney merchandise to Lebanese distributors or retailers. For example, one publisher held a U.S. license for Disney picture books, but some of its U.S. distributors were selling them to Lebanese distributors.

EXHIBIT 9.3 Key Demographic and Economic Data for Lebanon, 1992	
Population	3.4 million (76% urban)
Children 0–12 years	650,000
Children 13–18 years	320,000
Households	670,000
Surface area	10,452 square kilometers
Literacy rate	80%
GDP	US$6,460 million
GDP per capita	US$1,900
GDP distribution	
Agriculture	7%
Manufacturing	14%
Construction	7%
Trade	29%
Nonfinancial services	20%
Financial services	9%
Public administration	14%
Imports	US$3,565 million
Exports	US$510 million
Balance of payments	US$54 million

Exhibits 9.4A and 9.4B list some of DCPEME's licensees and their products; Exhibit 9.5 compares the retail prices for such products in Lebanon and in the United States.

Market Research in Lebanon

In early 1994, DCPEME commissioned focus groups of Lebanese parents with children under the age of 18 years to understand how parents entertained their children, which activities they encouraged, and which Disney products they liked and might purchase. The parents interviewed lived in Beirut and had household incomes among the top 25% in Lebanon. In addition, 200 children aged 8 to 18 years were interviewed to test awareness and appeal of Disney products. Research findings are summarized in Exhibits 9.6 and 9.7.

The studies revealed that parents viewed television as a way to stimulate their children's imagination—until the children were 8-years-old; beyond that age, television was considered more negatively—as a passive activity—although children were encouraged to watch cultural programs. Parents were much more positive about reading, starting to read stories to children as young as 1-year-old. Read-along tapes were not widely used given their limited availability in the market.

Plush toys (such as stuffed animals) were especially appealing to children aged 1 through 4 years, who formed very emotional relationships with these toys. Beyond the age of 4 years, most children switched to playing computer games, watching television, or engaging in outdoor sports. (Interestingly, Mattel's Barbie dolls retained their appeal for girls as old as 10 to 12 years.) Computer games, however, were not appreciated by parents; either the children purchased the games themselves or they insisted their parents buy them. In addition, parents felt that educational software for children was lacking in the market. Finally, teenagers were brand conscious in their choices of clothing and accessories. Examples of "fashionable" brands included Lacoste apparel, Sebago shoes, and Swatch watches.

	Country of		Retail sales	
Company	**origin**	**Product category**	**value ($)**	**Distribution type**
A	France	Picture books	175,000	Direct sales
B	U.S.A.	Picture books	165,000	Three distributors
	France	Apparel	20,000	Appointed distributor
C	France	Picture books	65,000	Direct sales
		Puzzles		
D	U.S.A.	Figurines	260,000	Several distributors
E	U.S.A.	*The Little Mermaid*		
		figurines	50,000	Appointed distributor
F	Italy	Toys	40,000	Several distributors
G	U.S.A.	Plushes	20,000	Appointed distributor
H	Spain	Puzzles	10,000	Several distributors
I	Japan	Video games	100,000	Appointed distributors
J	Japan	Video games	80,000	Appointed distributor
K	Belgium	Towels	85,000	Exclusive retailer
L	U.S.A.	Toothbrushes	80,000	Appointed distributor
M	France	Tapes, CDs	15,000	Several distributors
N	France	Rocking chairs	5,000	Exclusive retailer

EXHIBIT 9.4A Disney Licensees Distributing Products in Lebanon, 1993

Source: Distributors' estimates.

In cities of Western Europe, children began deciding what they wanted to do and play with as early as age 4 years; in Lebanon, the transition tended to occur around ages 7 to 8 years. Parents purchased gifts for their children on major holidays and for birthdays of their own children and of friends of their children. Sixty percent of parents also purchased small gifts for their children on impulse, including videotapes, drawing kits, picture books, and Lego games. These impulse purchases were more frequent when parents had only one child, when children were too young to express themselves verbally, when mothers worked full time, or when parents had been away on trips and felt a need to compensate for their absence. Thirty percent of parents purchased small gifts as rewards for good grades at school or for helping out at home. Parents with several children felt that if they gave a gift to one child without a specific justification, they would be pressured to purchase gifts for their other children as well. Parents were also concerned about spoiling their children.

Regarding familiarity with Disney, 30% of the parents had heard of the company through television cartoons or video movies, and 30% had been to a Disney theme park.

EXHIBIT 9.4B Retail Sales of Disney Products in Lebanon by Licensee Origin, 1993

Licensee origin	**Sales ($)**
Worldwide regional licensees	455,000
Nonworldwide licensees, selling through selected Lebanese distributors	485,000
Nonworldwide licensees, selling through wholesalers in other countries	230,000
Pirated Disney products (exclusively video)	650,000 to 1,200,000

Source: Company estimates.

EXHIBIT 9.5 Retail Prices of Disney products in Lebanon and the United States, 1993

Product	Lebanon retail price ($)	U.S. retail price ($)
Video		
"Sing Along Song" tapes (pirate)	5	12
"Disney Classics" tapes (pirate)	7	19
Publications		
Le Journal de Mickey magazine	1.60	—
Picsou (Uncle Scrooge) magazine	2.50	—
Disney Parade magazine	1.80	—
Disney Hachette picture books (e.g., *Snow White*), 90 pages	11	7
Fernand Nathan picture books (e.g., *Bambi*), 45 pages	7	—
Toys/Plushes		
Mattel's Footlights	14	—
Hasbro's Disney Babies (e.g., Goofy)	28	—
Educa's Maxipuzzle, 150 pieces	18	3
Computer Games		
Nintendo's Mickey's Dangerous Chase (GameBoy)	40	—
Nintendo's Aladdin (SuperNintendo)	100	70
Nintendo's Who Framed Roger Rabbit? (GameBoy)	35	—
Sega's Aladdin (MegaDrive)	80	60
Music		
Aladdin compact disc	22	22
Fantasia set of two compact discs	30	—
Pickwick's read-along tape	15	7
Pickwick's compact disk	27	15
Furniture		
Creapuzzle's rocking chairs	75	—
Mickey office chair made in Germany	250	—
Apparel/Accessories:		
Ties	40	28
School bags	20	13
Linen		
Sunday Junior's 1m 80 cm-wide sheets	52	—
Haplo's bath towel	20	—
Haplo's bath robe	75	—

The Disney brand was regarded as a high-value label, and interviewees believed that using Disney apparel and other merchandise enhanced people's self-esteem and perceived status. Many Lebanese had lived abroad during the country's civil war and were therefore aware of a wide range of Disney-licensed products beyond those legitimately distributed in Lebanon.

A Lebanese child's first contact with Disney characters usually occurred between ages 1 to 2 years, when parents began narrating Disney tales and children started watch-

EXHIBIT 9.6 Awareness of Disney Products in Lebanon[1]	
Product category	*% responding yes*
Magazines	60
Picture books	100
Read-along tapes	100
Videotapes	100
Television cartoons	100
Watches	73
Apparel	93
Toys	100
Computer games	0
School supplies	93
Home furnishing	67
Food	87

[1]DCPEME commissioned two focus groups involving 15 mothers and fathers of children under age 18 years. Respondents were asked: "In which of the following product categories do Disney products exist?" In fact, Disney products were marketed in all categories listed.

ing cartoons on TV. Disney values and characters were then developed through videotapes, picture books, and plush toys.

Product Categories

In order to decide which products—if any—should be introduced into Lebanon, Jeremy Carter reviewed DCPEME's research findings on Lebanese parents' reactions to various Disney products (see Exhibit 9.8). He also had collected preliminary data on Lebanese distributors' and retailers' margins by product category (Exhibit 9.9). With this information in hand, he set out to consider which product categories had the highest sales potential in Lebanon.

Apparel

This category included several product lines that varied in price/quality and age of the target audience. (Although Disney apparel was not sold legally in Lebanon, small quantities had been imported illegally.)

A high-end Disney line for teenagers would have to compete with such names as Benetton, Lacoste, Old River, and Compagnie de Californie. Lacoste, encountering piracy problems, had opened two stores in Beirut to enable customers to buy its genuine products and to educate the market on how to spot them. Carter was concerned that if Disney built a high awareness for its merchandise in Lebanon, it, too, would face imported pirate products. This scenario had already developed in East Asia.

Research participants had looked favorably upon the price levels of a medium-quality line of apparel: Disney T-shirts at $20 and sweatshirts at $30 represented prices that Lebanese customers found reasonable. One source of concern, however, was that

EXHIBIT 9.7 Selected Findings of DCPEME Market Study

During January and February 1994, personal interviews were conducted with 200 children (50% boys and 50% girls) aged 8 to 18 years. Children were interviewed at school. Place of residence was as follows: 45% in East Beirut, 45% in West Beirut, and 10% outside of Beirut.

- Arabic was the predominant language spoken at home for 58% of respondents, French was predominant for 23%, and English was predominant for 19%.
- Tom and Jerry were the characters preferred by 22% of the children, followed by Mickey Mouse with 8%. The overall distribution of first preferences was as follows (Disney characters are in bold):

Character Name	%
Tom and Jerry	22
Mickey Mouse	8
Bugs Bunny	7
Pink Panther	7
Donald Duck	6
Tintin et Milou	4
Asterix et Obelix	3
Aladdin	2
The Little Mermaid	2
Ninja Turtles	2
Lucky Luke	2
Beauty and the Beast	1
Peter Pan	1
Pinocchio	1
Snow White	1
Uncle Scrooge	1

- Sixty-six percent of respondents knew their preferred characters primarily from television, 12% from books, 9% from movie theaters, 9% from video, 3% from magazines, and 1% from computer software.
- Forty-four percent of respondents owned toys representing at least one of their favorite characters: 48% of these toys had been purchased outside Lebanon (mainly in Europe or the United States).
- Fifty-eight percent of respondents owned videotapes representing at least one of their favorite characters: 46% of these tapes had been purchased outside Lebanon and 64% were Disney tapes (either genuine or pirate).
- Thirty-one percent of respondents owned apparel depicting at least one of their favorite characters: 66% of this apparel had been purchased outside Lebanon.
- Ninety-two percent of respondents read at home, 17% of respondents had read the *Journal de Mickey* magazine: 38% of these children read it on a regular basis.
- Sixteen percent of respondents read *Piscou Magazine:* 50% of these children read it on a regular basis.
- Eight percent of respondents read *Disney Parade* magazine: 43% of these children read it on a regular basis.
- Sixty-seven percent of respondents had at least one video game at home, 44% of whom had Nintendo games and 25% of whom had Sega games. Forty-two percent of these games had been purchased outside Lebanon.
- Ninety-nine percent of respondents lived in homes with a television, 87% lived in homes with a video recorder.

EXHIBIT 9.8 Buying Intentions for Various Disney Products among Lebanese Consumers[1]		
Disney product	*Suggested retail price ($)*	*% who would buy*
Minnie T-shirt	23	40
Baby suit in jeans	27	80
Baby suit in cotton	27	60
Aladdin towel	30	33
Mickey slippers	15	40
Minnie tennis shoes	15	87
Mickey toothbrush	6	20
Aladdin plastic watch	8	33
Aladdin beach plastic glass	11	40
Donald Duck school bag	21	40
Donald Duck plush	30	33
Abu plush	38	7
Beauty doll	24	40
Read-along tape	11	67
Musical television	50	20

[1]This test was conducted in a focus group of parents of children aged 1 to 15 years. Focus group respondents were shown a variety of Disney products and were asked which they would purchase at the prices indicated.

These retail prices represented a 50% premium over U.S. retail prices for the identical products.

they perceived the value of such apparel by the added value *originality* would provide. On the other hand, T-shirts, sweatshirts, and accessories were often sold as gifts, and it was thought that gifts would represent a significant share of Disney apparel sales in Lebanon.

At the outset, Disney might work with international licensees to ensure product quality and creative standards. Although Disney apparel made by international licensees would find it hard to compete with low-priced, locally manufactured apparel or low-cost imports from Asia, the company would perhaps be able to penetrate the mass market with small accessories retailing at broadly affordable prices. The dollar sales of such products, if intensively distributed through many retail outlets, could be significant.

Publications

Although such French-language Disney magazines as *Le Journal de Mickey* and *Disney Parade* were legitimately being distributed in Lebanon, representing as a magazine category annual sales of about $20,000, picture books were the principal Disney publications. Many Lebanese children were able to understand Disney publications in

EXHIBIT 9.9 Distributor and Retailer Margins by Category		
Category	*Distributor margin (%)*	*Retailer margin (%)*
Apparel	20	30
Publications	10	20
Toys/plushes	15	20

French and English (see Exhibit 9.10), but because French was more widely taught as a foreign language than English in elementary school, sales of Disney publications in French were higher.

One major French licensee was distributing a 30-volume series of picture books featuring classic Disney stories like Snow White and Pinocchio; the series was carried by almost every Lebanese bookstore, and a licensee representative was responsible for replenishing inventory. Annual retail sales of Disney publications represented about 10% of the licensee's total sales in Lebanon, roughly $140,000. Its licensing agreement with Disney did not include Lebanon, but Disney did not oppose the sales: They helped increase Disney product awareness and introduce the stories and characters to young children. Another French publisher was also selling Disney stories; its license for Disney books in France expired in 1992 so DCPEME assumed that the publisher was liquidating remaining inventories of Disney books. Any picture book in French, however, faced competition from those starring such popular characters as Babar, Asterix, and Tintin, whose sales significantly outpaced Disney's.

One U.S. licensee sold Disney picture books in English through three local distributors; its annual retail sales in Lebanon were about $125,000. Price competition among the three was tough because there was no exclusive distributor for English-language Disney publications, and the licensee's publications were sometimes retailed at a loss.

Disney had signed licensing agreements with four publishers of books in Arabic. Several Lebanese book retailers had printing capabilities and wished to translate and publish Disney picture books and export them throughout the Arabic-speaking world. They argued that Lebanese printing quality was superior, citing an old proverb: "In the Arab world, Egyptians create stories, Lebanese publish them, and Iraqis read them!"

Plushes/toys

Although retail sales of plushes and "figurine"-type toys in Lebanon were estimated at $16 million per year, Disney products were not widely available, for several reasons. First, Disney plushes/toys faced strong competition from both branded and unbranded products in Lebanon. Fisher-Price, for example, whose products targeted the age 3-and-under set, were 30% cheaper than equivalent Disney items. Further, Fisher-Price regularly inserted product catalogs in local newspapers and ran promotions on children's TV shows, offering free samples. Disney advertising was almost nonexistent in Lebanon.

Second, one important Disney licensee in the plush category did not market in Lebanon; the other was restructuring its Lebanese distribution as a result of disagree-

EXHIBIT 9.10	Percentage of Lebanese Population Able to Understand Foreign Languages by Age			
	Disney target audience (%)		*Overall population (%)*	
	Under 12 years	*12 years and over*	*Under 12 years*	*12 years and over*
Arabic	100	100	100	100
French	70	80	50	60
English	20	60	10	30

ment over the kinds of merchandise the distributor received. Thus, in 1993, that Disney licensee selected another distributor for the Lebanese market, and the two were making ambitious plans for 1994.

Third, the category was limited to younger children, and Lebanese children rarely gave plushes as gifts to their friends.

Other products

Most Lebanese were unaware that Disney watches existed, although focus groups indicated that plastic watches retailing below $15 were perceived as affordable and unique. More expensive watches would have to compete with such brands as Swatch and Timex, both widely available in Lebanon. Other categories in which Disney licensees' presence was very limited included home furnishings and food products.

At the same time, all major Disney computer games were available for use on Sega and Nintendo systems, though Disney faced stiff competition from non-Disney action games. Nevertheless, Disney's latest game, Aladdin, had been the 1993 best-seller in Lebanon, selling out after a few weeks on the market. Retailers were also interested in "read-along" tapes, but compact disc sales were limited to the 5% of Lebanese households with CD players.

Character

The Disney characters most widely known and appreciated by Lebanese consumers were Mickey and Minnie Mouse, Beauty (of *Beauty and the Beast*), Snow White, and Ariel (of *the Little Mermaid*). Concurrent with the release of *Beauty and the Beast* and *Aladdin* in 1992 and 1993 respectively, DCPEME had concentrated its merchandising on the principal characters in these films—with great success. With the highly anticipated release of *The Lion King* in the summer of 1994, DCPEME had high hopes for the Lebanese market: Focus groups revealed that Lebanese youngsters liked animal-related plushes/toys, and boys especially appreciated the strength associated with lions.

Distribution

Fifteen Disney licensees had official distributors in Lebanon, but in many cases, their performance was not monitored closely because the country represented a small market. Given an improved political climate, licensees' interest in extracting more sales from Lebanon was expected to increase. Thus, one of DCPEME's distribution options was to rely on its licensees' current distributors while also encouraging its worldwide licensees not represented in Lebanon to sign agreements with one of these distributors. DCPEME would coordinate the distributors and encourage them to carry more Disney merchandise. Incentives might include establishing an advertising fund, sponsoring TV shows/special events, and offering Euro Disney entrance tickets and tour packages. A problem with this approach, however, was that current official distributors might not have the motivation or financial strength to distribute more Disney products, and might favor other products yielding higher margins. They also might not be the most appropriate to carry other Disney licensees' product lines; for example, Nintendo, a Disney licensee, had a Lebanese distributor that represented only Nintendo.

Another distribution option was to identify existing Lebanese distributors that might sell Disney products not yet present in the market. There were 10 top distributors in Lebanon in the product categories in which Disney competed; one carried a range of toy brands including Fisher-Price, Milton Bradley, and Matchbox. A methodical study of the product line expertise, distribution ability, and financial strength of such distributors would take 6 months. If DCPEME increased the number of its Lebanese distributors, it faced the challenge of coordinating and supporting organizations unfamiliar with Disney products.

In the case of either option, DCPEME would have to determine how to handle requests for exclusivity. Most distributors required exclusive rights in Lebanon for the items they carried because the market was too small to support competing distributors. Traditionally, DCPEME encouraged its licensees to test new country markets and distributors for a limited time before granting exclusive rights. Granting exclusivity to local distributors, however, might effectively combat diversion: Lebanese retailers could currently purchase Disney merchandise from U.S.- or European-Disney licensees' wholesalers and resell it in Lebanon.

Meanwhile, DCPEME had been contacted by several new distributors wishing to carry Disney products. One was an 18-store Saudi retail chain selling photographic and electronics equipment; it was interested in opening a Beirut store offering just Disney products and in acting as a distributor to other retailers. The chain had no previous experience in Lebanese retailing but recently purchased extensive space in Beirut for offices and a showroom, to be run by the current vice president of marketing, a Lebanese citizen. Despite being advised that it could not have exclusive rights for any Disney products or use Disney store signage or any Disney character name or logo, the Saudi retail chain negotiated exclusive rights with 11 Disney licensees to sell a variety of their products in Lebanon. This merchandise comprised apparel, toys, school supplies, and gifts items. Other Lebanese distributors could continue to purchase products not included in the agreement from the same Disney licensees.

A second distributor had acquired from Disney licensees not yet present in Lebanon the rights to sell some of their Disney products, and had opened a retail store in Beirut in December 1993; it also began advertising its Disney products (see Exhibit 9.11 for a sample). Other Lebanese companies—frequently startups with little marketing expertise—were thought likely to try to acquire rights for certain Disney merchandise from international Disney licensees not yet distributing in Lebanon.

Finally, DCPEME could license one or more Disney Corners within existing retail stores. The licensee would lease the space for each Disney Corner from a storeowner. A Disney Corner would offer the full array of genuine Disney products properly merchandised and would ensure both continuity of supply and the aggressive promotion of new character-related products as they were launched. A Disney Corner could be a landmark for Beirut residents, increasing awareness and stimulating gift-giving of Disney products, while reaffirming company values and enabling DCPEME to market product not carried by current distributors. Start-up costs for a 1,000-square-foot store-within-a-store were estimated at $125,000, including $30,000 of initial inventory. Inventory was expected to turn over four times a year and deliver a 30% gross margin. Beyond the costs, however, was the fact that opening a Disney Corner represented a serious commitment to a market whose potential had yet to be tested. Moreover, problems could arise with existing distributors of Disney licensees if DCPEME tried to direct all sales of Disney products through one or more Disney Corners where retail prices could be controlled.

EXHIBIT 9.11 Retailer Advertisement of Disney Products in Lebanon

ALL PURPOSE BAGS!
Hand and Back Bags to French quality & design.

Always look out for
more of our products,
a newer collection
in our next catalogue!

STICKERS ON RELIEF!
All surface 3-dimensional plastified fun
stickers ranging from 10 to 90 cm.
Made in Spain.

T. F. BOWLES₁₁₀
Mar Mikhael
Fattal Bldg. 3rd floor
Close to Fichet-Bauche
Tel/Fax:01-581757

DCP Organization in Lebanon

If DCPEME did decide to expand into Lebanon, should it set up an office in Beirut managed by full-time DCPEME employees, appoint a full- or part-time local marketing representative, or run Lebanon out of its Saudi office? An office would coordinate distributors' advertising and promotion efforts and mediate among them when necessary; ensure that DCPEME received all royalties to which it was entitled from sales of Disney merchandise; act to stop sales of pirated products or unauthorized imports; sponsor special promotional events; and in the long term, identify potential local manufacturers of licensed merchandise. Setting up an office in Beirut with full-time DCPEME employees would probably cost about $250,000 in the first year, whereas appointing and managing a half-time marketing representative would add perhaps $100,000 to DCPEME costs in 1994.

CONCLUSION

Jeremy Carter faced some tough choices. Should DCPEME enter the Lebanese market, and if so, how? Which products should be introduced, in what sequence, and through what distribution channels? How would copyrights, piracy concerns, and other protection issues be handled? Should Disney open an office in Beirut? The rewards in Lebanon seemed possible, but so did the risks.

CHAPTER

10 RECAPTURING MARKET SHARE

EMDICO (A)

On August 2, 1990, Iraqi forces invaded Kuwait. Fortunately, D. Srinivasan, marketing manager with Fuji Film's distributor in Kuwait, was visiting the United States at the time. However, when he returned to Kuwait in March 1991 after the end of Gulf War, he found his house ransacked. After several months visiting with his family in India, Srinivasan returned to the region late in 1991 as general manager of EMDICO (Emam Distribution Co., Ltd.) in Jeddah, Kingdom of Saudi Arabia (KSA). EMDICO was Fuji's newly appointed Saudi Arabia distributor.

In his new role, Srinivasan had to develop a marketing strategy to relaunch the Fuji film and camera product lines among others in Saudi Arabia. Srinivasan set out to convince management in Tokyo that they had made the right decision in appointing EMDICO. Their confidence would, he hoped, result in some monetary support to subsidize his marketing strategy and in the timeliness and availability of Fuji product shipments from Japan to Saudi Arabia.

THE KINGDOM OF SAUDI ARABIA

Founded in 1932 by King Abd Al-Aziz, the Kingdom of Saudi Arabia was a country one-third of the size of the United States with a population of 17 million in 1991.[1] The population had been only 3.2 million in 1950 and was expected to double by 2010. As shown in Exhibit 10.1, Saudia Arabia dominated the Arabian peninsula. Around 75% of the population lived in urban areas: The most important cities were Riyadh (two million) and Jeddah (two million). A quarter of the population were expatriates, principally Egyptians, citizens of other Arab countries, and nationals from the Indian subcontinent. Only one-quarter of the expatriates were accompanied by other family members,

---

[1] The combined population of the countries in the Middle East region, as defined by Fuji, was about 100 million in 1991.

Doctoral Candidate Yoshinori Fujikawa prepared this case under the supervision of Professor John A. Quelch as the basis for class discussion rather than to illustrate either effective or ineffective handling of an administrative situation. Confidential data have been disguised.

EXHIBIT 7.1 Map of the Arabian Peninsula

The Arabian Peninsula

THE EIGHT NATIONS OF THE ARABIAN PENINSULA: BAHRAIN, KUWAIT, OMAN, QATAR, SAUDI ARABIA, UNITED ARAB EMIRATES, YEMEN ARAB REPUBLIC, PEOPLE'S DEMOCRATIC REPUBLIC OF YEMEN.

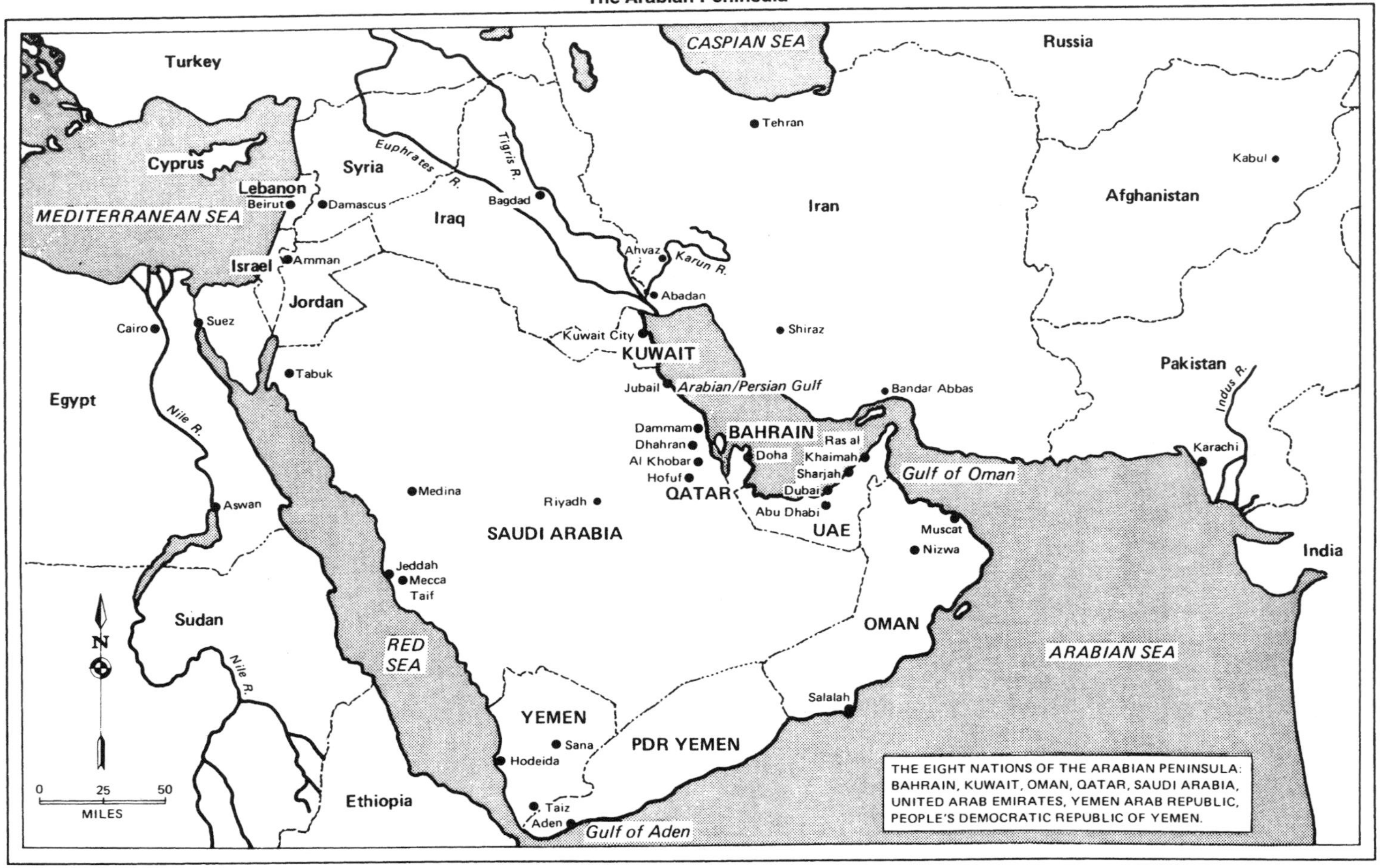

Source: Quentin W. Fleming, *A Guide to Doing Business on the Arabian Peninsula,* New York: AMACOM, 1981.

though the percentage was increasing. Arabic was the official language but English was widely used in business circles.

The age distribution of the 13 million native Saudis who lived in 3.8 million households was as shown in Table 10.1. Of Saudi households, 2.8 million included a husband, wife, and children.

The KSA GDP was SR 427.5 billion (US$114 billion) in 1992.[2] Saudi per capita income was higher than in all other Middle Eastern countries except Bahrain, Kuwait, and the United Arab Emirates. The petroleum sector, with a quarter of the world's proven oil reserves, accounted for 35% of GDP and most export earnings. Almost every Saudi household had a television, refrigerator, cooker, and washing machine. Ninety-two percent of households owned a car. Two-thirds of households owned stereo and video equipment. This level of affluence reflected the absence of any personal income tax and KSA government subsidies of utilities and public transportation as well as the availability of free education and health care.

The value of brand building, advertising, and market research was increasingly understood. International brands were sold freely through increasingly modern retail outlets (including 100 supermarkets among 17,000 food stores). However, media advertising expenditures were only SR 40 per capita in 1990 compared to almost $300 in the United States. As a result of the Gulf War, subscriptions to satellite television channels increased greatly.

The KSA constitution and government were based firmly on the teachings of the Islamic Koran. Alcohol was banned. Saudi Arabia was home to the pilgrimage center of Mecca and Medina. The faithful prayed toward Mecca five times daily. Every business had to close for half an hour at each of these prayer times. In accordance with the Muslim calendar, commerce was conducted from Saturday through Wednesday; Thursday and Friday were weekends.

Consumer behavior in Saudi Arabia was influenced heavily by Muslim prescripts. In a culture where family honor was defined by adherence to strict codes of conduct, women could not appear in public unveiled and they were not permitted to drive. Market research indicated that one-third of daily shopping decisions were made solely by Saudi husbands, one-third solely by Saudi wives, and one-third jointly. However, husbands made two-thirds of the actual purchases and only one in seven Saudi wives actually visited stores to purchase goods.

TABLE 10.1 Age Distribution of Native Saudis	
Age group (years)	**Percentage**
0–15	49
16–30	20
31–45	14
46–60	10
Over 60	7

Source: Arab News, December 15, 1992.

---

[2]One U.S. dollar was equivalent to 3.75 Saudi Riyals (SR).

TABLE 10.2 Film-Processing Speed Requested		
Speed	*Saudi Arabia (%)*	*United States (%)*
1 Hour	85	35
7 Hours	10	40
Overnight	5	25

Cultural norms affected the prevalence of photography. Women could not normally have their pictures taken or take pictures themselves. Weddings, however, would almost always be recorded, but only by women. Family portraits might also be taken at photo studios. However, concern that a stranger in a film-processing laboratory might see a woman unveiled or, worse, duplicate a photo being processed, limited this practice. For these reasons, a family that visited a photo studio for a portrait often preferred to wait until the pictures were developed.[3] Consumer surveys in Saudi Arabia and the United States found the following differences in speed of film-processing service requested (see Table 10.2).

On the other hand, the mix of subjects that consumers chose to photograph was similar in the two countries, as shown in Table 10.3.

TABLE 10.3 Selected Photo Subjects		
Subjects	*Saudi Arabia (%)*	*United States (%)*
People	60	70
Nature/landscape	15	15
Buildings	10	14

FUJI FILM BACKGROUND

Fuji Photo Film Co., Ltd., headquartered in Tokyo, Japan, was one of the world's leading manufacturers and marketers of photographic film, cameras, photo papers, and magnetic tapes. Net sales in 1990 were $8 billion.

Fuji organized its product lines into three groups: imaging systems (37% of worldwide sales), photofinishing systems (23%), and information systems (40%). The most important single product line was the Fujicolor series of color negative films and the biggest selling item was the Fujicolor Super HR 100, ideal for everyday photography. Fujicolor Super film was available in other speeds (HG 200, HG 400, and HG 1600). Fuji REALA was a color negative film that delivered colors as seen by the human eye. Fuji Chrome VELVIA color reversal film was for professional use. NEOPAN black and white film, used especially for sports and press photography, was available in three speeds.

The imaging systems group also offered a broad selection of cameras, from simple point-and-shoot compact cameras such as the FZ-5 and DL-25, to the FZ-3000 with its binocular-style body and dynamic 38mm to 115mm zoom lens. The range also included

---

[3]Partly as a consequence, there were only 28 wholesale labs in Saudi Arabia in 1991, compared to 3,400 in the United States. Wholesale labs collected films from retail sites such as photo studios and camera shops, developed and printed them at a lab, then redistributed the finished photographs to the retailers for customer pickup. The time between customer dropoff and pickup was typically 2 to 3 days.

sophisticated professional models. Fujicolor Quicksnap disposable cameras were launched in 1985, followed in 1987 by Quicksnap Flash and Quicksnap Marine. Also included in the product line was the FOTORAMA instant ID photo camera.

The photofinishing systems group sold photographic paper in a wide variety of surfaces and sheet sizes, photofinishing equipment, and chemicals. Fuji pioneered the development of a compact and durable minilab, the FA Compact II.[4] Although slower than the minilabs made by Kodak and Konica, it was more compact, better designed, and easier to service.

The information systems group sold materials and equipment for printing industries, medical imaging products, office automation systems, floppy disks, and computer tapes. Fuji was especially strong in digital medical X-ray imaging systems that it sold to large and mid-sized hospitals worldwide.

In Japan, Fuji's bright green packages were as ubiquitous as Kodak's yellow packages were in the United States. In 1990, Fuji accounted for 70% of film sales, 20% of camera sales, and 15% of magnetic tape sales in Japan.

Around 25% of Fuji's sales were generated outside Japan. Fuji's sales in the Middle East were around $150 million, 2% of Fuji's total revenues and 8% of Fuji's overseas sales.

Fuji typically entered new consumer markets with its film product line, followed by its cameras. Fuji often offered its basic products first, adding the more expensive and specialized items in its lines as demand increased. In Saudia Arabia, for example, 80% of Fuji film sales were of the popular 100-film speed, compared to 45% in the United States. Recently, sales of the FA Compact II minilab to photo studios and other outlets had helped Fuji penetrate the major cities of several developing markets, where Fuji often found itself playing catch-up to Kodak.

KSA MARKET STRUCTURE

As shown in Exhibit 10.2, around 6 million rolls of color film were imported annually into Saudi Arabia between 1984 and 1989. At 6 million rolls per year, the KSA film market was 2% the size of the U.S. market while Saudi Arabia's population was 7% that of the United States. The disparity was attributed to lower per capita disposable income and cultural constraints on picture taking. In 1990, the Iraqi invasion of Kuwait disrupted shipping in the Gulf and only 2.9 million rolls were imported. As part of the post war recovery process, some 4 million rolls of film were expected to be imported into Saudi Arabia in 1991, up 35% from 1990. This figure partly reflected the high level of inventories already held by distributors and retailers in Saudi Arabia.

No film or cameras were manufactured in Saudi Arabia. All were imported by Saudi distributors who each exclusively represented a single brand. They marketed the imported products to a variety of channels, typically taking a 15% margin on the selling price. In 1991, the KSA import tariff on film and cameras was 12%.

As shown in Exhibit 10.3, Kodak and Konica were locked in a tight competition for market leadership in film sales. Konica was also the number five brand in unit camera

---

[4]A minilab consisted of a film processor for developing the film and a printer that transmitted the images to photo paper. The word "minilab" was used interchangeably for a machine itself as well as for a store using a minilab machine on site. By 1991, there was one minilab for every 12,000 people in the United States.

EXHIBIT 10.2 KSA Film and Camera Markets: Industry and Fuji Imports, 1985–1995E

KSA market[1]	*1985*	*1986*	*1987*	*1988*	*1989*
Color film rolls (units)	6,200,000	6,135,000	6,170,000	6,760,000	6,060,000
Color paper (sq. m.)	3,700,000	4,040,000	3,900,000	3,800,000	2,000,000
Cameras (units)[2]	200,000	81,500	143,000	54,200	98,300
Minilabs (installations)	100	115	140	170	190
Fuji unit sales[1,3,4]	*1985*	*1986*	*1987*	*1988*	*1989*
Color film rolls (units)	560,000 (9%)	368,000 (6%)	553,300 (9%)	518,400 (9%)	545,400 (9%)
Color paper (sq. m.)	110,000 (3%)	202,000 (5%)	78,000 (2%)	80,000 (2%)	20,000 (1%)
Cameras (units)	2,000 (1%)	1,200 (1%)	1,300 (1%)	400 (1%)	900 (1%)
Minilabs (installations)	8 (8%)	10 (9%)	12 (9%)	14 (8%)	15 (8%)

[1]Estimates of imports by distributors into Saudi Arabia, based on the export figures in Japan Ministry of Finance, *Japan Export-Import Statistics 1991*. These are not estimates of retail sales.
[2]Volatility partly due to entry and withdrawal of foreign camera manufacturers.
[3]Percentage figures in parentheses are Fuji market shares.
[4]Target figures for 1992E–1995E were sales goals set jointly by Fuji management and EMDICO.

EXHIBIT 10.3 Brand Unit Market Shares (%) in Saudi Arabia: 1991

	Fuji	*Kodak*	*Konica*	*AGFA*	*Others*
Color film rolls	8	43	44	5	0
Color paper	9	46	43	2	0
Cameras[1]	2	2	5	0	91
Minilabs	7	43	40	3	7
Medical X-ray	60	20	5	10	5

[1]The leading camera brands in Saudi Arabia were Yashica (27% of unit sales), Canon (17%), Olympus (8%), Nikon (7%), and Konica (5%).

sales. Of the 2,400 outlets in Saudi Arabia through which film was sold, only 30 sold Kodak exclusively and 30 Konica. The remaining outlets were not tied to any one brand; few outlets, however, carried more than two brands of film. Cameras were sold by about 700 of the 2,400 outlets selling film.

As indicated in Exhibit 10.4, photographic studios accounted for 25% of film sales but only 5% of cameras. Camera and electronic stores retailed 65% of cameras and 30%

EXHIBIT 10.4 KSA Distribution Channels for Film and Cameras: 1991

	% film sales (units)	*% camera sales (units)*	*Total number of dealers*	*Number of Fuji dealers*	*Fuji dealer penetration*
Studios	25	5	1,542	308	20
Minilabs	35	20	216	66	30
Camera/electronics stores	30	65	218	22	10
Supermarkets	5	—	284	48	17
Industrial/hospital	—	—	460	46	10
Others	5	10	100	6	6
Total	100	100	2,820	496	18

EXHIBIT 10.2 (*continued*)

1990	1991E	1992E	1993E	1994E	1995E
2,900,000	4,000,000	5,500,000	5,600,000	5,800,000	6,000,000
2,025,000	2,500,000	3,000,000	3,100,000	3,200,000	3,300,000
80,000	60,000	115,000	120,000	130,000	136,000
214	230	250	300	380	460

1990	1991E	1992E	1993E	1994E	1995E
232,000 (8%)	320,000 (8%)	700,000 (13%)	800,000 (14%)	1,000,000 (17%)	1,200,000 (20%)
20,250 (1%)	25,000 (1%)	300,000 (10%)	400,000 (13%)	500,000 (16%)	660,000 (20%)
800 (1%)	1,000 (2%)	10,000 (9%)	15,000 (13%)	20,000 (15%)	22,000 (16%)
15 (7%)	16 (7%)	36 (14%)	60 (20%)	86 (23%)	110 (24%)

of film. One-third of film was sold by minilabs that provided on-premise processing in less than an hour. In addition, a few supermarkets served as convenient collection points for used films that were then sent to wholesale labs for processing.

There were 216 minilabs in Saudi Arabia in October 1991. The Konica distributor in Saudi Arabia had sold the most minilabs to date. The smallest Konica minilab sold for SR 250,000 and required the retailer to make a 50% down payment. Minilab models varied in the speed and quantity of film they could process at any one time. Most minilabs could process any brand of film and many sold two or more brands of film, not just the brand associated with the minilab. Profile information from a market research study on minilabs in Saudi Arabia is presented in Exhibit 10.5. Srinivasan also developed the economic projections shown in Exhibit 10.6 for dealer interested in buying the Fuji FA Compact II minilab. Srinivasan believed the breakeven point on the cheapest Konica minilab required the processing of 20 films per day versus 13 for the Fuji machine.

EXHIBIT 10.5 Profile of Minilabs in Saudi Arabia: October 1991

- Of the 216 minilabs in Saudi Arabia, 85% were in stand-alone retail outlets and 15% were in supermarkets.
- In 20% of the retail outlets with minilabs, more than one minilab was installed.
- Seventy percent of KSA minilabs were in photo studios, which typically derived 20% of their revenues from portrait photography.
- On average, 75% of a minilab's revenues were derived from photofinishing and 25% from retail sales. Of retail sales, 60% were from film, 20% from cameras, 10% from batteries, and 10% from items such as albums, frames, and videotapes.
- Eighty percent of all KSA minilabs were concentrated in Jeddah and Riyadh.

FUJI'S MARKET POSITION IN SAUDI ARABIA

Because Fuji film was sold in Israel, Fuji was blocked from doing business in the Middle East until the Arab boycott was lifted in March 1983. Meanwhile, Kodak had been selling in Saudi Arabia since the 1960s and Konica since the 1970s.

Once the boycott was lifted, Fuji asked Mitsui Corporation, a Japanese trading company, to identify exclusive distributors in all Middle Eastern countries. In 1984, Fuji

EXHIBIT 10.6   Sample Profit Planning for Prospective Minilab Owner

Assumptions			
(X) Model: FA COMPACT			
(A) EMDICO's selling price	SR	180,000	per unit
(B) Paper price	SR	12	per sqm dealer net
(1) Processing rolls[1]		20	rolls/day
(2) Working day		26	days
(3) Processing fee	SR	6	per roll
(4) Printing fee	SR	1.00	per print, 1 print = 10.2 cm * 15.2 cm = 0.0155 sqm
(5) Production ratio		90%	

Profit and loss calculation			
Monthly revenue			
(6) Film processing	SR	3,120	= (1) * (2) * (3)
(7) Printing	SR	18,720	= (1) * (2) * 36 prints * (4)
(8) Total revenue	SR	21,840	= (6) + (7)
Monthly expense			
(9) Paper	SR	3,869	= (1) * (2) * 36 prints * 0.0155 * (B)/(5)
(10) Chemical	SR	874	= 4% on total revenue
(11) Free film, album & envelope	SR	4,680	= (1) * (2) * SR 9.00
(12) Total expense	SR	9,422	= (9) + (10) + (11)
Margin			
(13) Gross margin (SR)	SR	12,418	= (8) − (12)
(14) Gross margin (%)		57%	= (13)/ (8) * 100
Fixed cost			
(15) Salaries	SR	2,500	Assumed
(16) Rent & utilities	SR	2,500	Assumed
(17) Minilab depreciation	SR	3,000	= (A)/60 months (5 years)
Profit			
(18) Net profit (SR)	SR	4,418	= (13) − (15) − (16) − (17)
(19) Net profit (%)		20%	= (18)/(8) * 100

[1]Breakeven film unit sales = 13 rolls/day.

itself appointed an exclusive distributor to represent its product line in Saudi Arabia. The selected firm already distributed several multinational company brands including the Japanese camera brands, Olympus and Pentax. However, according to one industry observer:

> Fuji's distributor never gave great emphasis to the Fuji line. It accounted for only 10% of their sales at most. They focused mainly on camera stores. Also, dealer service was not that great, stockouts, and late deliveries were common, and several dealers switched to competitive brands.

By the middle of 1991, Fuji's market shares in film, cameras, and minilabs in Saudi Arabia were estimated at 8%, 2%, and 7% respectively, as shown in Exhibit 10.3. Fuji penetration of distribution outlets was correspondingly low, as shown in Exhibit 10.4. The product mix of Fuji's KSA sales in 1991 is summarized in Exhibit 10.7.

Fuji management was concerned that the KSA distributor's performance was lagging distributor performance in other Middle Eastern countries. For example, Fuji had placed its equipment in only 16 out of 216 minilabs in Saudi Arabia compared to 35 out of 183 in the neighboring United Arab Emirates which had a population of only two million. Although the higher penetration of minilabs in the United Arab Emirates could be explained by higher per capita income and a more open society, the difference in Fuji's market shares was attributed to the relative competence of the distributors. In Iran, Syria, and Qatar, Fuji's share of minilab installations exceeded 30%. Exhibit 10.8 reports minilab installations in Middle Eastern countries by brand.

Early in 1991, Fuji management decided to change its distributor in Saudi Arabia. The market disruption caused by the Gulf War afforded a good opportunity. As one executive said:

> Our existing distributor did not respond well to the marketing challenges caused by the war. It seemed like a good time to start over, especially since a surge of economic growth was expected in the aftermath of the war.

Fuji's distributor in United Arab Emirates recommended to the general manager of Fuji's international marketing division that he contact Sheik Hani S. Emam whose distribution companies held exclusive sales and service contracts for several multinationals selling furniture, clocks, and other consumer products.

Fuji planned to publicly announce the appointment of EMDICO on December 7, 1991. Fuji management was concerned that the former distributor would launch a media campaign and file a breach of contract complaint with the Saudi government. Although Fuji management believed they had sufficient evidence of missed sales targets and poor service, BMW, in a recent similar case, had been required to pay compensation to its former distributor and its operations in Saudi Arabia had been frozen for several months while the dispute was resolved.

The situation was complicated by the fact that the existing distributor was holding SR 3 million of inventory (at distributor-selling prices), 90% in film and 10% in other products. About 30% of this inventory had not been paid for. Retail outlets supplied by the distributor were believed to be holding SR 5 million of inventories purchased from the distributor that would retail for SR 9 million. However, 20% of the Fuji film inventory in retail channels was believed to have passed its expiration date and a further 30% was set

EXHIBIT 10.7 Fuji Sales Mix by Product Line (Pre-EMDICO): 1991E	
Product line	***1991E (pre-EMDICO)***
Color film rolls	SR 2,080,000 (62%)
Color paper	500,000 (15%)
Cameras	90,000 (3%)
Minilabs	180,000 (5%)
Medical X-ray	500,000 (15%)
Total	3,350,000 (100%)

EXHIBIT 10.8 Minilab Installations in the Middle East: 1991[1]

Country	Fuji	Konica	Kodak	AGFA	Others	TOTAL	Population	Population per minilab
Bahrain	4 (11%)	7 (20%)	6 (17%)	10 (29%)	8 (23%)	35	550,000	15,714
Iran	30 (38%)	7 (9%)	28 (35%)	12 (15%)	2 (3%)	79	56,000,000	708,861
Jordan	5 (12%)	7 (17%)	28 (68%)	0 (0%)	1 (2%)	41	3,000,000	73,171
Kuwait	1 (2%)	3 (7%)	20 (48%)	8 (19%)	10 (24%)	42	2,000,000	47,619
Lebanon	8 (14%)	4 (7%)	29 (51%)	14 (25%)	2 (4%)	57	3,000,000	52,632
Oman	3 (6%)	9 (18%)	13 (26%)	8 (16%)	17 (34%)	50	2,100,000	42,000
Qatar	10 (38%)	10 (38%)	5 (19%)	0 (0%)	1 (4%)	26	500,000	19,231
Saudi Arabia	16 (7%)	89 (41%)	57 (26%)	31 (14%)	23 (11%)	216	17,000,000	78,704
Syria	25 (34%)	22 (30%)	23 (31%)	0 (0%)	4 (5%)	74	12,500,000	168,919
United Arab Emirates	35 (19%)	44 (24%)	49 (27%)	45 (25%)	10 (5%)	183	2,000,000	10,929
Total	137 (17%)	202 (25%)	258 (32%)	128 (16%)	78 (10%)	803		

[1]Countries listed are those included in Fuji's definition of the Middle East region.
Percentage figures in parentheses represent each brand's share in each country.

to expire within 3 months.[5] Some dealers had suggested privately to Srinivasan that they would appreciate EMDICO replacing the expired film with new stock at no charge.

THE 1992 MARKETING PLAN

Negotiations between EMDICO and Fuji management resulted in the market growth assumptions and sales goals for 1992 through 1995 summarized in Exhibit 10.2. Should these goals not be reached, Fuji reserved the right to reassign the distributorship after a minimum period of 2 years. Srinivasan's mission was to develop a marketing plan that would meet Fuji's objectives yet, at the same time, make money for EMDICO. Srinivasan estimated EMDICO's minimum 1992 general and administrative overhead associated with the Fuji distributorship at SR 400,000. He believed that EMDICO was well-placed to compete for 2-year government contracts to supply medical X-ray film to hospitals. His focus, therefore, was on improving Fuji sales to consumers that he expected would account for 80% of EMDICO's Fuji related revenues over the next 5 years.

Resolving the Issues

The Announcement

Opinions differed about how intensively the December 7 public announcement of EMDICO's appointment should be leveraged. A local agency proposed a press conference in Jeddah to which journalists and 300 top dealers would be welcomed by Srinivasan, his new management team, and senior Fuji managers from Japan.[6] Fuji's relaunch strategy would be announced at this event. The cost estimate was SR 120,000 plus an additional SR 30,000 if advertisements were placed in the major national newspapers. The proposed newspaper advertisement is presented in Exhibit 10.9. Alternatively, the announcement of EMDICO's appointment could simply be mailed to all dealers in Saudi Arabia at a cost of SR 10,000.

Geographical Coverage

Srinivasan had to decide where to focus his initial relaunch efforts and how rapidly to roll out nationwide, if at all. The three options he considered were to concentrate on Jeddah (which accounted for 23% of KSA film and camera sales and 18% of retail outlets selling film and cameras); to focus on the 10 largest cities in Saudi Arabia including Jeddah with a combined population of 13 million (and which accounted for 90% of KSA film and camera sales and 85% of retail outlets selling these products); or to launch nationwide. To meet the sales targets set by Fuji management, he was inclined to go national as soon as possible.

Communications

The 1992 communications budget depended on the geographical coverage and aggressiveness of the roll-out plan. Srinivasan believed his first priority should be to reestablish awareness of the Fuji brand. He therefore planned to use roadside signs (known as mupi boards) and billboards in the first half of 1992 and, possibly, to supplement these

---

[5]Fuji applied an expiration date 2 years from date of production to all its film packages. Beyond the expiration date, the quality of the film could not be guaranteed.

[6]It was estimated that half of these dealers would be among those already carrying Fuji.

EXHIBIT 10.9 Proposed Newspaper Advertisement for Relaunch

The technology that went into space and back is back.

FUJI FILM TECHNOLOGY, PROVEN IN SPACE, IS NOW BACK IN THE STORES.

FUJI is in the forefront of space exploration. Fuji films chosen by high science to vividly capture the mysterious beauty of deep space. Always with impeccable results.

Now, the same high technology that is being proven in space is made available to you - FUJI Films.

FUJI has a wide range of films for various applications to meet amateur or professional photography requirements. Each one guaranteed to provide sharp, clear and colorful reproduction always.

So, the next time you buy a roll of film, specify space-proven FUJI Films. And get pictures with a world of difference.

Sole distributor of Fuji products for the Kingdom of Saudi Arabia

EMDICO
EMAM DISTRIBUTION CO. LTD. w.l.l.
Kilo 11, Madinah Road, P.O. Box 1716, Jeddah 21441
Saudi Arabia, Tel: 691-7036/682-4294
Fax; 691-7036/691-8227.

TABLE 10.4 Monthly Advertising Costs by Medium, Depending on Geographic Coverage			
Media	*Jeddah (SR)*	*10 cities (SR)*	*National (SR)*
Roadside signs[1]	8,000	35,000	40,000
Billboards	10,000	46,000	56,000
Television	15,000	75,000	100,000
Radio	8,000	40,000	60,000

[1]Monthly costs for each medium to achieve 200 gross rating points (frequency times reach) under each geographic option.

with television and/or radio advertising in the second half of the year. He estimated the monthly costs shown in Table 10.4.

Organization

Srinivasan had already begun to recruit an entirely new sales and service organization. There was no shortage of qualified personnel and no inclination to hire any of the staff who worked for the former distributor. Srinivasan estimated the manpower requirements and monthly costs shown in Table 10.5. Costs included expenses and transportation. Sales managers would spend half their time selling and half their time supervising.

Srinivasan planned to place special emphasis on customer service. A computerized inventory management system was being installed to ensure timely and accurate deliveries of dealer orders. In addition, service engineers were needed to maintain and repair the minilabs that Fuji sold or leased to dealers. One service engineer (costing SR 2,000 per month) could typically cover 12 minilabs. The number of service engineers required would depend on how aggressively Fuji set out to install its minilabs at retail outlets. Fuji management offered to train EMDICO service engineers at no charge to the distributor.

Distribution

Srinivasan knew he had to correct Fuji's current low dealer penetration, but he had to decide on which dealers and channels to focus his sales efforts. He estimated that a salesperson could make five solid sales calls per day and that at least two calls would be necessary to persuade a dealer to carry the Fuji brand. The length of a sales call depended in part on the breadth of the product line to be presented. He was hopeful that the loyalty of all Fuji's current dealers could be reinforced and that some of the 100 dealers who had dropped the brand in the previous 2 years could be persuaded to sign up again.

Srinivasan believed strongly in point-of-sale signage. He planned to offer current Fuji dealers and new dealers outdoor store signs that would feature the dealer name and the Fuji name in the green, red, and white colors associated with the Fuji brand. Srinivasan estimated the average cost of these signs at SR 2,000. In addition, the annual cost of supplying each dealer with point-of-sale materials, brochures, and ceiling danglers

TABLE 10.5 Monthly Salaries and Number of Employees, Depending on Geographic Coverage			
Manpower (monthly salary)	*Jeddah*	*10 cities*	*National*
Sales staff (SR 2,000)	3	8	12
Regional sales managers (SR 6,000)	1	3	4

for inside the stores, and Fuji tape for the perimeters of shop windows and display cabinets, would be SR 600. Srinivasan planned to use the slogan "You can see it's Fuji" in Arabic and English on the in-store ceiling danglers. He also wanted to print special envelopes for Fuji film processed in Fuji minilabs with the slogan "Quality prints in record time." In addition, EMDICO delivery vehicles prominently carry the Fuji logo.

As part of the communications and distribution strategy, Srinivasan had all but decided to establish a flagship, company-run retail outlet to be called Fuji Image Plaza in the forecourt of the Safestway supermarket, the most modern, high traffic store in downtown Jeddah. The space would cost SR 15,000 per month and operating costs would be SR 5,000. The store would be run as a photographic studio, the full Fuji product line would be displayed and sold, and a Fuji minilab would process film and be available for dealer demonstrations. The initial investment in fixtures and equipment would be SR 180,000. A perspective view of the proposed store is presented in Exhibit 10.10.

Product Mix

Srinivasan had to decide whether the sales targets required him to launch the complete line of Fuji films (some 15 items) and cameras (12 models) as soon as possible or whether he should focus, at least initially, on selected, higher volume items (say 4 types of color film and 3 camera models). The latter approach might ease inventory management but send a negative signal that Fuji was not a full-line supplier.

Srinivasan was also considering three alternative product rollout strategies. The first was to simultaneously relaunch both film and cameras given that purchase of one typically stimulated purchase of the other. Advocates argued that promotions on cameras could be used to persuade dealers to stock Fuji film. The second option was to initially focus on rejuvenating film sales and to delay promoting cameras until at least the second half of 1992. A third option was to build the relaunch around minilabs sales on the grounds that dealers who installed Fuji minilabs would be inclined to stock and push Fuji film and cameras. The FA Compact II seemed like a marketable product, but Kodak and Konica might respond to any Fuji sales initiative by offering more attractive terms on their minilabs.

Pricing

The anticipated margin structure for Fuji film, cameras, processing, and minilabs is shown in Exhibit 10.11. Srinivasan was contemplating retail prices on Fuji film at about 5% below Kodak and 5% above Konica. Srinivasan had to take into account Fuji's current image in the market, the need to signal the brand's true quality, and the importance of not provoking a price war.

CONCLUSION

As December 7 approached, the date set for the public announcement of EMDICO's appointment, Srinivasan pondered his options. As indicated in Exhibit 10.2, Fuji management had set some ambitious sales goals for EMDICO from 1992 to 1995. This suggested the need for an aggressive relaunch of the brand beginning with a high profile press conference. On the other hand, the possible reactions of the previous distributor and of Kodak and Konica were a source of concern. Perhaps a lower profile relaunch and a gradual rollout were preferable. In either case, details of the marketing program for the relaunch had to be determined.

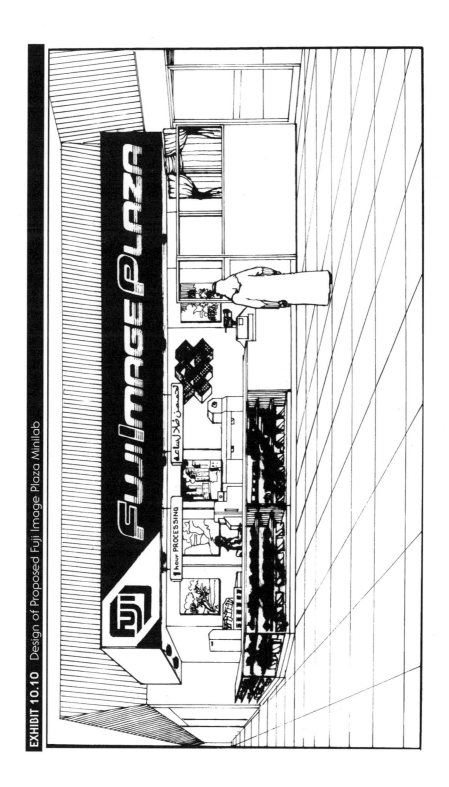

EXHIBIT 10.10 Design of Proposed Fuji Image Plaza Minilab

EXHIBIT 10.11 Typical Margin Structure for Fuji Products Sold in the Kingdom of Saudi Arabia

a. Film retail (e.g., Fujicolor HR100)

Retail selling price	SR	10.00
Less dealer margin		3.50
EMDICO selling price		6.50
Less EMDICO promotion		0.40
Less EMDICO margin		0.50
Fuji selling price[1]		5.60
Less Fuji variable costs		3.08
Fuji margin		2.52

b. Color paper (per one film development = per 36 prints = per 0.6 sqm color paper)

Retail selling price[2]	SR	42.00
Less dealer margin		25.65
EMDICO selling price[3]		16.35
Less EMDICO margin		1.64
Fuji selling price[3]		14.71
Less Fuji variable costs		8.09
Fuji margin		6.62

c. Camera (e.g., FZ-5)

Retail selling price	SR	133.00
Less dealer margin		43.00
EMDICO's selling price		90.00
Less EMDICO promotion[4]		12.50
Less EMDICO margin		14.50
Fuji selling price[1]		63.00
Less Fuji variable costs		34.00
Fuji margin		29.00

d. Minilab (e.g., FA Compact II)

EMDICO's selling price	SR	180,000
Less Finance charge[5]		14,300
Less EMDICO margin		25,700
Fuji selling price[1]		140,000
Less Fuji variable costs		97,000
Fuji margin		43,000

[1]Fuji selling prices to EMDICO include applicable transportation costs and import duties.
[2]Retail selling price of color paper includes processing fee (SR 6.00/film) and development fee (SR 1.00/print × 36 prints).
[3]Photo paper and chemicals.
[4]A camera promotion such as a free Fuji film and/or camera batteries would typically be offered with each purchase
[5]Finance charge was paid by EMDICO, not by a minilab owner. EMDICO planned to offer a bank-leasing program to prospective minilab owners. Under the program, EMDICO would receive full amount initially from a bank when a minilab sales was made. EMDICO would charge a minilab owner on a monthly basis and pay back to the bank with appropriate finance charge.

INDEX